The History of Charles County, Maryland

Written in Its Tercentenary Year of 1958

Margaret Brown Klapthor and Paul Dennis Brown

HERITAGE BOOKS
2009

HERITAGE BOOKS
AN IMPRINT OF HERITAGE BOOKS, INC.

Books, CDs, and more—Worldwide

For our listing of thousands of titles see our website
at
www.HeritageBooks.com

A Facsimile Reprint
Published 2009 by
HERITAGE BOOKS, INC.
Publishing Division
100 Railroad Ave. #104
Westminster, Maryland 21157

Originally published
Charles County Tercentenary, Inc.
La Plata, Maryland
1958

*The seal on the cover of this book was designed by
Frederick Tilp, circa 1954*

— Publisher's Notice —
In reprints such as this, it is often not possible to remove blemishes from the original. We feel the contents of this book warrant its reissue despite these blemishes and hope you will agree and read it with pleasure.

International Standard Book Numbers
Paperbound: 978-0-7884-0160-2
Clothbound: 978-0-7884-8233-5

Portrait in the Enoch Pratt Free Library, Baltimore, Maryland

CHARLES CALVERT, third Lord Baltimore. Son of Caecilius Calvert and the person for whom Caecilius named Charles County when it was established in 1658.

To

Charles County, God Bless You!

FOREWORD

The people of Charles County owe this account of the history of the County to the wisdom of the Charles County Tercentenary Committee who made its production one of the first projects of the celebration. It might be called a birthday present to the County and to its residents.

Compiling the history was primarily a labor of love for me. The County is my home and its long and proud history has fascinated me since I was a child. If I have succeeded in even partially presenting Charles County as I know it, it is because of the generous help I have received from many others who share my enthusiasm.

First a word of recognition to my father and co-author. To Paul Dennis Brown, who has been the County Agricultural Agent for thirty years, I owe much of my early interest in history and especially the history of my home county. To him we are indebted for the sections of this book dealing especially with agriculture, the industry of the county and transportation. It was he who searched the first records of the county in an attempt to locate the first County Courthouse. His knowledge of the geography of the county was a great help in identifying and locating places long since passed into oblivion. His intense interest in the whole project and his willingness to assist in the research on any phase of the subject were of inestimable value in completing the history.

But we received help from many others too, and individual recognition and thanks are due to all of them. The whole staff of the Charles County Public Library, especially the Chief Librarian, Miss Doris W. Holmes, made the facilities of the library available to us and shared with us their own considerable knowledge of Charles County History and legend. Similar recognition must also be paid to Mr. James W. Foster, Director of the Maryland Historical Society and his staff and to Dr. Morris Radoff Archivist of the Maryland Hall of Records and his staff.

I was greatly assisted in sections dealing with the history of the Catholic Church in the county by Miss Virginia Mudd of Pomfret, Maryland and Miss Mudd's notes from the *Port Tobacco Times* were also especially helpful.

Mr. Samuel L. Ward of La Plata very kindly made his notes on Charles County History available to me and it was in these notes that I found references to many things included in the book which I had not found elsewhere.

Mr. Peter Vischer of Port Tobacco shared his research on "Habre de Venture," the Stones and allied families, including much information on the general history of the county.

Mrs. Rudolf Carrico furnished valuable information on the Carrico family, the Marshalls of "Marshall Hall" and the Harris family of "Mt. Tirzah."

Mrs. Young Wright sent references on her home "Aquinsick" including data on the Neale family, descendants of Capt. James Neale of "Wollaston Manor", who lived at "Aquinsick" in the 18th century.

Mr. Robert Barbour shared his knowledge of the history of Port Tobacco and especially its period as the County Seat of Charles County.

To Miss Miriam Matthews we are indebted for information on "Mt. Carmel" and the story of the nuns who established the first convent in English America.

Mr. Frank P. Hamilton very kindly lent us his copy of *History of Maryland* by J. Thomas Scharf for the duration of our research. This book is a basic reference on state history and difficult to obtain outside of libraries.

The Reverend William Horrigan, S.J., Chaplain of the Restorers of Mt. Carmel also helped both on this subject and the general history of the Catholic Church in Charles County.

Others to whom we owe our thanks for their share in the book are Judge John Dudley Digges, Chairman of the

Charles County Tercentenary Committee, Mrs. William Carlyle Turner, Miss Dorothy Posey, Mrs. Thomas P. McDonagh, Mrs. Frank Jack Fletcher, Mrs. James W. Wills, Mr. Henry M. Bain, Jr., Mr. Don Levine, Mr. Eugene Jenkins, Mrs. Carol Rollins and Mrs. Ben Walker, the Executive Secretary of the Tercentenary Committee. Mrs. Samuel Linton and Hon. Leander McCormick-Goodhart.

Finally, a word of gratitude to our respective families who contributed to this book by their unfailing interest in the History and by their understanding cooperation during every phase of its creation.

To all of these, then, are due the thanks of not only the authors but of all those, who reading this book, find the History of Charles County a pleasure and a source of information in the years to come.

M. B. K.

ABOUT THE AUTHORS

This book, *The History of Charles County, Maryland*, first published in 1958 in observance of the county's three-hundredth year, is reprinted in memory of its co-authors, Margaret Brown Klapthor and Paul Dennis Brown.

P. D. Brown was born in Somerset, Kentucky, in 1892. Together with his wife, Margaret Berry Brown, and one young daughter, he moved to Charles County in 1919, to manage Causine's Manor, a 750-acre farm in Bel Alton. In 1929, he took on the position of County Agent with the University of Maryland Extension Service, and in that capacity was able to serve Charles County not only in providing agricultural expertise but also in helping to establish and maintain the county library, fair, and hospital, as well as bringing electrification to the area. In addition, he was knowledgeable in local history and interested in historic houses. He was the recipient of many professional and community service awards at the time of his death in 1974. Given the primary importance of agriculture to Charles County, no one was better qualified than he to address that topic in this commemorative book.

Margaret Brown Klapthor, his second daughter, was as ideally suited to treat the general history of the county. She was born in Henderson, Kentucky, in 1922. After graduating from college, she worked for the Smithsonian Institution in the Division of Civil History. She married Frank Klapthor in 1956, and only then moved from the county to Washington, D.C. Shortly thereafter, having left her Charles County home and living on Capitol Hill, she wrote this history. Her writing career really began in 1935 with an essay that won a national contest, and that she read over the radio from Rochester, New York. She continued to write and publish in her area of specialization, the First Ladies and the Presidential Collection at the National Museum of American History, until the time of her death in 1994. In addition to producing many books and articles, she curated several highly acclaimed exhibitions. Her life's work was to obtain and consider the facts, and to tell their interesting story. She brings us, her readers, together within a shared framework -- the place and names known well to many -- and she brings the facts of history to life in these pages.

Mary Berry Brown Moore, the authors' sister and daughter, and the rest of our family are grateful to Heritage Books, Inc. for this opportunity to remember two individuals so dear to our hearts. We who knew them derive great pleasure from the reprinting of this book; and we hope that you will, too.

TABLE OF CONTENTS

	page
FOREWORD	v
CHAPTER I *In the Beginning — The Seventeenth Century*	1
CHAPTER II *Growth and Development — The Eighteenth Century*	43
CHAPTER III *Maturity — The Nineteenth and Twentieth Centuries*	101
AGRICULTURE	149
IN CONCLUSION	162
NOTES AND REFERENCES	163
APPENDIX #1 *Old Charles County*	167
APPENDIX #2 *Charles Countians of Prominence*	169
BIBLIOGRAPHY	172
CENSUS OF 1790	179
INDEX	197

LIST OF ILLUSTRATIONS

CHARLES CALVERT, THIRD LORD BALTIMORE....*Frontispiece*

Group I .... *following page 22*
    MAP OF CHARLES COUNTY, CIRCA 1670
    HOUSE ON "SARUM"
    SURVEYOR'S SKETCH OF THE CHARLES COUNTY COURTHOUSE, 1697
    VIEW OF PORT TOBACCO VALLEY AND PORT TOBACCO RIVER

Group II .... *following page 59*
    GENERAL WILLIAM SMALLWOOD
    "SMALLWOOD'S RETREAT"
    THOMAS STONE
    "HABRE DE VENTURE"

Group III .... *following page 92*
    DANIEL OF ST. THOMAS JENIFER
    "THE RETREAT"
    JOHN HANSON
    ROBERT HANSON HARRISON

Group IV .... *following page 104*
    POTOMAC RIVER BRIDGE
    "ROSE HILL"
    PATUXENT RIVER AT BENEDICT
    DURHAM CHURCH

Group V .... *following page 130*
    THE LINCOLN CONSPIRATORS
    CHARLES COUNTAINS WHO AIDED BOOTH
    OBITUARY OF ROBERT FLOYD
    MATTHEW HENSON

Group VI .... *following page 149*
    NATIVE TOBACCO COMPARED WITH MARYLAND TOBACCO
    SCENES FROM THE STATE TOBACCO WAREHOUSES
    METHODS OF TRANSPORTING TOBACCO
    METHODS OF TRANSPORTING TOBACCO

CHAPTER I—IN THE BEGINNING

THE SEVENTEENTH CENTURY

In 1634 a Jesuit missionary in the wilderness that was then the infant colony of Maryland writes thus to his Superior in Rome "... on the third of March ... we turned our course to the north to reach the Potomeack River ... Never have I beheld a larger or a more beautiful river. The Thames seems like a mere riverlet in comparison with it; it is not disfigured with any swamps but has firm land on each side. Fine groves of trees appear, not choked with briers or bushes and undergrowth, but growing at intervals as if planted by hand of man, so that you can drive a four horse carriage wherever you choose, through the midst of the trees." He continues his letter accordingly, "We have been here only one month and so the remaining particulars must be kept for the next voyage, but this I do say that the soil seems remarkably fertile; in passing through the very thick woods, at every step we tread on strawberries, vines, sassafras, acorns and walnuts. The soil is dark and not hard, to the depth of a foot and overlays a rich, red clay. There are lofty trees everywhere except where the land has been cultivated by a few persons. Numerous springs furnish a supply of water. No animals are seen except deer, beaver and squirrels which are as large as the hares of Europe. There is an infinite number of birds of various colors, such as eagles, cranes, swans, geese, partridges and ducks. From these facts it is inferred that the country is not without such things as contribute to the prosperity or pleasure of those who inhabit it."[1] This description of the Maryland Countryside was further elaborated in an account of the colony of the Lord Baron of Baltimore which Cecil Calvert himself compiled from reports by travellers who had returned from the new world. He states "The situation of the Country is excellent and very convenient. The climate is serene and mild not oppressively hot like that of Florida and Old Virginia nor bitter cold like that of New England, but preserves so to speak, a middle temperature between the two and so enjoys the advantages and escapes the evil of each." In describing the colony in greater detail the account goes on to mention all of the wonders the prospective settler will find in Maryland. The tidal waters provide in abundance shad, cod-fish, herring, trout, mussels, to mention only a few. The country is thickly wooded with many hickory trees, mulberry trees, alder, ash, chestnut, cedars, laurel, pine, sassafras, cypress trees, 80 feet high, and oak trees so tall and so straight that beams 60' long by $2\frac{1}{2}$' wide can be made of them. The glowing account continues with a description of vines and fruits; fox grapes, wild cherries, peaches, gooseberries, plums, mulberries, chestnuts, walnuts, strawberries and raspberries. As for vegetables he specifies lupines, peas, beans and grains. The wild life of the area includes muskrats, martens, weasels, eagles, partridges, wild turkeys, blackbirds, thrushes, red and blue birds, swans, geese, cranes, herons and ducks.

Even allowing for the enthusiasm of the man who was attempting to sell this new colony of Maryland to emigrant settlers the description of the part of the Colony which was being settled in 1634 might almost be that of Charles County a little over three hundred years later. For the County of Charles which may be found on the map of Maryland directly north and a little west of St. Mary's County is most typical of the tidewater area which was the first part of the State to be settled.

The recorded history of the area from which Charles County, Maryland was created can be said to start with the first visits of white men to the area. The very first white men to view the land were probably Spanish missionaries, as it is known that their voyages along the Atlantic coastline as early as the 16th century might have brought them this far. However, our first detailed account comes from Capt. John Smith of Virginia who in 1608 set out to explore the country surrounding the Chesapeake Bay for information about the resources and quality of the land. In a small open boat in the company of seven gentlemen and seven soldiers he made two voyages of discovery that took three months and navigated about 3,000 miles. In the course of these travels he sailed up the Potomac River to the falls above Georgetown. Smith says the reason for the voyage was "to search this mine (which they hoped was a silver mine) ; also to search what furr, . . . and what other minerals, rivers, rocks, nations, woods, fishing, fruits, victuall, and what other commodities the land afforded; and whether the bay were endless or how farre it extended; of mines we were all ignorant, but a few beavers, otters, bears, martins and minks we found, and in divers places that abundance of fish, lying so thick with their heads above the water, as for want of nets (our barge driving amongst them) we attempted to catch them with a frying pan; but we found it a bad instrument to catch fish with."[2] In his account of the journey Capt. John Smith mentions specifically an Indian tribe which he called the "Toags" which are identified as the tribe living in the vicinity of Maryland Point and are more commonly known as the "Doages". He also mentions the Indian village of "Potopaco" and gives its number of inhabitants as 20 men.

In 1632, Capt. Henry Fleet, adventurer and Indian trader while on a trading voyage along the creeks and tidal streams of the Potomac records that he came to the town of "Patobanos" and arranged with the Indians there that all the Indians of the region would save their furs and beaver skins for him as they had begun to appreciate the benefits of trading with him. It seems certain that in the period between the voyages of Capt. John Smith and that of Capt. Henry Fleet a certain amount of trade had flourished and the goods of European orgin, copper, glass beads and other similar objects were traded to the Indians of the Potomac River for their produce.

The Indians in this area were Algonquins and they were included within the territory commonly called the Powhatan

Confederacy. A state of peace existed among the tribes in the Confederacy but they were continually defending themselves against the depredations of the war-like Susquehannocks who lived to the north around the head of Chesapeake Bay.

Father Andrew White in his first letter to Rome describes the Indians in some detail "The natives are very tall and well proportioned; their skin is naturally rather dark, and they make it uglier by staining it, generally with red paint mixed with oil to keep off the mosquitoes, thinking more of their own comfort than of appearances. They disfigure their countenances with other colors too, painting them in various and truly hideous and frightful ways, either a dark blue above the nose, and red below, or the reverse. They generally have black hair which they carry round in a knot to the left ear and fasten with a band, adding some ornament which is in estimation amohng them. Some of them wear on their foreheads the figure of a fish, made of copper. They adorn their necks with glass beads, strung on a thread-like necklace."

"They are clothed, for the most part, in deer skins or some similar kind of covering which hangs down behind like a cloak. They wear aprons round the middle, and leave the rest of the body naked. The young boys and girls go about with nothing on them. The soles of their feet are as hard as horn and they tread on thorns and briers without hurt. Their arms are bows, and arrows three feet long, tipped with stag's horn or a white flint sharpened at the end. They shoot these with such skill that they can stand off and hit a sparrow in the middle; and in order to become expert by practice they throw a spear up in the air, and then send an arrow from the bow string and drive in into the spear before it falls. But since they do not string the bow very tight, they cannot hit a mark at great distance. They live by means of these weapons and go out every day through the fields and woods, to hunt squirrels, partridges, turkeys and wild animals . . ."

"They live in houses built in an oblong oval shape. Light is admitted into these, through the roof, by a window a foot and half long; this also serves to carry off the smoke, for they kindle the fire in the middle of the floor and sleep around the fire . . . They live for the most part on a kind of paste, which they call 'Pone', and 'Omini', both of which are made of Indian corn; and sometimes they add fish, or what they have procured by hunting and fowling."[3]

The peaceful nature of the Indians who were living in Charles County reflected the bountiful nature of the area in which they lived. The water and the fertile land provided them with all their needs. Wild game and seafood were plentiful and they even practiced a sort of crude farming. They lived in small tribal or family groups near tidal streams. To this day they are remembered by the names of the streams on which they lived. Familiar ones are the Mattawoman, Chicamuxen, Nanjemoy, Picawaxen, Wicomico, Patuxent, Pomonkey and Port Tobacco.

In recent years excavations along Port Tobacco River by William J. Graham and on Nanjemoy Creek by the Smithsonian Institution have yielded valuable information about the Indians of the region. Graham found and excavated eight villages and camp sites in the Port Tobacco area. The Smithsonian Institution worked on the west side of Nanjemoy Creek near Friendship Landing. The excavations in burial grounds produced a wealth of material other than skeletal remains. Wampum, peake, and roanoke used for trading and decorations were found in the graves, as well as pot sherds, beads and copper ornaments. The areas also yielded artifacts including stone hoes, axes, arrow heads and broken pottery. An earlier excavation at Marshall Hall yielded weapons, pottery, mortars and wampum.[4]

As Port Tobacco is the Indian village most often mentioned in the contemporary records and as it has been so well documented by Mr. Graham it may be taken as a prototype of the other villages in the county. Consider the wisdom with which the site was selected. The valley of the

Port Tobacco is narrow and bounded by comparatively high hills on either side. The river entrance is commanded by an impressive height at Chapel Point rising 120 feet above the river. The valley itself is level and well drained with a gradual slope to the river. It is fertile and well suited to agriculture with the primitive tools the Indians had developed. The tidal portion of the river abounded with edible fish and the surrounding woods supplied berries, fruits and an abundance of wild game. Oysters and crabs were plentiful. Never failing springs of good water were found in many places on both banks of the river. The land and its resources were suited to the type of life the Indians lead. The members of the tribe did not all live in a common village but in a number of smaller groups relatively close together. The largest group in the Port Tobacco area seems to have been at Old Warehouse Landing.[5]

At the time Captain John Smith sailed up the Potomac in 1608 he estimates 20 Indian warriors at "Potopaco" which probably represents a total population of from 100 to 200 persons. However it may be that this estimate is low as the Jesuit missionaries attached great importance to this tribe. In 1642 in the Jesuits' report to Rome they say "the town, called Portobacco, to a great extent received the faith with baptism. Which town, as it is situated on the river Pamac (the inhabitants call it Pamoke) almost in the center of the Indians and so more convenient for excursions in all directions that we have determined to make our residence; the more so because we fear that we may be compelled to abandon Piscataway on account of its proximity to the Sesquehannoes, which nation is the most savage and war-like of these regions and hostile to Christians."[6] Among the prominent converts for that year is listed "the young Queen of Portobacco".

The mission which was established at Port Tobacco in 1642 only lasted approximately two years as in 1644 the Reformists gained power in England and Captain Richard Ingle of London attacked the Jesuit headquarters at Port Tobacco. Father Andrew White and Father Thomas Copely were taken back to England in chains.

By the time of the restoration in the colony of Maryland to the Calverts, the Indians had disappeared from their homes along the Port Tobacco River, according to the Woodstock letters. Within 5 or 10 years after Father White left them the Port Tobacco Indians had disappeared, probably absorbed into the Piscataway tribe which retained its entity longer than any other tribe in the region. The disappearance of the Indian was a direct result of the steady advance of settlements by the white colonists who within that same short period of time moved into Indian territory and claimed it as their own. There was never any recognition in Maryland of Indian titles to land and patents were taken by the colonists directly from the Lord Proprietary. From 1649 to 1660 all the land along the Port Tobacco River was patented and within another twenty-five years there were no Indians left in the valley of the Potomac.[7]

Despite the rapid and complete disappearance of the Indians as a separate racial group in the Charles County area in the 17th century we still have today in the county a reminder of its orginal inhabitants. There lives in Charles County today a group of people of mixed racial origin who call themselves "We-Sorts". It appears they are mainly of White and Indian blood with an occasional strong infusion of the Negro element. These people have many of the physical characteristics of Indians. They too like to farm, and they are able hunters, guides, and fishermen. Their name, based on the phrase "we sort of people" indicates their clannish attitude and until the nineteen thirties they were a group unto themselves. They had separate school buildings in the public school systems. The group is 100% Catholic and at St. Ignatius Church on St. Thomas Manor, where most of them are communicants, they had a separate section of pews set aside for them on the ground floor of the church behind the white section.

That these people trace their beginnings back to the "Free Colored" in the county seems indicated by the fact that most of the "We-Sort" names of the county can be found on the Census Roll of 1790 in that category. When the Negro slaves were freed at the end of the Civil War it was necessary for this group who had been called "Free Negroes" to invent a term to designate themselves as a separate group and it was then that the term "We-Sort" came into being.[8]

The same fertile land that had provided a living for the Indians attracted the colonists who came to Maryland and within a short time they began to spread out from the original settlement at St. Mary's City. They followed the river and went up the tidal creeks and bays. The earliest settlements on the land that is now Charles County were on the Wicomico River and its valley but before long there were people on the Port Tobacco River and on the Nanjemoy and finally even up to Mattawoman.

The Lord Proprietor of the Colony divided the land into Proprietary Manors, and afterwards out of these manors, were granted the individual manors as large tracts of land and plantations and farms as smaller ones. Grants were made at an early date long distances from the center of population in St. Mary's City. Thus we find that in 1638 Thomas Copley, one of the Jesuit priests in the colony, was granted land on the east side of Port Tobacco Creek and in 1642 James Neale received patent for 2,000 acres on the west side of the Wicomico River. Neale's grant was to be called "Wollaston Manor". In 1649 Nicolas Cawsin was granted 1,000 acres "upon Patowmeck River between Cedar Point and head of Portobacko Creeke" and that same year the grant of land made to Thomas Copley was transferred to Thomas Matthews and was given manorial right under the name of "St. Thomas Manor." In 1651, 1,600 acres around Newport was made into a manor called "Westwood" and given Thomas Gerard. By 1654 three more manors had been granted in the area—one of 5,000 acres on Nanjemoy Creek to Governor William Stone, to be called "Poynton Manor", which was given in consideration of his good and faithful services to the Proprietor. Another in the same area, 3,000 acres to be known as "Rice Manor" was granted to Lieutenant William Lewis; and Thomas Cornwallis, one of the great landholders of the Maryland Colony, was granted 5,000 acres at "Mattawoman Neck" with manorial rights.

The names given to the Proprietary Manors from which all these grants were made were Zachia Manor, Pangiah and Calverton Manor. The constitution of Zachia Manor predated the creation of Charles County and its name is to be found only in the letters of Charles Calvert or in the land surveys of the area. The records of surveyors had to place every plot surveyed within a given manor. The smaller political subdivision of these great proprietary manors were called "Hundreds". The following hundreds are recorded in the area to become Charles County; Wiccommico Hundred in 1642; Pykawaxen Hundred in 1649, Riverside Hundred in 1653, Chingamuxen Hundred in 1653 and Nanjemoy Hundred in 1657. These dates are taken from the first patent within the territory.[9]

With a constant influx of people into the area the Lord Proprietor and the Governor were soon receiving complaints that the distance to the St. Mary's Courthouse was too great for the efficient transaction of business. On April 13, 1658 the Governor's Council ordered the erection of a new County to take care of these more distant settlements. On May 10, 1658 the Honorable Josias Fendall, Governor of the Province issued the following proclamation in the name of Lord Baltimore; "Caecilius Absolute and Prop^e of the Provinces of Maryland and Avalon, Lord Baron of Baltimore: to John Hatch, James Lindsey, Henry Adams, Edward Parks, James Walker and Robert Hunley Gent^n . . . All th^t tract of Land of this o^e Province of Maryland Bownded with West Wicocomoco Ryver, up to the head thereof and Sowth wth Patowmeck ryver from the mouth of Wicocomoco up as high as any Plantaon under o^e govermt is now seated, and from thence wth a right line drawne from such plantaon as afores'd to the head of Wicocomoco Ryver [is erected] into a County" to be named "in honou^e of our only son and heir apparent, Charles Calvert, Esquire. Gyvuen under the great seale of this our province of Maryland, this Tenth day of May in the 26 yeare of Our Dominion over the s'd province and in the yeare of o^e Lord 1658. Wittnes o^e Right Trusty and wellbeloved Josias ffendall Esq'r o^e Lieut^t of the sd province" and signed "Josias ffendall".[10]

The wording of the Proclamation actually gave the new county an elastic boundary as the boundary was undoubtedly intended to move northward as the land grants moved up the river. The vague boundaries existed for the first 37 years of the county. It was not until 1695 when a General Act of the Assembly created Prince George's County that the county lines were clearly defined. At that time it was clearly stated that Charles County was to begin upon the upper side of the Indian and Bird (now Budd's) Creeks where the upper bounds of St. Mary's County ended and "extend itself upward as farr as Mattawoman Creek and branch and bounding on the said Branch by a straight line Drawn from the head thereof the head of Swanson's Creek in Putuxent River including all that Land lying on the upper part of Bird's Creek and Indian Creek Branches where St. Mary's County ends to the lower side of Mattawomans Creek and Branch and Swansons Creek and Branch between Putuxent and Potomock Rivers as aforesaid."[11]

The orginal Proclamation setting up Charles County seems intended to include all the land west of the Patuxent. It is likely, however, as the area, which later became Prince George's County, was settled that the official business of settlers living in the watershed of the Patuxent River was transacted in Calvert County because of the convenience of water transportation. Probably only that section of Prince George's County lying in the watershed of the Potomac should be considered as part of the early Charles County.

The men who were appointed commissioners were required to swear "that as Commis^e of the County of Charles the Proceedings of the Provincial Court [12] they were required to swear "that as Commis^e of the County of Charles you shall do equal right, to the poore as to the rich, to the best of your cunning, witt and power and after the presidents and customes of this province and Acts of Assembly there of made And th^t you hold your sessions or courts as you are directed in your commission or according to Acts of Assembly providing in that behalf. And all fines and amerciements that shall happen to be made and all forfietures which shall fall before you, you shall cause to be entered without any concealment and certify the same to his Lordship's Receiver of this Province, ye shall not debarre or hinder the persecution of Justice or take any gift, bribe or fee to the intent or delaying of Jedgment but shall behave yourself justly and truly to the best of your understanding and power as long as you shall be by lawful authority discharged therefrom."

The years immediately prior to the establishment of Charles County had been years of political struggle and actual warfare in both the Mother Country and the Colony of Maryland caused by the fight for power between the Puritans and the adherents of the King. Lord Baltimore's loyalty to the King placed the Colony in Maryland in jeopardy each time the Puritans gained some measure of power. One of the most interesting incidents in this struggle for power took place in Maryland shortly after the establishment of Charles County and many of the most prominent citizens of the new Country were directly involved. The Province had been restored to Lord Baltimore in 1657 by Oliver Cromwell and the Lord Proprietor appointed Josias Fendall as its Governor. Governor Fendall lived in the area which was proclaimed as Charles County and it was through him that Lord Baltimore had issued the proclamation for the establishment of the County. It appears from the records that Governor Fendall, despite his oath of allegiance to Lord Baltimore, conceived a plan for enlarging his own authority at the expense of the proprietary and attempted to assume the position of a governor appointed by the people, through their representatives in the Lower and Upper Houses of the Assembly. The government of the Province was still in an unstable condition after the Ingle Rebellion and the Puritan Uprising and Fendall saw an opportunity for personal power which he seized, aided and abetted by his fellow citizens of Charles County. The contributing cause of the rebellion seems to have been taxation. An act had been passed by the Assembly of 1647 granting the Proprietor a duty of 10 shillings on every hogshead of tobacco exported from the Province. This act was the cause of the complaints and dissatisfaction which gave Fendall his opportunity. Actually Lord Baltimore had wished to make the duty only 2 shillings per hogshead but Governor Fendall wickedly concealed it from the people. At Fendall's instigation the Lower House of the Assembly claimed themselves to be a lawful Assembly without dependence on any power in the Province and further claimed themselves as the Highest Court of Judicature. On March 13, 1659, Fendall came out in the open, taking the position that the burgesses could make and enact laws by themselves and publish them in the name of the Proprietor; that such laws would be in full force provided they were agreeable to reason and not contrary to English laws.

Philip Calvert, brother of Lord Baltimore, who was secretary to the Upper House declared that the Burgesses could not enact laws without assent of the Lord Proprietary or the Governor. A poll of the Council showed a tie vote. Fendall then expressed his willingness to sit with the Lower House as Governor on their terms. Calvert and Baker Brooke, members of the Council "departed the howse and given in these words or to this effect 'that you may, if you please, wee shall not force you to goe or stay' " uttered by Governor Fendall.

Fendall found his principal support among his friends of Charles County but his rebellion was short lived. It collapsed in May, 1660, when Charles II returned to the throne and the Proprietor was restored to the favor of the courts.[13]

Four proclamations are found in the Charles County Court Minutes of November, 1660. The first is the announcement by Philip Calvert, new governor of the Province, of the restoration of Charles II. The second is a Proclamation of the King requiring all the inhabitants to assist in putting down the Fendall rebellion. Next Philip Calvert announces his appointment as Governor and last is the proclamation by the new Governor of a general amnesty and pardon for all Charles County persons engaged in the late mutiny and sedition except Josias Fendall and John Hatch, who were both given qualified pardons shortly afterward.[14]

The Provincial Court on December 11, 1660, ordered "all acts and orders entered in the time of the defection of the Government from his Lorship, being the 5th of March, 1659 be null and of noe force and that the same be forthwith razed and torn from the records."

In some unknown manner the Charles County Court records of this period were not destroyed as ordered and they are the only County records in the State that cover this period. As such they are valuable source material for students of the Rebellion.

As a matter of fact the Court Records of Charles County are a tremendously interesting document of the people of the County and the way in which they lived. The first page of the First County Record Book begins "Records for Charles Countie within the Province of Maryland. It being erected into a Countie by the Hon'ble Josias Fendall, esq. and Gov'r of the Sayd Province May 1658".

There is a wide variation in Court Records of the Maryland Counties depending on the legal knowledge and training of both the Judges on the Bench and the Clerks who kept the records. Charles County records reveal both the Clerks and the Bench were men of superior attainment who left records in good legal form and of a fullness seldom attained by the other counties.

County Court Justices or Commissioners were selected by the Governor from the most prominent men in the county in numbers varying from six to ten. The first man selected was the Chief Justice and the term of office of the justices was at the Governor's pleasure. At least one of the first three or four named was required to be present or Court could not be held.

These Justices or Commissioners had not only judical powers but administrative powers as well. They were empowered to try criminal cases not involving loss of life. Civil cases were limited to those involving not more than 3,000 pounds of tobacco or the equivalent of about £20 sterling and all other cases above these went before the Provincial Court. Judgement was by majority vote of the Court with an occasional justice dissenting. The first definite reference in these County records to a grand jury is to be found in the October, 1662, session of the Charles County Court where a "Jury of Inquest of 12 members presented several offenders for swearing, bigamy, Sabbath breaking and hog stealing."

Administratively, County Courts fixed the levey, the poll tax, authorized public expenditures. They set pay for soldiers, salaries for ferry operators and other County employees. They had jurisdiction over the care for the poor, sick and those of unsound mind. Other duties involved establishing and paying bounties on wolves and wild cats.

They had legal custody of orphans and appointed constables, also supervision of roads, employed ferry operators, licensed ordinary keepers and had complete control of the fiscal operations. These duties of administration were not unlike those now vested on the Board of County Commissioners.

So much for the organization of the County. What did the Commissioners do? How did they do it? The Court records reveal much about the life of the County. Their judical job was the same as the Courts of today: to keep law and order, and to see that justice was administered. To accomplish this the dignity of the Court must be rigorously upheld. The records contain a number of citations for contempt of Court. Usually a public apology was sufficient to settle citations for contempt. However, in June, 1660, one

John Chenman of Charles County was fined ten pounds of tobacco, for profanity in the Court room.

August 19, 1658, Thomas Baker was hailed into Court for calling Justice Job Chandler "A spindel-shanked Doge". The court bound Baker over on his good behavior. In later records the same Baker appears as a Justice who was driven off the bench, when charged with hog stealing. However, hog stealing in that day usually meant the shooting of ear-marked hogs running at large in the forests. This was a sport engaged in by both servants and planters until the Assembly made it a misdemeanor.

In the May 12, 1659, session of the Charles County Court "supened" Robert Troop, Edmund Linsey and Joseph Linton before them to declare who it was who had called Justice Capt. John Jenkins "Captain Grindstone", perhaps a reference to his hardness as a Justice. No action was recorded in this contempt case. There was comparatively little theft of household goods or property in the early days, because the colonists had so few personal possessions to steal.

Interestingly enough the early court records of Charles County abound with names that are still familiar to the county today. Liber A which was kept by the Clerk George Thompson with the exception of several months in 1660 written by Thomas Lomax contain references to names such as: Beane, Belaine, Borman, Carpender, Causeane, Chandler, Clarke, Gray, Hawkins, Harrison, Harris, Hungerford, Jarbo, Lomax, Matthews, Mitchell, Neale, Newman, Posey, Pope, Rawlins, Robinson, Robsson, Sanders, Simpson, Smoote, Swann, Thompson, Linton, Wade, Wheeler, among others.

There is no record of where the first Court of the newly erected Charles County was held on May 25, 1658. The second meeting of the Court was held at Humpherie Atwikses on June 4. George Thompson was appointed Clerk of the Court and "James Linsey, Henrie Addames, James

Walker, Edward Parks" were the commissioners who were present. The Court met at stated intervals all through the next two years, probably at Humphrey Atwikses, and not until the Court of February 12, 1660, do we find another definite reference to the place in which it was held. The Court record for that date states "Court adjourned until March 12, 1660 and appoynted to bee held at Clement Theobals hows".[15]

The Charles County Court before 1675 seems to have met at inns or in private houses without exception. Various listings in the County levies show payments to innkeepers for this purpose. In 1671 the levy shows the Edmund Lindsay (Lendsey), the Port Tobacco innkeeper and planter was paid 1,000 pounds of tobacco "for the trouble of his house for keeping court";[16] and the following year Benjamin Rozer, the sheriff, received 450 pounds of tobacco "while court was kept at his house".

It seems to be true that the people of the county actually called these homes in which court was held "court house" as in testimony before the Court on February 9, 1663 "Thomas Hussey sayeth he being subpoined by Will Robbins to a Court held in Charles County the 12th of May last past and being in a loft att the Court house". In the same case one George Harris also testified to "being in a loft in Court House.[17]

In 1663 the Assembly ordered County Commissioners of each county to build stocks and a pillory near the courthouse and a ducking stool at some convenient place and also to provide irons for burning malefactors. The one with the letter H was for hog stealers, one with R for runaway slaves, one with M for murderers and T for thieves. These marking irons were in the hands of the Sheriff who administered the court sentences. Counties failing to comply with these orders were subject to a fine. In compliance, the Charles County Commissioners ordered the sheriff to build stocks, a pillory and a whipping post at the place where court was kept and a ducking stool at Popes Creek.

In 1672, the County levy shows that 10,000 pounds of tobacco was provided for Henry Moore to build a court house but this does not seem to have ever been done so it is assumed that Moore did not fill his part of the bargain.

An act of the Assembly of 1674 required each county in the Province to erect or provide a suitable court house and prison. Prior to that time the safekeeping of prisoners was in the hands of the sheriff leaving him to keep them as best he could under the circumstances. Charles County then authorized from the County Levy of October 6, 1674, 20,000 pounds of tobacco to Mr. John Allen for building a Court House and prison.

On November 11, 1674, the record directs that John Allen "shall have payment" for what he has done, and over and above the "Former bargaine" about the Court house and prison shall be paid to him out of the next year's County levy. This same session of the court records the Deed of Sale for the property and contains a detailed description of the buildings:

"Mr. John Allen acknowledges this ensueing Deed of Sale for a Court house & prison with an acre of Land belonging thereunto being a parcell of a tract of land scituate & being in Charles County Called Moores Lodge to Mr. Henry Adams and Mr. Thomas Matthews one the behalfe of the Right Honorable the Lord Proprietor for the publicke use of the Inhabitants of Charles County for a Court house for his Lordship's Justices to hold court in & a prison house to secure prisoners in when thereunto Comitted

"To all Christian People to whom these presents shall come Greetinge I John Allen of Charles County in the Province of Maryland Gentleman, For & in Consideration of twenty thousand pounds of good sound Merchantable tobacco raised in the said County by a publicke levy & to me in hand paid, the receipt whereof I doe hereby acknowledge & therewith to be Fully paid, Contented and satisfied, have granted, bargained & sold, & by these presents doe grant bargaine and sell unto the Right Honorable Caecilius absolute Lord & proprietary of Maryland & Avalon Lord Baron of Baltemore & his heires & Successors for ever, One acre of Land being parcell of a tract of Land scituate in Charles County aforesaid Called Moores Lodge distant from the head of Portobacco about foure miles, & one dwelling house scituate upon the said acre of Land, twenty & five foot in Length and twenty & two foot in breadth, with a porch tenne foot long & eight foot wide thereunto Adjoyneing with a roome over the first roome and another over the said porch, & a shead behinde in breadth twelve foot & a halfe or thereabouts, divided with a partition into two roomes, with two bricke Chimneyes (that is to say) the one to be built in the Lower roome of the said house & the other upon the same foundation in the upper room thereof, with all necessary & Convenient doores, locks, keyes, bolts, latches, hinges, staircases, staires, windowes, window frames, Casements & glasse to be well glazed & put in the said frames throughout the said house above & below, & all the roomes to be well plankt on the floores, the lower roome to be well wainscotted, the upper roome well daubed & sealed with mortar white limed & sized, & the shead sealed & lined with riven boards, And alsoe one other house to be built neare unto the said house & upon the said acre of Land three foot within ground at the foundation to be twenty & five foot long and fifteene foot wide within, & of sufficient strength for a prison, the first room entering to be eight foot in height from the lower floore, & a partition in the middle thereof, with a loft or Garrett over all the said roome & both the floores of the said roome & loft to be well plankt & the said loft to be six foot high & sealed and lined with riven boards, Together with free Egresse and Regresse to & from the said house for all persons at all times, The said dwelling house to be Compleatly finished for a Courthouse forthwith in manner mentioned, And the said house for a prison to be finished as aforesaid before the last day of May now next ensueinge, To have & to hold the said acre of Land & houses & all & singular the before graunted premises thereunto belonging with their & every of their appurtenances from mee the said John Allen & my heires for ever, unto the Right Honorable the Lord Proprietary aforesaid his heires & Successors forever, To & for the publicke use of his & their County of Charles County in Maryland aforesaid & the Inhabitants thereof for a Court house for his Lordships Justices to hold Court in & a prison to secure prisoners when thereunto Comitted, And to & for these very purposes for ever And I the said John Allen for myselfe my heires Executors and Administrators doe hereby Covenant promise & graunt to & with the Right Honorable the Lord Proprietary afore said his heires & Successors, That I the said John Allen, my heires Executors, Administrators, or Assignees shall & will from time to time & at all times hereafter maintain provide a keepe or Cause to be maintained Provided and kept a publicke ordinary or house of entertainment neare unto the said Court house & prison, for the Convenient entertainment of his Lordships Justices & all other persons whatsoever at any time thither lawfully resortinge: And shall & will keepe and Cause to be kept the said Court house & prison in good and sufficient repair for ever except their foundations shall happen to decay with rottonesse ....." And the deed was signed by John Allen and dated the 10th day of November, 1674.

This full account in Liber F of the Charles County Court Proceedings is followed by a memorandum that "full & peaceable possession and seizin of the said house was given by the within named John Allen to Mr. Henry Adames, Mr. Thomas Matthews and Mr. Ignatius Causine, three of his Lordships Justices.

It seems conclusive that this first Court House of Charles County was not in the town of Port Tobacco. The original deed of sale says that the parcell of the tract of land called Moores Lodge was four miles from the head of Port Tobacco River. Further evidence of its inland location is found in the Act of the Assembly of 1727, authorizing the new courthouse to be built at Port Tobacco, which states that "the place where the Court House now stands is <u>so remote</u>

from any landing that the charge of bringing materials together by land carriage for that end (building the new Court House and prison) will be much greater than if the same was to be built at the head of Port Tobacco Creek."

A search of the land records seems to indicate that Moores Lodge on which the original Court House was built was probably on one of the branches of Zekiah Swamp, Clarke's Run, which is about three miles south of La Plata and three miles east of Port Tobacco perhaps in the vicinity of the farm called "Johnsontown" near the Charles County Fair Grounds.

Though John Allen obligated himself, his heirs, his executors, etc., to keep the Court House and prison in good repair "for ever except their foundations shall happen to decay with rottonesse" evidence shows that he soon shifted his burden to other shoulders. Sometime before 1687 he sold his land, and his obligations to keep the Court House and the Ordinary to Thomas Hussey.

In March, 1687, at the meeting of the Council of Maryland, the Commissioners of Charles County presented a petition which had been drawn up at a meeting of the County Court on the 10th day of January, 1687, by Commissioners Capt. Ignatius Causeen, Capt. William Barton. Mr. Henry Hawkins, Major John Wheeler, Mr. John Courts and Mr. Randolph Hanson. They stated that because Thomas Hussey refused to keep the ordinary at the Court House at the price of liquors set by the Court, the Court had licensed Mr. Philip Lynes to keep it and they ordered Thomas Hussey to give up the key to the Court House and the acre of land belonging to it by virtue of the original deed of sale. They asked the Provincial Court to grant an order for laying out the acre of land belonging to the Court House to the best advantage for the public good and the accommodation of the court. They also requested that additional land be laid out adjoining the court house from that part of his Lordship's forest not yet patented, as much as the Council thought advisable.

At the same meeting of the Council Philip Lynes submitted evidence that despite a warrant forbidding anyone to obstruct the passage of supplies and provisions to the Court House pending a decision in the present dispute about the "Court House Lott", Thomas Hussey did attempt to keep out Lynes and his employees.

The Council ordered the Sheriff of Charles County to bring Thomas Hussey before the Council on the first day of the next Provincial Court to answer the contempt charges and they directed the Sheriff not to let Hussey out on bail unless he would give good security for his appearance at the appointed time and promise to behave in the meantime.

Thomas Hussey forthwith appeared before the Provincial Council in April. In answer to the charges against him, he advised the Council that in January when the Commissioners set the price of liquor for the ensuing year, they set it so low that he chose to let his license fall rather than try to keep the Ordinary as he was obligated to do by the purchase of land. However, he says that as he realized the necessity of an inn for accommodating the County at court time and as the Court house was remote "from any other place" fit to serve as such, he offered to put in his place an "honest person" who would fill the requirements and take over his obligation which he assumed when he purchased the land from Capt. Allen. According to Mr. Hussey, the Commissioners refused his offer and granted the license for the Ordinary to Mr. Lynes, meanwhile petitioning the Council to lay out the acre of land for the Court House. Hussey continues to the effect that he esteems "Public Profit" before "his private Convenience" and is willing for the land to be laid out, just so it does not take more than the acre which is the County's right and he promised that he would give free access to the land. He complained that Lynes chose to take upon himself the authority of setting his own bounds to the Court House acre and threatened to take away Hussey's dwelling houses in the acre.

After hearing Mr. Hussey's testimony, the Council ordered the Deputy Surveyor of Charles County to survey and lay out the lot or acre of land on which the Court House was standing including in the acre the Prison, Pillory and Stocks and so far else as the acre needs to extend to make it convenient to "wood and water" without prejudicing the dwelling or other houses belonging to Thomas Hussey which are adjacent to the Court House. The surveyor was directed to return the plot of the survey to the Council with all convenient speed.

They cleared Hussey of the charges brought against him by Lynes but said that there was cause for complaint against him for hindering and molesting Lynes in erecting and building a kitchen for the Court House. Hussey promised not to trouble Lynes any further and he was dismissed, paying his charges and the fees "hereabout accrewed."[18]

Unfortunately no records seem to have been kept for the Provincial Council for the years between 1689 and 1692 because of chaotic conditions in the Colony during its change of status from a Proprietary Colony to a Royal Colony so the report of the survey is not available.

It is even possible that the survey was not made immediately because in the year 1697 we find in the Charles County Court Records the surveyor writing to the Commissioners as follows:

"To ye worshipful ye Justices of Charles County Whereas by virtue of agrement Act of assembly relating to lands for courthouse and by your worships command I have survaid and laid oute of a tract of land belonging to Thomas Hussey of Charles County and joining the court, three acres beginning at a locust post number 1 and thence running northwest and by north, for length 30 pearch, to a locust post number 2, and thence running south west by west for breath sixtene pearch, to a locust post number 3, and thence running north eastward by south for length of 30 pearch, to locust post number 4, and thence running north east by east for breadth sixtene pearch, to affor said locust post as may further appear by a platt here of as follows—September ye 10th 1697—" The surveyor's report is followed by

CHARLES COUNTY as it appears on a map in Circa 1670 in the Public Records Office in London.

Photo by Constance Stuart Larrabee, Chestertown, Maryland

HOUSE ON "SARUM," Manorial grant to Joseph Pile from Lord Baltimore in 1680.

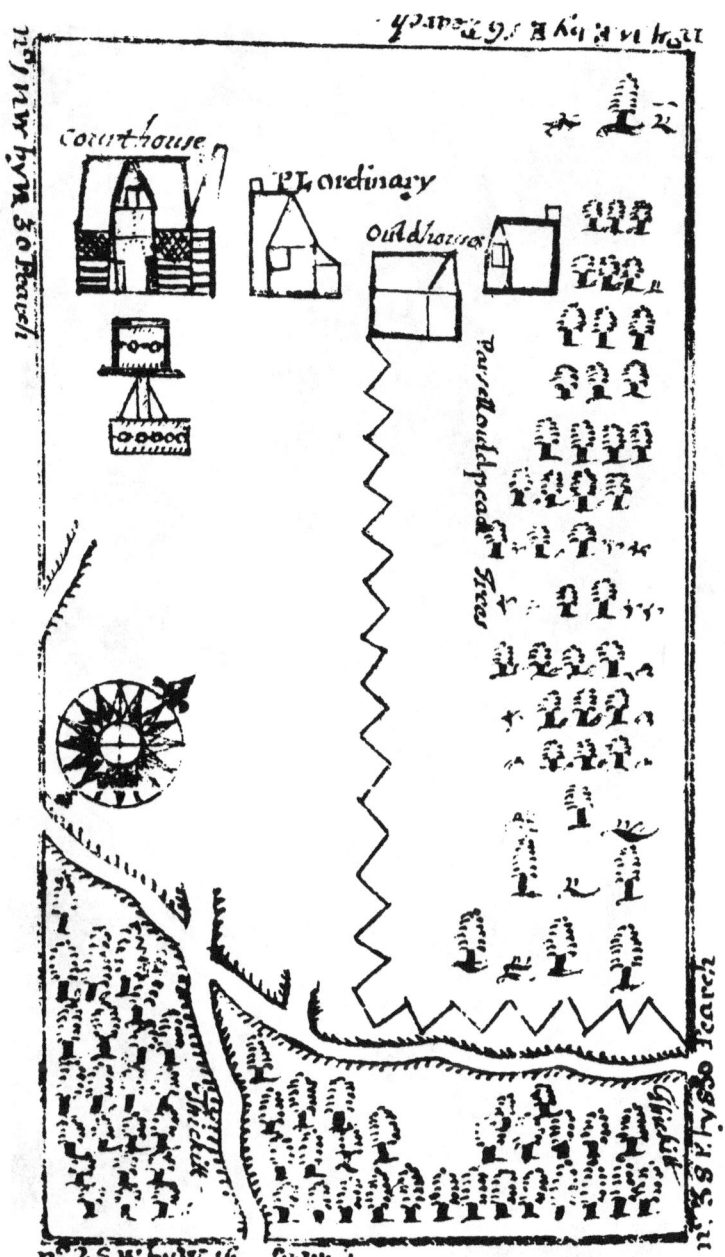

From *Charles County Records, Liber A, p. 277*

SURVEYOR'S SKETCH of the Charles County Courthouse and the area in which it stood made in the year 1697. This Courthouse was built on land then owned by Thomas Hussey which was four miles from the head of Port Tobacco River on the North branch of Zekiah Swamp.

Photo by *Constance Stuart Larrabee, Chestertown, Maryland*

View of the Port Tobacco Valley and Port Tobacco River taken from Mulberry Grove.

a sketch of the courthouse and the area in which it stood.[19] The small, rather primitive building surrounded by its out buildings, peach trees and beyond that the wilderness gives a good indication that Charles County almost 50 years after its establishment was still in many ways, a frontier community.

While on the subject of the first courthouse it is interesting to note that the "King's Arms" were purchased for it in 1701 and "Barrs" were added in 1709. A later ruling in 1721 forbade all liquor by retail at or withing half mile of the Courthouse "without a license by this Court".

All this time the County was growing in population. It is a matter of interest to see what manner of people these were and how they lived. What was their economic status and what were the general problems they faced? Fortunately there is a wealth of recorded material to answer these questions.

Men of considerable means came in search of adventure and to take advantage of the religious freedom offered in the new Colony. They brought with them indentured servants, some of whom were skilled artisans, carpenters, brick layers, blacksmiths and others. There was also a solid core of English middle class persons who gave the colony stability and as always there was also a small element of the criminal class who sought to escape the heavy hand of justice at home.

They settled along the waterways which thread the County. Cabins and huts were close to the water edge and in the scattered clearings stood the more pretentious homes of the manors. The first houses were built of wood and bricks were used only in the chimneys. There is ample proof that most of the bricks used in construction in the Colonial period were made at or near the site of the building. This is contrary to the general idea that all bricks used in the houses and churches were brought from England as ship ballast. Ships of that day were small and cargo space was needed for other valuable items in addition to bricks and other building materials. The record of the Provincial Court, 1653 show a case in which a man named Cornwallis agreed to transfer to Cornelius Canada, brick maker, 300 acres of land on the Patuxent in payment for 36,000 brick, "good, sound and well burned". One-third were to be made that year in the Patuxent or Potomac and the balance to be delivered at Canada's plantation by June 1654.

In *Archives of Maryland* the early records mention one house 20 by 25 feet and another 20 feet square. A house owned by Paul Simpson was only 15 feet square, built of logs, floored and lofted with deal boards, lined with riven boards. Furnishings were few and very plain and candles were used for light and fire places for heat. Table utensils were of wood or earthen ware and pewter, while kitchen utensils were from brass, copper or iron. All the cooking was done at an open fireplace. The wearing apparel of the 17th century colonist was in most cases as meager as the living quarters and its furnishings. It was the custom in those days upon the death of a colonist to file an inventory of all his possessions. The inventory of the estate of Captain Robert Wentour is as follows: one Portugal cap, one sea cap, old freze suit, serge suit, cloth suit, bareskin suit, buff coat, short coat lined with plush, pair freze britches, old gray coat, Holland jacket and canvas doublet. Captain Wentour was a member of the Governors Council and as such must have been a man of above average means. It is not likely that at this early date there was much if any weaving of fine cloth in the colony. And if it had to be imported it was, of course, high in price.

Communication between the widely scattered homes was difficult. There were narrow trails through the forest to St. Mary's City, to the Patuxent and north to Annapolis. Travel was on foot or by horseback following the marks on blazed trees. Water transportation was the most comfortable and the safest method but it was slow. Small boats privately owned plied up and down the Potomac and across to Virginia.

One of the first acts of the Charles County Court was to establish a ferry over Wicomico River. On June 4, 1658, at the second meeting of the Court it was ordered by the Governor's Council and the County Commissioners that one Samuel Harris should keep a ferry over "Wicokomeko" River from Metompkin Point to the end of Trews March (marsh). The County agreed to pay him yearly "900 Thousand" pounds of tobacco and the County contracted with Goodman Smote to build the ferry boat for 700 pounds of tobacco. Quite often the ferry operator also kept an ordinary or inn for the accommodation of the travelers who used his ferry.

Official letters or proclamations in the Province were sent from house to house until they were safely delivered as directed. Every house holder was required by law to relay public mail to the next plantation within one half hour after receiving it. Failure to do so made him liable to a fine of 100 pounds of tobacco. In cases of emergency special messengers were drafted to deliver dispatches. It was not until near the end of the Proprietary period that public post was established.

On May 20, 1695 a proclamation was made of an agreement entered into with Captain Perry to be post between the Potomac and Philadelphia eight times a year. Starting from Newton's Point, on the Wicomico, to the Potomac, he was to go by Allen's Mill (now called Fresh), Benedict-Leonard Town and across the Patuxent to Annapolis. The stages were to start the last Monday in June. This route was one of the links in the chain established to connect Williamsburg to Philadelphia.[20] This same year a post route and a road was established from Port Tobacco through Upper Marlboro by the Ferry at London Towne on South River to Annapolis and on to Philadelphia.

Sundays and Court days saw great activity from all the countryside. Especially for Court days the public house was crowded and all nearby homes had visiting relatives and friends. After Court was adjourned festivities were in order. Because of the isolation in which many of them lived the colonists made the most of every opportunity while traveling.

Seventeenth Century Charles County people were not immune to illness. The nature of the illnesses is not too clear. However, from meager descriptions malaria may have been the most common. Ague and fevers are mentioned in a number of cases. It was not uncommon on many of the river farms to have summer houses on a part of the property well back from the river, which is a reverse of the modern day practice. This was no doubt an effort to get away from the mosquitos that came up from the marshes and river and creek shores. An example of such summer houses was one at Causine's Manor, not standing now, but whose foundations may be found in the field ajoining the road to Chapel Point. The present house on Brentfield farm on the road from Faulkner to Popes Creek was the summer house, while the foundation of the main house, or winter quarters, on that farm are almost down at the river shore.

Much of the early records are concerned with suits pertaining to the treatment of the sick in the County and they contain a wealth of information on those who guarded the health of the County. It is not surprising with the crude methods of diagnoses and treatment that many of the colonists did not survive. Doctors, Chirurgeons and lay practitioners appear in suits to collect bills, and in suits for malpractice, and civil cases. There is no way to determine if these men were qualified, but it seems unlikely many of them had received professional training for their services. Perhaps the reader can form his own conclusion from the following account of one Dr. John Meekes, who styled himself as a "Chirurgeon of London", and was also a storekeeper in Charles County.

It involved a suit against Mrs. Anne Haggat, administratrix of Humphrey Haggat.

The bill presented by Meekes' "atturney" William Price reads as follows:

"To the Worshipful Commissioners for Charleses Countie the humble Petition of John Meekes Sheweth

"That Humphery Haggat deceased stands indebted to your Petitioner for phisick administred to his wife and him upon his death bed; the sum of 1840 lb of tobacco and Caske and also for sugar sent for to your petitioner as by his noat may appear the sume of 246 pounds of tobacco for which your Petitioner humbly Craueth your worships to grant him an order against the Relict and Administratrix of the sayd haggats Estate for the sayd debt and hee shall as in duty bound Pray & c

"Mr. humphery Haggat his bill of Phisick december the 23th Ao 1662 sent for by Mr Humphery Haggat to his wife shee then beeing sicke and lambe I used thees meanes to her:

25 day one dosse of purging Pills	lb	0030
26 day one dosse more of the licke Pills	lb	0030
27 day one portion of mixtur	lb	0040
28 day let blood in the foote	lb	0050
29 day 1 dose of Purging pils	lb	0030
30 day 1 large plaster for the payne in her hippe	lb	0020
1 parcell of Oyntment to Embriate for her disease	lb	0030
for one fortnights time going and cumming back afoot	lb	0400
Before this was administred by me thay sent for medicins by thear man Thomas Steed I sent it according to thear order.		
Euecroticem cum duplix slipticon Paracilue Emplaister Adherna and Diapalma: and oyntment at	lb	0100
3 dosses of troches of mir at	lb	0120

860

"March the 29 Ao 1663 sent for by Mr. humphery haggat beeing sick of a violent bloodie flux I did cum to him April the second day Appliation used to him

2 Restringent Portions used that day at........lb	0080
1 supositer at night to Cause Rest........lb	0030

next day
I Cordiall portion........lb	0040
2 Restringent Boloses ....lb	0080
1 Cordiall bolus more........lb	0040
1 Cordiall portion at night........lb	0040
1 subpositer at night more as before to .Cause Rest. ....lb	0030

next day
1 Restringent glister at........lb	0040
2 Cordiall boloses ....lb	0080
1 subpositor at night used asbefor to Cause Rest. ....lb	0030
1 Cordiall giuen him in the night........lb	0040
1 parcell of oyntment for his hips........lb	0020

next day
1 Restringent Portion in the morning at..lb	0040
2 portions of Restringent meanes left with him ....lb	0060
1 parcelle of Cardamims and sum lef to bee used in his drincke for his use........lb	0030

Boate hands and time for four days and Visit........lb 0300

                                                        980
                                                        860

        The total sum........lb 1840"

The total bill of 1840 pounds of tobacco for this vast and forbidding array of medicinals, to say nothing of the blood letting is not high by present day standards. But what of the results? Mr. Haggat died. Mrs. Haggat lived to enjoy life as the wife of the prominent planter Richard Fowke and Dr. Meekes collected his bill.

Other doctors mentioned are John Stone, probably the son of Governor Wm. Stone; Dr. Matthew Gaidge and one Dr. Jacob, alias John, Lumbroso. Lumbroso appears as a physician, attorney, planter and keeper of an ordinary. He was a Portuguese Jew who was a remarkable charcater answering to many civil and criminal suits against him. Perhaps most amazing of all we find a practicing woman physician appearing in these same records. Mary Doughtie Vanderdonck had a regular practice in the middle of the 17th century and she was not reluctant to carry her debtors into court.

Usually the burial was on the home plantation where the deceased had lived. Officials looked with disfavor on excessive burial expenses, as they were the first costs to be defrayed out of the estate. Friends and relatives were provided with black mourning ribbons, and a funeral dinner was generally given with beer and liquor served. These were just as legitimate an expense as the digging of the grave, the coffin or canvas bag and the winding sheet.

In Charles County one James Lee was made one of the overseers of the estate of a widow, Mrs. Joseph Lenton. Lee made the arrangements for the funeral. As was the usual custom Lee purchased the following items: Two pounds of gun powder to fire muskets at burial, three barrels of beer for the wake and the necessary black ribbon for the friends and relatives. The total cost of these items was twelve hundred pounds of tobacco. When Francis Pope, who was the administrator of Joseph Lenton's estate, refused to pay the bill, suit was brought in the Charles County Court. It was dismissed because Lee failed to show that Mrs. Lenton's deceased husband had made him an executor.

This did not clear the situation, however, because Lee brought a second suit at which he apparently proved he had been appointed. In this second suit Geo. Thompson was the attorney for Pope and he asked that the jury be given these instructions:

"First, to inquire whether at an ordinary planters wife's funeral it be not ridiculous to shoot, as they do at a young soldiers death.

"Second, to inquire whether at the time of the funeral it be Christian-like for some few neighbors to be gathered together and instead of showing a mournfulness for the loss of a friend and neighbor, to turn to their carousing cups to the quantity of three barrels of beer to the value of nine hundred pounds of tobacco.

"Third, to inquire whether or not it be most unreasonable that James Lee should charge three hundred pounds of tobacco for a boat and hands to fetch this same drink.

"Fourth, to inquire whether or not it be absurd that Lee should charge the administrator of the deceased with thirty-six yards of black ribbon at twelve pounds of tobacco a yard, when the whole world may imagine that it was but a dolorous countenance to disguise his rejoicing beat."

The foreman of the jury, Thomas Lomax, announced a verdict in favor of Lee.

The role of the Colonial Militia in Maryland directly effected the lives of the people who lived in Charles County. In June and July of 1658 the militia of the Province had been reorganized and in the new Charles County the earliest mentioned captain was Joseph Jenkins. James Lindsey was Lieutenant. The local captains were required to list all residents 16 to 60 years of age who were able to bear arms and from these lists enough men were to be picked to make up trained military bands for the protection of the colonists. The captains were also obligated to inspect the arms of the householders and see that each family had its proper outfit. They were to hold monthly musters and fine absentees. These fines collected could then be used to buy drums and colors for the militia and "after such provisions was made, to make the company drink at their meetings to muster."[21] Even as late as 1675-1676 we find record of Giles Cole and Stephen Cawood of Charles County killed in fighting the Susquehannock Indians.[22]

Lord Baltimore continued to bestow manor grants in the Charles County area until almost the end of the Century. In 1664 Henry Darnall was granted 1,000 acres in Benedict Hundred which was known as "Darnall's Manor". In the same Hundred Nathaniel Truman, Gent. was granted 1,000 acres in 1665 which was called "Manor of Truman's Place". The next grant was in 1667 when Thomas Allanson received 1,000 acres in Chincamuxen Hundred as "Christian Temple Manor". A 2,000 acre manor called "Friendship" was granted to Bennet Hoskins in Port Tobacco Hundred in 1672. "Rice Manor" in Nanjemoy Hunderd which had escheated to the Proprietary was resurveyed for Jesse Wharton in 1675. The 2300 acre property was then renamed "Wharton Manor". A manor grant of 3,333 acres in Benedict Hundred was granted Major William Boarman in 1676 and called "Boarman's Manor" and lastly "Sarum" was granted to Joseph Pile in 1680. The manor consisted of 1160 acres in Newport Hundred.[23] These manors together with the ones listed earlier in the chapter account for all the manors granted in Charles County except for one of undetermined date held by Job Chandler who held manorial rights jointly with his brother-in-law Simon Oversee on an unnamed tract of land perhaps somewhere in the Port Tobacco area.

The many waterways which thread Charles County made major seaports unnecessary. Every planter could have his own landing and many did. However, the Maryland Assembly in 1669 created seaports with the plan of serving the thinly settled neighborhoods. From these places tobacco and grain could be shipped to foreign countries and at them merchandise goods and commodities from the mother country could unload. Proper excise taxes on imports and exports could be collected at these specified ports for the Proprietary and for the Colony. Before 1669 the ports of entry on the West Shore had been St. Mary's City, Chaptico and Port Tobacco.[24] We do find early records of a community in the Port Tobacco area which grew up with "Chandler's Hope", the patent of Job Chandler, as it focal point and is sometimes referred to in the records as Chandler's town or Chandlee'stown. This was the only place with any concentration of population for many years.

However, the erections of towns by legislation was a hobby with the lawmakers and land speculators in the Province. Some of these towns were laid out where a village already existed. Others were laid out on open ground because the people needed a market or a port or because the site was promising. None of these towns grew with any rapidity but many of them grew steadily in conformity with the needs of the growing population.

The pattern of erection was generally as follows: Commissioners were appointed to agree with the owner of land for a tract of 50 to 100 or more acres which was then staked off and divided into lots of an acre each, intersected by proper streets, lanes and alleys. The lots being numbered and priced, the owner was allowed to select one lot and the rest were divided among the "taker-up" who received the free-hold in consideration of a yearly quit-rent usually one penny to the Lord Proprietary.[25]

Such an Act for Advancement of Trade was passed by the Assembly in November of 1683. "And in Charles County on diggs his purchase in Wiccocomico River formerly ffendalls on the Creeks and on the Church Land on the East side of Portobacco Creek neere the mouth of the Creeke and on Stumpe necke near Chingemuxen on Mr. Reddish his land. Commissioners appointed for buying and purchasing said Towne Lands, Ports and Places of the now owners and possessors—Coll. Wm. Chandler, Mr. Edw'd Pye, Mr. Thomas Burford, Mr. Henry Adams, Mr. Ignatius Causiene, Capt. James Neall, Copl. Humphery Warren, Mr. John Wheeler, Capt. Wm. Barton, Mr. Rob't Henley, Mr. James Tyne, Mr. John Stone, Mr. James Smallwood, Mr. John Bayne, Mr. Joseph Cornall, Mr. Wm. Smith, Mr. John Gouge, Mr. Henry Hawkins, Mr. John Reddish, Mr. Robert Payne, Mr. Jno Munn, Mr. James Wheeler, Mr. Edw'd Sanders, Mr. Edwd Mings."[26]

The results of the Commission of 1683 were reported to the General Assembly in 1684. Two towns were established as ports in Charles County. They are not named but the locations are given as follows: "At the Head of Port Tobacco Creek, near the Church there" and "At the mouth of Nanjemoy Creek at, or near, Lewis' Neck."

Benedict - Leonardtown, now known as Benedict, was also erected in Charles County in 1683. It was named for Benedict Leonard Calvert, the 4th Lord Baltimore.[27]

The religion of the colonists was one of the most important phases of their life in the new world. The colony of Maryland had been founded by Lord Baltimore as a place of refuge primarily for persons of the Roman Catholic faith. The records of the Catholic Church in Charles County begin long before the establishment of the County. You will perhaps remember that it was in 1639 that Father Andrew White of the Society of Jesus converted the Queen of the Potopaco Indians and 130 of her subjects. He then made that Indian village his home for most of his stay in Maryland. It was while he was living there that he composed his catechism in the native dialect and compiled a dictionary and grammar of the language. Father Thomas Copley joined Father White at Port Tobacco about 1643. About 1644 Capt. Richard Ingle, acting under orders from the Puritans in England, attacked the modest establishment of Father Copley and Father White and took them back to England in chains.

The mission was restored to Father Copley in 1648 and a year later he acquired St. Thomas Manor under the usual "conditions of Plantation" with all manorial rights. Because of the uncertain political affairs of both the Province and the Mother Country, Father Copley transferred the deed of the manor to Thomas Matthews, one of the prominent Catholic settlers of the Colony. The transfer of the manor grant from Father Copley to Thomas Matthews reads as follows: "Know ye that whereas Thomas Matthews of our Province of Maryland gentleman hath assigned to him 4,000 acres of land from Thomas Copley, esq. —do give, grant, enfeoffe and conform unto the said Thomas Matthews All the parcell of forest Land lying on the north side of Potowmeck River neere unto a Creek formerly called Portobacco Creek But now St. Thomas Creek. And we do by these patents will and appoint that the said recited Parcells of Land shall from henceforth bee one entire manor and bee called by the name of St. Thomas Mannor That he may hold, use and enjoy within the said Mannor, a Court Leet and Court Baron . . . Given under our great Seal of our province this 25th of October Anno Domini 1649."[28]

The grant contained 3,500 acres of land on the west side of the Creek and 500 acres on the East side which included the land known today as Chapel Point and St. Ignatius Church.

Thomas Matthews held the land in trust for the Society despite the fact that it was legally his and in 1662 when Lord Baltimore was once again in firm control of the Province, Thomas Matthews returned St. Thomas Manor to the Society of Jesus through Father Henry Warren, S.J. The Mission was permanently established by Father Warren in 1662 probably in a house with Chapel attached, on a cove between Deep Point and "Fort" (Fourth) Point. It was also called "Olde Chapell", hence the name Chapel Point today. The records seem to indicate that from 1662 on there have always been Jesuit priests in residence at St. Thomas Manor attending to the spiritual needs of the Catholics over the whole area of the County and expanding going to the north as the settlers moved on. In 1673 the report of the Jesuit Fathers in Maryland to the Provincial of the Society in Rome mentions two Franciscan fathers who had arrived to work in the Mission field with the Jesuits. These Franciscan priests, the first to come to English America, are credited with establishing the mission at Newport which was the beginning of St. Mary's Parish of today.

The Act of 1692 established the Church of England as the official religion of the Province and Catholics in the Province were barred from all civil rights. Despite the difficulties under which they then labored, the Jesuits living at St. Thomas Manor continued to care for the spiritual welfare of the Catholics of the county. Two records surviving to our times attest to the continued vitality of the mission despite political persecution. In 1695 a church bell was installed at St. Thomas by Father William Hunter, S.J., and he established the first Mission Stations in the countryside about St. Thomas.

The early roots of St. Mary's Church in Bryantown may be traced to a chapel on the farm of Maj. William Boarman called "Boarman's Rest" of which there is record as early as 1696. This mission is one of those established by the Jesuit fathers at St. Thomas and was known as Zekiah Chapel.

In 1697, a terrible pestilence broke out among the people of the lower counties. While the disease was raging the Catholic priest went from house to house helping the sick and administering to the dying. In consequence, the Lower House sent a message to the Governor complaining that "the Papish priest of Charles County do, of their own accord, in this raging and violent mortality in that County, make it their business to go up and down the County and to person's houses when dying and frantic and endeavor to seduce and make proselytes of them and in such condition boldly presume to administer the sacrament to them" and they asked the Governor to issue a proclamation to restrain their behavior.[29]

Right from the very beginning there were almost as many Protestants in the County as there were Catholics. Many of these were of decided Presbyterian tendencies and to mention a few who can be definitely indentified with the meager records which we have today: Walter Beane, or Bayne, his brother Ralph, and Governor William Stone were evidently members of that church. For awhile there does not seem to have been any church organization but private meetings conducted by laymen were probably held in various houses. The arrival of the Rev. Francis Doughty in Charles County in 1657 establishes the date of the organized existence of Presbyterianism in Maryland, and indeed in the new world.

Francis Doughty first appears in America in 1637 in Massachusetts. There he preached the Presbyterian doctrine until he was forced to leave the colony by the established church. He emigrated to New Amsterdam where again he gathered a congregation of the English inhabitants of the place. This time he ran into difficulties of a political character as his daughter Mary married Adrain Van der Donk, principal lawyer of the colony and political rival of Stuyvesant. Van der Donk died in 1655 and upon the death of his powerful Protector, Doughty, his daughter and other members of his family moved into the "English Virginias". He left for Maryland in August, 1657, where he purchased land from Giles Thompkins in Charles County. Here he at last enjoyed the religious freedom which he had so long sought. He married Governor Stone's sister Ann and seems to have made his headquarters at Nanjemoy where Governor Stone lived. It seems likely that he gathered a Church at that place and though an old man he was still vigorous enough to go about the country teaching and baptizing. It is interesting to note that it was Doughty's daughter Mary, who as Mary Doughty Van der Donk (or Vanderdonck), and later as the wife of Maryland's Hugh O'Neill, practiced medicine in Charles County in the seventeenth century.

There is no record of the place or date of Doughty's death. His work in Charles County was continued by the Reverend Matthew Hill who established himself in Charles County in 1669. In a letter back to England at that time Hill states that the people among whom he has been called to labor are "a loving and willing people". He says that "under his lordship's government we enjoy a great deal of liberty and particularly in matters of religion". He asks for some books and adds that he will have to wait for any salary until the tobacco harvest "Which is the only current money in our province".

Hill married Edith, the daughter of Walter Bean or Bayne, and he obtained grant of an estate which he called "Popleton" and which is still called by that name. He signed himself "Matthew Hill, Gentleman." Hill encountered trouble with the growth and strength of Quakers in the Colony and he was further handicapped by poor health. He died in 1679 leaving orphan children and considerable estate including a library of seventy volumes.

With the labors of Doughty and Hill, there was a period of some twenty years when Charles County had an organized Presbyterian group. It has been customary to regard Somerset County where Frances Makemie ministered in 1683 as the cradle of the Presbyterian Church in America but it is now evident that over a quarter of a century earlier Presbyterianism had begun in Charles County with the coming of Francis Doughty and had been maintained successfully by Matthew Hill.

After Hill's death the history of the Presbyterian Church in Charles County is almost unknown. It seems likely that church organization continued as the government in the individual church was the board of elders. Laymen worked to keep the church together until a minister could be found. This condition of affairs continued until the 18th century.[30]

In 1689 when William and Mary came to the throne of England, the regime of Lord Baltimore in the Province of Maryland was again in difficulty. William who felt that Proprietary Colonies were dangerous took the government of Maryland into his own hands and appointed a Royal Governor leaving Lord Baltimore possession of only his land and his personal revenues. Lionel Copely was appointed governor of the Colony in the King's name and one of the first things he did in 1692 was to have the Assembly pass an act establishing the Protestant religion of the Church of England as the established religion of Maryland.

This action was not unpopular in the colony itself as in 1689 we find a petition from the Protestants of each county in the Province asking the King to take such action, among the Colonial papers in the British Public Records Office.

On November 28, 1689, an address was sent to their most Excellent Majesties King William and Queen Mary by some of the inhabitants of Charles County. It is headed "The humble Address of the Gentlemen, Merchants, Planters, Freeholders, and Freemen their Majesties Protestant Subjects in Charles County in the Province of Maryland" and states "Wee your Majesties most faithful and loyall Subjects reflecting upon that greate transcendant happiness, that hath crowned the wishes of all your Protestant Subjects in your Rightful Succession to the Imperial Crowne of these Realms, have thought it our duty in particular to prostrate ourselves before your most gracious Majesties in an humble recognition of the same, acknowledging these tyes of an infinite gratitude by which we are ever bound as well by our owne natural dutye to your most sacred persons for that great deliverance of which Almighty God has blest you in makeing the glorious Instruments of the Protestant Religion, to the great comfort and rejoicing of us and our Posterity.

"Wee make bould to assure your most Excellent Majesties, that notwithstanding the Eendeavors and discouragements of the Popish party here to withdraw us from our Allegiance, wee still resolutely persist to own and justifie your Majesties with Sovereign Right and Dominion to this Province of which wee are Members together with the Protestant Religion of which your Majesties have been such Eminent owners and Defenders, in the mean time attending your most gracious pleasure towards a Settlement under a Protestant Government in this your Majesties Province, whereby our Religion, Lives, Liberties, and Properties may be secured, we daily pray the Divine Providence to protect your Majesties against all your Ennemies that you may be a lasting and strong Sanctuary for the Protestant Interest and be at last Crowned with the just reward of your glorious undertakings in the possessions of an immortal and Eternal Diadem.

Hum. Warren
James Smallwood
William Hawtan
Hen. Hardy
Chas. Shepherd
John Wilson
Osborne Lomax
John Wincott
Joseph Manning
Philip Lynes
Robert Thompson
Stephen Mankin
Wm. Stone
Joseph Bullox
George Plebe
Will. Hutchinson
Edward Middleton
Michaell Mynock
Jno. Marten
Rwa Newman
Will. Frost
Henry Hawkins
Edwd Philpott
Benjamin Posey
Mathew Dyke
Edward Rookewood
George Breet
Wm Taylor
Wm Spikeman
Jno Cornish
Rich Wade
John Ratcliff
Robert Powel
John Payn
George Newman
James Turner

Edward Turner
Peter X ad
Robert Powell
Randolph Hinson
John Addison
Richard Newton
John Gibbs
Alexander McKarter
Fra. Adams
Ralph Shawe
Tho. Parker
Tho. Wakefield
Edwd Cerston
James Kingsbury
Richard Land
Thos Whichaley
John Courby
Jos Allward
John Goasby
Wm Barton Sinr
John Gumey
Jon Callock
Rich. Dodd
James Thomson
Jon Cage
Arthur Eathey
John Knolewater
Henry Franklin
Henry Belcher
Valentine Hill
Hugh Bawden
Law. Rochefort
S Deyzer
Gilbt Clarke Vicecom
Comitat

Maryland.
1689."

Under the new law the ten existing counties were divided by the county justices and freeholders into parishes. In Charles County the only church in existence before the

Establishment Act was Christ Church at Port Tobacco with the Reverend Mr. Moore as minister. A church at the head of Port Tobacco Creek is spoken of previous to 1684. Mr. Moore died in 1692 and he was succeeded in 1694 by the Reverend George Tubman who remained as pastor until 1701.

The following Episcopal Parishes were established in the County in 1692-93; William and Mary or Pickawaxon; Port Tobacco; Nanjemoy or Durham; and Piscataway or St. Johns. The County was divided into seven hundreds, the lower part of William and Mary Parish, upper part of William and Mary Parish; the east side of Port Tobacco, the west side of Port Tobacco; the lower part of Nanjemoy Parish and the upper part of the same Parish; the upper part of King and Queen Parish, Benedict being joined to part of King and Queen Parish.

The report to the Assembly for 1694 included the following information on Charles County parishes. William and Mary and Port Tobacco already have churches built, Nanjemoy has a church in progress and Piscataway has a church agreed for. All the parishes want ministers and vestrymen are needed in every parish.

In 1696 the religious census of the Province sent to the Bishop of London showed William and Mary Parish and Port Tobacco Parish had 250 Tithables and an income of 10,320 pounds of tobacco with the incumbent minister for both parishes being the Reverend George Tubman. "Nanzemy" had 175 tithables with 19,000 pounds of tobacco.

Mr. George Tubman was reproved by the Reverend Thomas Bray who had been appointed comissary of the Province by the Bishop of London. He was charged with being a "polygamist", having married a wife in this country and already having one in England. Tubman protested to the Council that he had never married the English woman but had lived with her before becoming a minister and that he could produce proof of his claim if given an opportunity.

The Reverend Dr. Bray reprimanded him severely and gave him until November 1701 to produce his proof. No more is heard of Mr. Tubman after that date and it is not known whether he died or left the state for want of the proper evidence.

CHAPTER II—GROWTH AND DEVELOPMENT
THE EIGHTEENTH CENTURY

The Charles County of the eighteenth century was a settled community. All aspects of frontier life had disappeared from the area. The people were living in a society which was well defined according to the economic status of the individual. This is the century which calls into being the "great houses" which can still be found in the area. It is also a century of "great men"—men called into prominence by the demanding times in which they lived. Charles County's claims to national recognition find their basis in this century. For this reason it is worth careful consideration and study.

The first glimpses of the century follow much the same pattern as the end of the previous one. The way of life of the colonists changed slowly.

A census taken in 1712 shows that at that time Charles County had 933 masters and taxable men, 783 white women, 1507 children and 724 Negroes. The masters of families and taxable men are generally reputed "fitt to beare arms, being persons from 16 years and upwards, of which there are not many old and decrepit".

The first Negroes in Charles County are said to have been imported in the 17th Century by Francis Pope whose land grant on the Potomac River included Pope's Creek. The tobacco economy which was the life blood of the county demanded a cheap and expendable labor and more and more slaves were brought in to fill the demand. Undoubtedly at the time this census was taken, almost all the Negroes in the county were in the slave category, but during the eighteenth century there were an increasing number who were given their freedom and they created another class of society which is listed on later censuses as free colored.

Education is another interesting aspect of life in the colony which must be considered. During the 17th century education was a private matter which each man solved for himself and his family to the best of his ability. The wealthy colonists sent their sons back to England to be educated or imported tutors for them and for the rest of the colonists, education was only a rudimentary type confined to the home or to a few private schools set up by the more enterprising of the educated.

Late in the 17th and very early in the 18th century, laymen's libraries were established by the Reverend Thomas Bray as a part of his program to strengthen the Church of England in the colonies. They were designed for inhabitants of isolated districts and were intended as an antidote against the preaching of Quaker missionaries. In 1701 such a library was sent to Pickawaxen.[1]

In 1698 the constables in all the hundred were ordered to take exact account of schools and return information on the schools and the teachers to the Assembly. On the basis of this report, in 1723 the Assembly authorized schools for the 12 counties then comprising the Province. These were to be free schools and the funds for their support were levied by a tax of 20 shillings, in addition to what had been paid before for every Irish Catholic servant and for every Negro imported into the province.

With the establishment of the Church of England as the official church of the province, its ministers very quickly assumed the leadership in education. In 1724 the Bishop of London requested all clergymen to report on instruction of youth in their parishes. Robert Scott, the Rector of All Faith Parish, which included part of Charles as well as St. Mary's County, replied, "I have no public school in my parish for the instruction of youth but we are going about it."

The Reverend William McConchie of Port Tobacco and Durham parishes reported, "As yet there are no endowed schools in my parish though there are seven or eight private schools".

About 1724, the Reverend Hugh Jones became pastor of William and Mary Parish. The parish was 30 miles long and 10 miles wide and necessitated services at two places. So anxious were his parishioners to increase his meagre salary that they petitioned in vain the Maryland Assembly to allow the justices of Charles County to add substantially to the poll tax on Protestants in their parish, during the time he was minister. During the Commissary visitation in 1731 he gave account of his stewardship among numerous Negroes of the community—how he constantly examined them on their faith and expounded to them "the catechism upon Sunday after the second lesson" so that he had several classes of them that could give as good an account of their faith as the white youth "whom he catechised on all holidays". He tells how he baptized Negro adults after instructing them in their duty, baptized their infants when brought to church and married such as applied to him for that purpose.[2]

About 1753 the Reverend Isaac Campbell, rector of Trinity Parish, opened a private school in his residence which continued in operation until 1784.

The teachers in the early non-religious private schools were all to often men of little learning and ability. They were in many instances indentured servants. The children learned little and the school buildings were used for other purposes.

In response to the Act of 1723, there was a movement to merge the funds received in the four lower counties on the Western Shore.

Finally, in 1774, the free schools of St. Mary's, Charles and Prince George's Counties were united, their funds were pooled and a school for the three counties was ordered to be erected at "The Cool Springs", to be known as Charlotte Hall School in honor of Queen Charlotte of England. In 1798, Calvert County also joined the merger. A few years later, the funds belonging to Calvert and Prince George's County were withdrawn.

At the meeting of the board in 1774, Charles County was represented by the following trustees: The Reverend Isaac Campbell, Messrs. Francis Ware, Josias Hawkins and Dr. James Craik. The next meeting was not held until 1782 because of the intervening Revolutionary War. The school has been in continuous operation since January 1, 1796.

The year 1727 saw the establishment of Port Tobacco, or Charlestown as it was officially named, as the county seat of Charles County. In that year, the Assembly authorized the erection of a "Courthouse and Prison on the East side of Port Tobacco Creek at a place called Chandler's Town", stating that the place where the existing courthouse stood was so far impaired, ruined and decayed that there was a necessity for a new one. The distance of that courthouse from convenient river transportation prompted the move to the head of Port Tobacco Creek. Accordingly, in 1728, a town of sixty acres was authorized at the place where the "Courthouse is now building" and was named Charlestown. The Justices contracted with Messrs. Robert Hanson, and Joshua Doyne to build the Courthouse, prison, stocks, and pillory for 12,000 pounds of tobacco.

From that date on until the end of the 19th century, Charlestown, or Port Tobacco as it continued to be called by the people of the county, was the center of the social and political life of the community. It was the only town of any size in the county. It was the center of commerce for the whole area as a short distance down the Creek was the Naval Port of Entry where goods were weighed and marked and where the ships unloaded the luxuries and necessities which were so dear to the colonists' hearts, and where they were loaded again with hogsheads of tobacco for England. The spot still bears today the name "Warehouse Landing" reminiscent of its eventful past.

The social life of the town revolved around sessions of the general court with the people gathering from all over the area to stay in the inns and ordinaries of the town or stopping with their relatives who lived in the town. By the last part of the century, several large hotels were in operation, one with 25 large bedrooms, a dining room seating 200 people, a breakfast room, card room, double parlors, and kitchen plus the proprietor's suite with living and bedrooms and the servants quarters.

In 1752, the actor Thomas Kean, who with his theatrical company played in Williamsburg, Annapolis and other metropolitan areas, came also to Port Tobacco where he and his group presented "The Beggar's Opera" to a full house, no doubt.

War and military exercises, and membership in the colonial militia still remained one of the main occupations and recreations of the men of the community. In 1740 when Governor Ogle ordered a call to arms for the so-called "Expedition Against Cartagena", a recruiting officer gathered a group from Port Tobacco which included Capt. William Chandler as officer.

In 1748, the militia of the county included the following:

Horse Soldiers

Under command of Capt. Arthur Lee	73
Under command of Capt. Allen Davis	73
Under command of Capt. William Hanson	78
	224

Foot Soldiers

Under command of Capt. William Theobold	108
Under command of Capt. Richard Harrison	182
Under command of Capt. John Thomas	82
Under command of Capt. Barton Warren	102
Under command of Capt. Samuel Chunn	90
Under command of Capt. Francis Ward	136
Under command of Capt. John Stoddert in Prince George's County but now annexed to Charles County by late Act of Assembly.	61
	761

Total in all 985

And the report was signed by George Dent, 18 February, 1748.[3]

The reference in the last part of this report points to an important boundary change made in the Charles County line in 1748 by Act of the Assembly. At the request of certain inhabitants in the lower part of Prince George's County, a new boundary was drawn between Prince George's and Charles transferring some of the land in question to Charles County. The boundary was defined as "A line drawn from Mattawoman run in the Road commonly called the Rolling Road, that leads from the late Dwelling Plantation of Mr. Edward Neale through the lower Part of Mr. Peter Dent's dwelling plantation until it strikes the Patowmack River at or near the bounded Tree of a Tract of Land whereon John Beall, junior lives(standing on the Bank of the aforesaid River at the lower end of the aforesaid Beall's plantation)". With this change, the shape and area of Charles County became the same that exists today.

The preoccupation of the Couny with military service is further demonstrated during the French and Indian War. In the spring of 1758, Governor Sharpe ordered companies of militia from Kent, Calvert, Baltimore, Charles and Prince George's County to patrol the western frontier. This order was resisted by the Lower House of the Assembly as an encroachment on their powers on the part of the governor; but Sharpe paid no attention to their resolutions and with his usual spirit and energy placed himself at the head of two hundred men in August and marched for Fort Cumberland to relieve the Virginia troops who were garrisoned there under George Washington. Soon afterwards, a working party from Fort Cumberland, to which 81 Marylanders were detailed, went to reconnoitre the enemy's position at Fort Duquesne. In a sortie before the fort the Marylanders lost 27 privates, one officer and one-half of their whole force was missing. Captain Ware, Lt. Rily and Ensign Harrison, who is probably the Harrison of Charles County previously listed in the militia, brought off the remaining Marylanders in safety. This seems to have been the only engagement of the French and Indian War in which we can assume Charles County men participated.

It was during this part of the century that people in the different English colonies were beginning to feel a bond of kinship one with the other. The experience of fighting side by side with militia men from other states, as they had so recently done, made the colonists conscious of the possibility of uniting for the mutual good of all. This feeling of mutual assistance which was growing in America, is also apparent in other things. On May 6th, 1760, Governor Sharpe issued his proclamation commending to the benevolence and charity of the good people of Maryland, their distressed fellow subjects of the town of Boston, who were suffering by the great fire which broke out in that town on the 20th of March and destroyed 174 dwelling houses and as many warehouses, shops and other buildings to the value of 100,000 pounds. In response to this appeal, the people of Charles County donated 173 pounds, 2 shillings and 8 pence.

Improved roads and better transportation in general both within the colony and across its borders kept people posted on the conditions throughout British Colonial America. The correspondence of Governor Horatio Sharpe tells of establishing " a rout from Annapolis in Maryland to the several parts of that Province where it might be proper to settle Post Offices—And from Upper Marlboro southward to Port Tobacco in Charles County—30 miles". His proposal was endorsed October 20, 1764.[4]

The number of ferries across the Potomac River increased greatly until they were sometimes only a few miles apart and great competition existed between them. Between 1745 and 1747 there were six ferries over the Potomac which carried on a keen rivalry in their advertisements in the *Maryland Gazette*. Richard Harrison and Robert Dade had rival ferries at Nanjemoy. Both advertised good boats and constant attendance. Charles Jones advertised a ferry at lower Cedar Point calling attention to his good boats, and skillful hands and pointed out that his route was by 18 to 20 miles the nearest way to Williamsburg. George Dent advertised his ferry as being better than Thompson's which he claimed was dangerous. Dent also boasted a marked road from Port Tobacco to his ferry. Colonel Richard Hooes ran a ferry from the Virginia shore to Cedar Point and in 1720 he charged 2 shillings for transporting a man plus 2 shillings for his horse.

Just as the transportation of the colonist on land depended largely upon the horse, so did much of his recreation. In the period prior to the Revolutionary War, Maryland horses ran advertised matches at Port Tobacco and at Newport in Charles County and on the list of members of the Maryland Jockey Club, we find such familiar names as Benjamin Stoddert, Col. John Hoskins and Samuel Harrison.

In 1766 Lord Baltimore ordered the Proprietary Manors in the Province to be sold. In Charles County he still owned the remaining lands of Calverton Manor containing 3,412 acres, Pangiah Manor containing 1,001 acres and Zekiah Manor which contained 5,304 acres. The prices received for this land varied from 20 to 30 shillings per acre.[5]

Another sign of the coming demand for self government was the great interest taken in county elections. Liquor flowed freely on election days but it was considered bribery for the candidates to treat the voters. On October 14, 1771, the Lower House of the Assembly considered a petition from Charles County complaining of the election of Captain Francis Ware and Josias Hawkins charging them with "treating". The objection was sustained and the Speaker signified "their attendance was no longer required".

In 1765, the Stamp Act was passed by the British Parliament and received the royal assent. It provided that all bills, bonds, leases, notes, ship's papers, insurance policies and legal documents to be valid in the courts must be written on stamped paper which was to be sold by public officers. The Act was received with great indignation and a determined resistance in which the people of Charles County joined the people of the province and the province joined with the other 12 colonies. It was finally necessary for the British to repeal the Act, but Parliament continued to assert their right to levy taxes on the colonies and it wasn't long before equally unpopular taxes were placed on various trade goods including tea.

In protest, the colonists agreed not to import anything taxed by Act of Parliament and Non-Importation Associations were organized in 1768 for the purpose of investigating and reporting violations of the agreement. Charles County had such an Association which was organized in October, 1768. In November several packages of taxed goods landed in Charles County contrary to the terms of the agreement. The owners of the goods were warned by the Association and the goods were shipped back to England.

By 1774 the feelings of the colonists were running so high that a shipment of tea into Boston brought about the Boston Tea Party and in retaliation the British proclaimed a blockade of Boston harbor prohibiting any goods being landed or shipped at that point. As soon as the news of the blockade reached the other colonies, they were indignant. In common with many of the other counties in the colony of Maryland, a meeting of protest was held at the courthouse in Port Tobacco on June 14, 1774. There it was resolved that no goods were to be imported from Great Britain after August 1st, that the county would join in breaking relations with Britain. They agreed to send deputies from the county to Annapolis to join in the meeting of protest which the Colony was holding. The County people agreed that they would break off trade with any colony, town or county which refused to associate in the project and the County was urged to adopt measures to protect their liberty. The deputies appointed for the Annapolis meeting were Walter Hanson, William Smallwood, Josias Hawkins, Francis Ware, Joseph Hanson Harrison, Thomas Stone, John Dent, Daniel Jenifer, Robert T. Hooe, Gustavus

Richard Brown, Thomas Hanson Marshall, Samuel Love, James Forbes, Phillip Richard Fendall, Zephaniah Turner, James Key and James Craik with John Gwinn as their clerk. From these men was appointed a committee of correspondence to receive and answer all letters or in an emergency to call a county meeting.

Such a meeting was called at Port Tobacco on November 18, 1774, to vote for representatives to the Continental Congress. With Samuel Harrison as Chairman the meeting elected a committee to act and represent the county and to execute any association agreed upon by the Continental Congress. The committee consisted of Walter Hanson, William Smallwood, Josias Hawkins, Francis Ware, Joseph H. Harrison, Thomas Thornton, Isaac Campbell, John McPherson, Henry Fendall, Thomas Stone, George Dent, Gustavus Richard Brown, Daniel Jenifer, Samuel Love, John Dent, James Craik, Robert T. Hooe, James Key, Thomas Hanson Marshall, Zephaniah Turner, Kenelm T. Stoddert, Thomas Marshall, Peter Dent, Richard Clagett, Richard Speake, Ignatius Luckett, Francis Mastin, Burdet Hamilton, John Keybert, Reuben Dye, Henry Davis, Warrent Dent, William Winter, Jr., John H. Stone, Robert Sennett, Gerrard B. Causien, George C. Smoot, John Marshall, Joseph Joy, Thomas Harris, Jonathan Yates, Jezrell Penn, Moses Hobart, Gerard Fowke, William McConchie, Richard Barnes, Richard R. Reeder, Samuel Stone, Jr., Edward Smoot, Stephen Compton, Theophilus Yates, John Brue, Samuel Jones, Edward Warren, James Maddox, James Campbell, Benjamin Philpot, Walter Winter, John Parnham, Samuel Turner, Hezekiah Dent, William Compton, Zachariah Chunn, Charles S. Smith, Robert Young, Joseph Anderson, Henry S. Hawkins, John Hanson youngest, Bennet Dyson, Benjamin Fendall, Samuel Harrison, youngest, Notley Maddox, George Keech, George Dent, Jr., John Stone, Walter H. Jenifer, John N. Knott, Francis B. Franklin, Alex McPherson, Jr., Thomas McPherson, John McPherson, William Hanson, Benjamin Cawood, Jr., Charles Mankin, Belain Posey, John Muschett, Hoskins Hanson, Walter Hanson,

Jr., John B. Meeke and Pearson Chapman. It was a committee of 100 men, the best known citizens of the county, but any seven members of the committee had the power to act for the whole group.

At this meeting it was also resolved "That Samuel Hanson, Walter Hanson, Dan. Jenifer, Thomas Stone, Robert T. Hooe, James Craik, James Key, Walter Hanson Jenifer, John H. Stone and Zephaniah Turner, be a committee of correspondence for this county, and that any five have power to act." Also "That it is the sense of this meeting, that Samuel Hanson, William Smallwood, Josias Hawkins, Francis Ware, Joseph H. Harrison, Thomas Stone, Daniel Jenifer, John Dent, George Dent, Robert T. Hooe, Samuel Love, and Thomas Hanson Marshall ought to attend the next provincial meeting on the 21st instant, and have full power to represent and act for this county."

By this time the attitude of the people was distinctly war-like and in December 8, 1774, the delegates to Annapolis set up amounts to be raised by various counties for the purchase of arms and ammunition and Charles County's assessment was £800.

Accordingly at a meeting at Port Tobacco on the Second Day of January, 1775, the inhabitants of Charles County read, considered and unanimously approved the proceedings of the last Provincial Convention and they ordered the proceedings of the County meeting to be published in the *Maryland Gazette* as follows:

"*Resolved, unanimously,* That Captain George Dent, Samuel Hanson, William Smallwood, Josias Hawkins, Francis Ware, Joseph H. Harrison, Thomas Stone, Daniel Jenifer, Robert T. Hooe, John Dent, Samuel Love, Thomas Hanson Marshall and Philip Richard Fendall, Be, and are by this meeting appointed Deputies to represent this county in the next provincial Convention, to be held at the City of Annapolis, and that any three or more of them have power and authority to act for and bind this County.

"*Resolved,* That a general subscription, to be managed and conducted by gentlemen in each hundred of this county, will be a most agreeable and effectual method to collect what remains to be made up of the sum of money appointed to be raised in this County, by the last Provincial Convention.

"*Resolved therefore,* That the following gentlemen do forthwith open subscriptions in the respective hundreds for which they are appointed, to be offered to every free person in each hundred, and subscription taken, viz.:

"Piccawaxen Parish—Mr. Samuel Love in the Lower Hundred, and Captain George Dent in the Upper Hundred.

"Port Tobacco Parish—Mr. Josias Hawkins, and Capt. Francis Ware, in the East Hundred, Mr. Samuel Hanson, Jr., in the Upper Hundred, Mr. Daniel Jenifer in Cedarpoint Hundred, and Mr. Robert T. Hooe, in Port Tobacco Town.

"Durham Parish—Captain Joseph H. Harrison, in the Lower Hundred, and Mr. William Smallwood in the Upper Hundred.

"King George Parish—Captain John Dent, for the part within this County.

"Trinity Parish—Mr. Belain Posey in the West Hundred, Doctor John Parnham, in the East Hundred, Mr. Alexander McPherson in Bryantown Hundred, and Mr. Robert Young, in Benedict Hundred.

"*Resolved,* That it is the duty of the said gentlemen to note, and return to the committee of this County, a list of such persons (if any there be) who are able, and on application refuse to subscribe, that their names and refusal may be recorded in perpetual memory of their principles.

"*Resolved,* That the said gentlemen do, as soon as possible, collect the subscriptions to them respectively made, and pay the same to Philip Richard Fendall, Esquire, Treasurer, to be applied by the committee of this County to the purpose mentioned in the tenth resolve of the last Provincial Convention.

"*Resolved,* That the gentlemen appointed to take subscriptions for the purpose aforesaid, do collect the subscriptions already made to the Town of Boston, and also do obtain additional subscriptions for the relief of the brave sufferers in that distressed Town, as can be got, and that the whole may be made in readiness to be sent as soon as possible.

"It is recommended by this meeting that the inhabitants of this County, in forming themselves to their respective Hundreds, as much as can with convenience be done, the following gentlemen, to wit: Philip Richard Fendall, George Dent, jun., Daniel Jenifer Adams, William Harrison, John Skelton, John Lancaster, James Neale, Walter Rye, Thomas Sims, Joshua Sanders, Henry Boarman, John Craig, Robert Gill, Jun., John Moran and George Tubman, are added to the Committee of Observation for this County".

In the midst of all the political turmoil there comes a charming, firsthand account of Charles County as viewed by the eyes of a visitor. Dr. Robert Honeyman in his journal now the property of the Huntington Library relates that he reached Port Tobacco an hour before sunset on March 2, 1775.

"When I got there I went out into a field by the town and saw a company of about 60 gentlemen learning the military exercise—Port Tobacco is about as big as New Castle (Delaware) and is seated between hills at the top of Port Tobacco Creek which two miles below falls into the Potomac, and only carries small craft now. There are six stores in the place, four of them Scotch. Near the town is a Roman Catholic Chapel, very elegant with a fine house adjoining where live four or five Jesuit priests. They have a fine estate of 10,000 acres and two or three hundred negroes. There is also a very pretty church of freestone with an organ in it. There is also a warehouse for tobacco."

Men drilling on the green and the delegates elected at the county meetings were quickly followed by instructions from the convention organizing the Province and the counties for military action.

On January 1, 1776, the Maryland Convention appointed Thomas Stone and Francis Ware, both of Charles County among others "for raising clothing and victualizing forces in the Province and to report regulations on governing troops". The Convention then elected officers to command the Maryland Line. For the 1st Battalion, William Smallwood was elected Colonel and Francis Ware was elected Lieutenant Colonel. The 1st Company was captained by John Hoskins Stone.

The Convention also authorized the raising of seven independent companies. The First Independent Company was from Charles and Calvert Counties. The captain was Rezin Beall, First Lieutenant, Bennett Bracco, Second Lieutenant John Halkerston and Third Lieutenant Daniel Jenifer Adams.

For home defense the Convention divided the Province into military districts. The First Military District was composed of St. Mary's County, Charles County, Calvert County and Prince George's County with John Dent of Charles County appointed as Brigadier General of the whole district. One half company of 50 men were stationed in Charles County. The militia officers for Charles were as follows: Upper Battalion — William Harrison, Colonel; Colonel Samuel Hanson of Samuel, Lt. Colonel; Kenelm Truman Stoddert, 1st Major; Samuel Hanson, Jr., 2nd. Major; Walter Hanson, Quartermaster.

Lower Battalion—Josias Hawkins, Colonel; Robert T. Hooe, Lt. Colonel; John Marshall, 1st Major; John Harris, 2nd Major; John Nathan Smoot, Quartermaster.

It is interesting to note conditions under which men served at the time of the Revolutionary War. The pay of the common soldier for one month was $5.50, the Sergeant got $6.50; a lieutenant received $18.00; a captain $26.00. By the time a man reached the rank of Lieutenant Colonel he was entitled to $40.00 plus $20.00 for expenses and the Colonel received the grand sum of $50.00 plus $30.00 expense money. The daily rations consisted of 1 pound of beef or 3/4 pound of pork, 1 pound flour or bread, 3 pints of peas per week or other vegetables, 1 quart of Indian meal per week, 1 gill of vinegar and 1 gill of molasses per day, 1 quart of cider, small beer or gill or rum per day; three pounds of candles per week each hundred men, 24 pounds soft soap or 8 pounds hard soap per week per 100 men.[6]

In the meantime the feeling of independence was growing in the County. By June, 1776, the County Committee sent specific instructions to their delegates at the State Convention advising them of their wish to have the Maryland delegates at the Continental Congress vote for separation from Great Britain and establishment of a Confederation of the Colonies for their common good. The instructions were addressed by the freemen of Charles County to Josias Hawkins, Thomas Stone, Robert T. Hooe, Joseph H. Harrison and William Harrison who represented them at Annapolis as follows:

"Reasons for the mode of voting and determining questions by a majority of counties, have not appeared to us to exist since the last general election; therefore we charge and instruct you to move for, and endeavor to obtain a regulation for voting individually, and determining questions by a majority of members, and not of counties in the future. And as we know we have a right to hear, or be informed, what is transacted in convention, we instruct you to move for, and endeavor to obtain, a resolve for the floors of the House to be kept open in future, and that on all questions proposed and seconded, the yeas and nays be taken, and, together with every other part of your proceedings, published, except such only as may relate to military operations; questions which ought to be debated with the doors shut, and the determinations thereupon kept secret.

"The experience we have had of the cruelty and injustice of the British government, under which we have too long borne oppression and wrongs, and nothwithstanding every peaceable endeavor of the united colonies to get redress of grievances, by decent, dutiful, and sincere petitions and representations to the King and Parliament, giving every assurance of our affection and loyalty, and praying for no more than peace, liberty and safety under the British government, yet have we received nothing but an increase of insult and injury, by all the colonies being declared in actual rebellion; savages hired to take up arms against us; slaves proclaimed free, enticed away, trained and armed against their lawful masters; our towns plundered, burnt, and destroyed; our vessels and property seized on the seas, made free plunder to the captors, and our seamen forced to take arms against ourselves; our friends and countrymen, when captivated, confined in dungeons, and, as if criminals, chained down to the earth; our estates confiscated, and our men, women and children robbed and murdered; and as at this time, intead of commissioners to negotiate a peace, as we have been led to believe were coming out, a formidable fleet of British ships, with a numerous army of foreign soldiers, in British pay, are daily expected on our coast to force us to yield the property we have honestly acquired and fairly own, and drudge out the remainder of our days in misery and wretchedness, leaving us nothing better to bequeath to posterity than poverty and slavery; we must for these reasons declare that our affections for the people and allegiance to the Crown of Great Britain, so readily and truly acknowledged till of late, is forfeited on their part. And as we are convinced that nothing virtuous, humane, generous or just, can be excepted from the British King or nation, and that they will exert themselves to reduce us to a state of slavery by every effort and artifice in their power, we are of opinion that the time has fully arrived for the colonies to adopt the last measure for our common good and safety, and that the sooner they declare themselves separate from, and independent of the Crown and Parliament of Great Britain, the sooner they will be

Portrait by Robert Edge Pine, National Gallery of Art,
Washington, D. C., Mellon Collection

GENERAL WILLIAM SMALLWOOD
Major General of the Maryland Line, Revolutionary War.

Smallwood's Retreat, reconstructed home of General William Smallwood near Marbury, Maryland.

Photo by Herbert S. Copeland, Accokeek, Maryland

Portrait by Robert Edge Pine, The Baltimore Museum of Art

THOMAS STONE
A Signer of the Declaration of Independence for Maryland.

Photograph by Constance Stuart Larrabee, Chestertown, Maryland. Courtesy of Mr. and Mrs. Peter Vischer

HABRE DE VENTURE, home of Thomas Stone near Port Tobacco, Maryland.

able to make effectual opposition, and establish their liberties on a firm and permanent basis. We, therefore, most earnestly instruct and charge you to move for, without loss of time, and endeavor to obtain positive instructions from the Convention of Maryland to their delegates in Congress, immediately to join the other colonies in declaring that the United Colonies no longer owe allegiance to, nor are they dependent upon the Crown or Parliament of Great Britain, or any other power on earth, but are, for time to come, free and independent States; provided that the power of framing government and regulating the internal concerns of each colony be left to their respective Legislatures; and that the said delegates give the assent of this province to any further confederation of the Colonies for the support of their union, and for forming such foreign commercial connections as may be requisite and necessary for our common good and safety. And as the present government under the King cannot longer exist with safety to the freemen of this Province, we are of opinion a new form of government, agreeable to the late recommendation of the honorable Continental Congress to all the United Colonies, ought immediately to be adopted."

These instructions must have been especially gratifying to Thomas Stone who was to represent Maryland at the Continental Congress and to sign the Declaration of Independence in her name. He had the assurance of the approval and backing of his fellow citizens of Charles County when he took that decisive step. The Declaration of Independence was adopted July 4, 1776. On July 19 a motion was passed that all members of the Congress should sign it and on August 2nd the Maryland delegation including Thomas Stone signed the document.

The joy with which the citizens of Southern Maryland greeted the Declaration of Independence may be guessed when we read the enthusiastic account of how the first anniversary of the Fourth of July was celebrated in 1777. Though this delightful description is probably of St. Mary's County as it was written by Sister Mary Xavier Queen whose childhood home was "Bushwood" in St. Mary's County, much the same festivities were certainly taking place in neighboring Charles County at this time. In quoting her grandmother the Sister says that a barbecue dinner was held in every district of the County and a grand ball followed the big dinner that night. The site for the dinner and dance were selected long in advance and the land was plowed and then rolled and beaten until it was hard as marble and suitable for dancing. The long tables were set with lambs, pig, duck and chickens donated by the people and cooked to perfection. The celebrants met at 10 A. M. and danced until 12:30; dinner lasted until two and after a short recess they danced until five and had supper. The ball started at eight and the company danced until 12. Then after a light refreshment of cake and lemonade, the dance resumed until daylight. Grandmother continues "I made two fine linen dresses for the occasion and three pairs of sheepskin slippers. One pair was trimmed with blue satin ribbon, another pink and the third white. I danced out the blue before dinner, and the pink ones in the afternoon and the white ones at night. One of my dresses was striped with blue and pink and the other was pure white.[7]

During the next years all the efforts and activities of the citizens of the county were directed toward the war. Many of the men were fighting in the Maryland Line under General Smallwood and their service extended the full length of the war; their first major battle being the Battle of Brooklyn when the Maryland troops covered the retreat of the rest of Washington's army, and last engagements being fought in the southern campaign ending with the Battle of Yorktown.

Meanwhile those who remained at home were also busy and active in the cause of the Revolution. One of the most fascinating stories of this period of County history is the attempt of John Hanson, Jr., and Walter Hanson, Jr., to erect a powder mill which was to supply all of the gunpowder needed by the State of Maryland during the War. They agreed to build the mill on a run of water that empties itself into a branch called Clark's Branch and near the main road leading from Port Tobacco to the old bridges on Zekiah Swamp. This run is identifiable today by the name "Powder Mill Run" and it is located between Spring Hill and Newtown. The mill was to be capable of manufacturing at least 800 pounds of gunpowder a week and also the Hansons agreed that they would make the salt petre belonging to the public into gunpowder at the rate of 60 shillings common currency. They were lent 500 pounds for this purpose on June 4, 1776, by the Treasurer of the Western shore of Maryland which they agreed to pay back with 4% interest within two years. The men were quite serious about the venture and one of them went to Philadelphia to learn all he could about the latest methods of manufacturing gunpowder. The money began to run short and on November 27, 1777, they were granted a further sum of 500 pounds by the Assembly. This time they were required to give a new bond because of the omission of a penalty in the first bond.

On November 23, 1789, John Hanson, Jr., submitted a bill to the Assembly which listed provisions, work, work done by the blacksmith and brandy furnished the men working in water—the whole coming to 2 pounds, 9 shillings. A good bit of the work had been done by this time as on November 9, 1789, G. B. Causin inspected the work and found everything had been completed except for the refining house. A description of the mill shows that it was quite an establishment. The houses which were erected were 40' 9" by 18'; two stories high, with a sawed oak frame, shingled roof, plank floor $1\frac{1}{4}$" thick, tongue and grooved. A barreling house and refining house are mentioned specifically. The water wheel was 20 feet in diameter and the mill race was 7' deep and 12' wide.

In 1790 John Hanson, Jr., sent a memorial Petition to the General Assembly of Maryland. It was written by him in behalf of himself and Sarah Hanson, relic of Walter Hanson, deceased. It outlines the story of the mill as follows: They entered contract with the Council of Safety for the

State of Maryland for a powder mill and agreed to manufacture powder for the State at a set price. For this purpose a sum of 1000 pounds common currency was lent them by the Committee of Safety. They began to erect the mill immediately but they were not able to complete it because

1. As Militia Captains they were often called from home in service of the militia.
2. Five of the men they employed disappointed them by enlisting in the army.
3. Finding all the salt petre and sulphur belonging to the state advertised for sale by the Intendant they concluded it would be needless to complete the mill and they stopped work.

The petition continues stating that the Hansons tendered the money lent them for the purpose and at that time they advised the Assembly that if salt petre and sulphur would be furnished them they would complete the work immediately. In view of the fact that the Assembly did not bother to answer them they now respectly petitioned that the bonds be cancelled.

The Assembly reported on this petition that the bonds were to be delivered and that upon delivery to the State's agent, the buildings on which the money was expended were to be rejected. The story of Charles County's powder mill ends with the notation that May 30, 1790 Belain Posey tendered the money to cover the bonds to the Assembly. This ended the story of the powder mill and the first venture into industry attempted in the County.[8]

The whole-hearted support of the people of Charles County in the movement for independence is further emphasized by reading the list of Signers in Charles County of the Oath of Allegiance to Maryland in 1778. The Oath was taken before the Magistrate and required the citizen to repudiate allegiance to England and swear allegiance to the State of Maryland. It was signed by over 2000 men in Charles County and the list contains many of the family names surviving to the present time. To mention only a few we find Dent, Boone, Turner, Mudd, Cox, Quade, Clements, Barnes, Sanders, Padgett, Cooksey. The entire list may be found in Charles County Records, Liber X No. 3, 1775-1778, folios 641-651.

As the scene of the war moved south, the people of the county began to feel the actual touch of the war. British warships were in the Potomac River, and in 1781 the raids of the British along the river were constant and residents of the area were in a continual state of alarm. On May 31, 1781, we find George Mason of Gunston Hall in Virginia writing to his friend Pearson Chapman who lived at "Chapmen's Landing" in Charles County that he was preparing to move into Maryland farther from the river. He sent his valuables to Mr. Chapman with a letter saying that "The rapid march of the enemy obliges me to send as many of my effects as I can readily remove to Maryland and I expect to follow immediately with Mrs. Mason and my daughters. I must therefore beg the favour of you to permit all the things I send to be put into your dwelling house for safety until I can carry them up to my son William's house at the head of Mattawoman which I shall do with all possible expedition."⁹ Son William's place at the head of the Mattawoman was "Araby" which he had inherited from his grandmother, the Widow Eilbeck whose daughter Ann was George Mason's first wife.

The efforts to levy monies to pay state expenses and help to liquidate the public debt during the war led to many inequalities among the states. Virginia had discriminating laws and higher import and port duties than Maryland. Because of this, in November, 1777, the Continental Congress recommended that Maryland, Virginia and North Carolina appoint commissioners to meet at Fredericksburg in January, 1778, to regulate and ascertain the price of labor, manufactures, internal produce and commodities imported from foreign countries, also to regulate charges of inn holders.

This conference at Fredericksburg was not successful but as a result of it, Virginia requested a joint commission of Maryland and Virginia to meet to discuss the rights of each in the use and navigation of the Chesapeake Bay, the Potomac and the Pocomoke Rivers. In December, 1777, the Maryland Assembly appointed Daniel of St. Thomas Jenifer and Thomas Stone both of Charles County together with Samuel Chase, as commissioners to meet with the Virginia Commissioners at Alexandria in February, 1778.

Another attempt was made made in January, 1785, and Jenifer and Stone were appointed on the new committee. The meeting was set for Alexandria in March but at the solicitation of George Washington, it met instead at Mt. Vernon on March 28. The Virginia committee consisted of George Mason, and Alexander Henderson and it is assumed that Washington also took an active part in the deliberations. This time the commissioners did come to an agreement and the rules and regulations they laid down at that time have existed with little change until this very day.

Throughout the period of the Revolutionary War we find men of Charles County playing an important part in organizing the government of the state and also that of the nation. John Hanson, who was born in Charles County, was elected a delegate to the Continental Congress in 1780. He was the strongest exponent of the stand adopted by Maryland that the Articles of Confederation should not be ratified until all the states would cede their western lands to the United States as public domain. Upon the acceptance of this principle by all the states, the Articles of Confederation were adopted on March 1, 1781, and the United States of America became officially a nation. The first election of a president was held by the Congress in November of that year and John Hanson was chosen "President of the United States in Congress Assembled". He served as the presiding officer of that body during the difficult days following the end of actual fighting of the war and the attempt to gain a peace settlement. John Hanson as the presiding officer of the Congress officially received General Washington after the surrender at Yorktown and expressed to him the gratitude of the Congress. When his term of office was drawing to a close in 1784, John Hanson issued a Thanksgiving Day Proclamation setting aside the last Thursday in November as a day of Thanksgiving and Prayer. His proclamations suggested for the first time, this day, which has since been followed.

Special mention should also be made of Daniel of St. Thomas Jenifer who also served as Intendant of State Revenue, delegate to Congress and as one of Maryland Delegation to the Constitutional Convention in 1787, signed the Constitution of the United States.

The coming of peace brought with it the usual problems as the army disbanded and as the people of the country made the adjustments necessary to convert to a peacetime economy. This was especially difficult because of the close ties which had existed between England and this country and the fact that so many American business interests including the tobacco trade was still dependent on cooperation between the recent enemies.

In 1786 a number of lawsuits were filed by British creditors against Maryland debtors for amounts that had been owed since before the Revolutionary War. A gentleman named Alexander Hamilton who was representative of the Glasgow firm, James Brown and Company, filed about 100 such legal actions in Charles County through his attorney John Allen Thomas. As may well be expected, there was widespread hostility against these actions. On June 12, the first day of the June Term of Court in Port Tobacco, a mob of about 100 men crowded into the courtroom and "in a riotous and tumultous manner" demanded that the attorney Mr. Thomas strike his name from the suits so they could not be tried. The judges felt that the bringing of this great volume of litigation by a single company against people who could not pay would result in county-wide distress. Chief Judge Walter Hanson said he was reluctant to commit so many debtors to prison especially "at a time when debts to a most enormous amount that have lain dormant ever since the beginning of the war are now called for with such rapidity that the jails must be filled with wretched and unhappy debtors." On the advice of the Judges, who were Walter Hanson, John Dent and Samuel Hanson, Jr., especially on the advice of Judge Dent, the lawyer Thomas withdrew his name from the suits and the mob dispersed.

Hamilton wrote to his employers in Scotland that his life had been threatened and that he believed that he had only escaped bodily injury by being absent from the Court on that day. He continues that "as there is a chance of my being assassinated, I have made my will and taken precautions to protect the company's rights."

Mr. Thomas protested to the Governor but after investigation, William Smallwood, who was then Governor of Maryland, and the Council exonerated the three magistrates from any taint of complicity in the case.

The ringleaders of the riot were however severely reprimanded and fined and Governor Smallwood issued a proclamation forbidding any such disturbances in the future. No other outbursts of this sort occurred and after the ratification of the treaty of peace with Great Britain and the establishment of the Federal Government, the British creditor seeking redress through the courts had a much easier time.[10]

The first official United States Census was taken in 1790. The Census was taken by listing the heads of the families living in the County and then listing the free white men under 16 years of age, the free white women, other free people and the slaves. This list is a complete record by name of the persons who were living in the County in that year, and the information given on the list is valuable in many ways. The total population of the County proved to be 20,613, only a few thousand less than the present population. This is broken down as follows:

Heads of families 2,043
Free white men including heads of families 2,565
Free white men under 16 2,399
Free white women 5,160
Other free people 404
Slaves 10,085

The incidental information imparted by the list is as interesting as the statistics it contains. For instance, Gerard B. Causin, who was probably still living on Causin's Manor, had 75 slaves to work his 1000 acres. We find General Smallwood had 56 slaves at Smallwood's Retreat and we know that his yearly crop of tobacco was 3,000 lbs. according to the records of Durham Parish.

As we have seen, the Act of 1692 established the Church of England as the official church of the colony of Maryland and professed Catholics were barred from all civil rights. This condition was not rectified until the State of Maryland by its Constitution in 1776 granted freedom of religion to everyone in the State. Despite the conditions under which they worked, the Jesuits living at St. Thomas Manor managed to keep the church alive during this period and even established the first mission stations in the County at this time. A count made by the Sheriff of Charles County in 1708 showed 709 Catholics in the County. The only other County in the State with such a large Catholic population was St. Mary's County. Father George Hunter who was pastor of the Church at St. Thomas Manor for a period of over 25 years during the last half of the eighteenth century kept his congregation growing. It is even recorded in his account book about 1755 that he paid an organist for the church at St. Thomas Manor 20 pounds a year, the organ having been bought in Philadelphia for 50 pounds. Father Hunter lived to see his church enjoy the religious freedom granted by the State. He died at St. Thomas Manor in 1779 and is buried there in the Priests' Graveyard beside the church. During the period of restrictions, Mass was often said in private homes in the county, where often a separate room was maintained as the "Priest's Room".

The Mass was celebrated in the main room of the house and it was attended by all the family, the servants and neighbors within travelling distance. The Priest would arrive on Saturday evening, bringing his vessels and vestments. He would hear confessions that evening, say Mass the next day, distribute communion, have religious instructions for the children and baptize babies and converts. Then he would go on to the next "station" and minister there, often visiting a number before returning to St. Thomas.

Confirmation of this custom is to be found in the will of Anthony Neale son of Capt. James Neale of Wollaston Manor. Anthony died in 1722 and his will was probated in 1723. To his son Edward Neale he left half the dwelling plantation "Aqueenseek" and "including silver chalice and rest of church stuff to remain in said dwelling house for use of family".[11]

As early as 1763 Father George Hunter purchased land for an outlying mission church and it was in that year that the church acquired "Pomfret Chapple Land". A small frame chapel was built on the land not far from the location of the present church at Pomfret and Mass was said there twice a month. By 1786, one of the priests at St. Thomas was also assigned to take care of Newport, Cobb's Neck and the southern part of the county.

Many of the wealthy Maryland Catholic families sent their children to Europe, Belgium and France to be educated and a number of them entered religious orders. In this way, a supply of priests was maintained for Maryland Catholics. By 1696, Robert Brooke, who was the first native-born American Jesuit, had returned to his native land to work in the mission field. From that time on, there was a steady increase in the number of vocations from among the young people of the colony of Maryland. The roster of the Jesuits serving at St. Thomas Manor contains names like Father Matthew Brooke, Father Thomas Digges, Father Bennett Neale, Father Ignatius Matthews, Father John Boone, Father John Boarman, Father Augustus Jenkins.

When Father George Hunter died in 1779, Father Ignatius Matthews became pastor of the parish.

It is about this time that we get a wonderful contemporary description of Port Tobacco and St. Thomas. J. F. D. Smythe, who published an account of his "Tour in the United States of America," in London in 1784 says "Port Tobacco is not larger than Piscataway, neither of them containing more than forty or fifty houses, but it carries on a much more considerable trade which consists of some wheat, but chiefly tobacco."

"Near the town of Port Tobacco upon a commanding eminence overlooking the Potomack is a seat belonging to the late society of the Jesuits in occupation of a Roman Catholic priest named Hunter in a situation the most majestic, grand and elegant in the whole world. The house itself is exceedingly handsome, executed in fine taste and of a very beautiful model; but imagination cannot form the idea of a perspective, more noble, rich and delightful than this charming villa in reality is. And as the best description I could give of it would come so far short as even to disgrace the place itself, I shall not hazard the attempt."

One of the most interesting family groups in the late 18th century was the Neales whose family home was Chandler's Hope at Port Tobacco. With a strong Catholic heritage behind them, starting with Captain James Neale of Wallaston Manor, and with their religion made more precious by the ban under which they were forced to practice it, we finally find a branch of the family producing a generation devoted entirely to the religious life. By the 1750's the four boys, Benedict, Edward, Charles and Leonard were all attending the boarding academy which the Jesuits had established at Bohemia Manor, in Cecil County on the Eastern Shore of Maryland.

Then, one by one, as they came of age, they were sent to Europe for further education at the Jesuit schools in France and in Belgium. There they entered the religious life and three of them returned to this country to aid the work of the Church at a time when their services were most important.

Leonard Neale studied at Bruges and Leige and entered the Society of Jesus at Ghent in 1767. He labored for a time in the mission field in British Guiana and returned to this country in 1783. To his great joy, his first congregation was in his home neighborhood, as he was sent first to St. Thomas Manor. But he was soon needed in more important work and we find him in Philadelphia at the time of the yellow fever epidemic in 1793. As Bishop-elect and co-adjutor of the Church in America, he was appointed President of Georgetown College in 1799. The remainder of his remarkable career as it influenced the Church on a national basis will be discussed in the next Chapter.

One of Archbishop Neale's brothers, Father Charles Neale, was instrumental in bringing the Carmelite nuns to this country, and he served the rest of his life as their priest, living near the Monastery and ministering to both the sisters and the people of the surrounding country. When he died in 1823, he was acting as the Superior of the Jesuit Mission in America.

The younger brother, Father Francis Neale was Vice-President of Georgetown College in 1799, then made President in 1809. While President of the college, he also served as Master of the Novices and Pastor of Holy Trinity Parish in Washington. He was replaced as President in 1812 and again served as Vice-President. Francis Neale was the only survivor of the group of American Jesuits trained at Leige who lived to see the Jesuit Mission in America promoted to the status of a Province in 1833.

In the like manner, many daughters of the Catholic families of the colony of Maryland had followed religious vocations in Belgium and France because monastic life was outlawed in England and in the colonies. The English penal laws against Catholics were in force until the Revolution. A Charles County girl named Ann Matthews had entered the religious life in Belgium and for sixteen years, as Mother Bernardina Theresa Xavier, had been Prioress of the Carmel at Hoogstraeten. With the end of the Revolutionary War, she began a correspondence with Mother Mary Margaret Brent, Prioress of the Carmel at Antwerp, discussing the founding of an American Carmel. Mother Bernardina's two nieces, Sister Mary Aloysia of the Blessed Trinity (Ann Theresa Matthews) and Sister Mary Eleanora of St. Frances Xavier (Susana Matthews) joined with her in that hope. Father Ignatius Matthews, Mother Bernardina's brother, who was already in America wrote and urged them to come. Father Charles Neale, S.J., already mentioned, who was cousin of Sister Mary Margaret Brent agreed to take the nuns to America. The matter was brought to the attention of Bishop Carroll, the head of the church in America, who was most enthusiastic and promised the nuns and their project a welcome.

Accordingly, the three native-born Charles County sisters and a fourth nun, Subprioress Mother Clare Joseph of the Sacred Heart, who was Frances Dickenson from England, sailed for Maryland under the protection of Father Neale on May 1, 1790. It was a long and difficult journey for the gentlewomen, accustomed as they were to the sheltered life of cloistered nuns. By July 9 they were off the shores of Charles County and they disembarked at Brentfield, the home of Robert Brent who was brother of Mother Mary Margaret Brent of Antwerp. They stayed for a few days at the home of Ignatius Matthews while Father Neale sought more suitable quarters. As a temporary expediency they then proceeded to Port Tobacco and took up residence in Chandler's Hope, the unoccupied house of Father Neale's family.

As the house at Chandler's Hope was not basically suited to be used for the monastic life, Father Neale continued to look for quarters and he negotiated to exchange his property for a much larger one about two and a half miles north of Port Tobacco. This land he gave to the Carmelites for their permanent quarters. The buildings were started at once and though not completed, the nuns moved into them on the feast of St. Theresa of Avila, the Holy Foundress of the Carmelite Order, October 15, 1790. This was the first convent of religious women to be established in the United States.

The community was largely self-sufficient, as the monastery farm produced wheat, corn, tobacco, vegetables and fish were abundant from the nearby river. There was also a water mill on the property. The farm was operated by Negro slaves brought by new members as they joined the community. The Sister's own sheep supplied wool for their clothing.

Father Neale remained with the group as their chaplain. He also served as pastor for people of the surrounding countryside, as members of the Pomfret parish often went to Chapel of Mt. Carmel for Mass.

The religious community flourished in numbers but it became increasingly difficult to support the group from the produce of the farm and the buildings in time became in need of repairs. Father Neale died in 1823, Mother Bernardina had died some years before and in 1830 Mother Clare Joseph passed away. In 1831 the Archbishop ordered the transfer of the convent to the city of Baltimore and Mt. Carmel was deserted. It is maintained today as a religious shrine and as an historical site of importance by a devoted organization known as the Restorers of Mt. Carmel.[12]

As indicated by the educational activity discussed earlier in this century, the Church of England continued to grow in strength during this period as the established church of the colony. Public tax money supported the minister so the wealth of the parish could be used to build and maintain the houses of worship. Most of the handsome little brick Episcopal churches to be found in Charles County today date from this era.

Port Tobacco Parish continued to be important because it embraced the county seat. It was one of the few parishes in the County which had ministers for the whole of the century. Two with exceptionally long records are Reverend William McConchie, who served from 1711 to 1742 and died at the post, and the Reverend John Weems, who came in 1787 and served until 1821. About 1755, the elder Dr. Gustavus Brown, a prominent member of the parish, offered to give an organ to the church if the parish would support an organist.

Trinity Parish was created by the Assembly in 1744. It consisted of those parts of King and Queen Parish and of All Faith Parish which were in Charles County, the boundaries being Zachiah Swamp, the Wicomico River, the St. Mary's County Line, the Patuxent River and the Prince George's County Line, making an area of some 199 square miles. The old Newport Church was then standing on Gilbert Swamp. The vestry was organized in 1750 and the Reverend Isaac Campbell presented his letter on July 16, 1751. The site of the present church was selected at a parish meeting in October of the same year. The church was completed in 1756 and in 1769 the parish also completed a brick building at Benedict as a chapel of ease.

The most famous minister of the parish was the Reverend Hatch Dent who began as a reader and was ordained and became the second rector of the parish in 1786. He had served as an officer in the Continental Army and he was also the first principal of Charlotte Hall School.

In accordance with the church's policy of education, the brick vestry house built at Trinity was also used as a school house. It is said that William Wirt, afterwards Attorney General of the United States who took part in the Aaron Burr trial, attended school here.[13]

Interesting evidence of the disrupting influence of the Revolutionary War on parish life in Charles County is found in the minutes of Durham Parish dated April 25, 1791. The entry is headed "Easter Monday" and states "Whereas there has been no Vestry in Durham Parish for about three years The people of said Parish are desirous that all Parochial affairs, particularly the approaching ruin and destruction of the church, unless some necessary steps be taken, Do meet on the day after Easter, April 25, 1791 and appoint General William Smallwood, Major William Truman Stoddert, Captain F. Speake, Capt. William F. Adams, Capt. John Mitchell, Francis B. Franklin, Capt. Garner, William Jeremiah Gray, William Jones, Walter Hanson."

On May 9, 1791 the above appointed Vestry met and the parish members pledged 30,750 pounds of tobacco and 177 pounds, 16 shillings to "restore the spirit of their religion and the flourishing state Durham Parish was in previous to the late glorious revolution".

The Presbyterian congregation in Charles County seems to have combined with that in Prince George's County for the 18th century. In 1704 there is a record of a full-fledged Presbyterian Church with a pastor and a large congregation at Patuxent which is just over the line in Prince George's County. A few years later the church was given a lot in Upper Marlboro by Colonel Ninian Beall, who was an elder of the church and the mainstay of the Western Shore congregation. The deed for the property lists as trustees of the church sixteen men from both Charles and Prince George's County. Even in 1719 when the Presbyterian Church at Bladensburg was built and the Marlboro parish was divided, it still included part of Charles County. Names reveal a strong Scotch element in the congregation, as indeed there were many persons of that nationality in the colony, most of them in the mercantile business.

The communion service which was made in 1707 and used in the church at Patuxent, was sent on to the church in Bladensburg and is still in use by the successors of that congregation now located at Hyattsville.

This century also saw the beginnings of Methodism in Charles County. There were no churches established but it was the custom for a minister to come to a community, find a private home in which he could hold services, and if he drew a congregation from the neighborhood, he would then make this house a place in which services were held at regularly established intervals. Each minister took care of a number of communities which was called his circuit and the minister himself was called the "circuit rider".

In the early 1700's Methodists in Charles County were part of a circuit consisting of St. George's Island, Piscataway, Horse Head, Bethel and Piney Point. Some homes in Alexandria, Virginia, were in the same circuit and the whole belonged to the Virginia Conference. The circuit rider, traveling by boat and on horseback, visited each community two or three times a year, preached to the people, attended conference and brought back to the community his report on the conference. Between 1780 and 1785 the circuit was transferred from Virginia to Baltimore, Maryland, and it remains a part of the Baltimore Conference today.

It is about this time that we find a published reference to one of the circuit riders who came to Charles County. In a book written in 1848 by the Reverend Henry Smith called "Recollections and Reflections of an Old Itinerant" he says "Thence to Oxen Hill, Piscataway, Col. Beal's in Clark's (Charles) County and so on to Chickamuxen on Sunday. Thence through Port Tobacco and on towards Leonardstown."

It might be well to glance again at the way the people of Charles County were living by the end of the eighteenth century. Many of the handsome large houses which are preserved and treasured as homes today had been built by that time and the people of substance who lived in them enjoyed a pleasant, congenial social existence. The Stone papers in the Maryland Historical Society contain many letters from the younger members of the Stone and Craik families telling of a pleasant round of parties and visits and fun among the younger generation.

Fragmentary records of a Debating Society organized in Port Tobacco in 1788 are among the papers. Gerard B.

Causin, Daniel Jenifer, Nicholas Peers, Valentine Peers, Zephaniah Turner, Michael Jenifer Stone and Thomas Howe Ridgate were the members admitted at the second meeting. The Society met at six P. M., debated until 9, ate at nine and adjourned at ten. By the general consent of the Society, the meeting could be lengthened to eleven o'clock.

A Frenchman who traveled in Maryland in 1791 leaves us the following information on the food and eating habits of the people in the State. He records that for breakfast he was given ham, broiled chicken with a cream sauce, slices of bread spread with butter, tea and coffee. Lunch consisted of eggs, chicken, ham and weak wine, cabbages and potatoes which are served as they are taken out of the boiling water and flavored with melted butter.

Bayard also gives us a wonderful description of tea as it was customarily served late in the afternoon, "A mahogany table is brought forward and placed in front of the lady who pours the tea. Vessels of silver contain the coffee and the hot water. The hot water is used to weaken the tea or to wash the cups. A servant brings in on a silver tray, or a tea service, the cup, the sugar bowl, the cream pitcher, round slices of buttered bread and slices of smoked cured meats which are presented to each person and which must be held on the lap. Frenchmen are greatly embarrased when in one hand they hold the cup and saucer and with the other they must take slices of bread and butter and smoke-cured meat cut in very thin slices. An elderly American to whom this method of serving was inconvenient after taking a cup in one hand and slices of bread and butter in the other, opened his mouth and told the servant to fill it for him with smoked venison." He also says that care is taken to place the spoon in a way that it indicates whether you wish another cup.[14]

The real story of Charles County during this exciting period of history might be said to be the story of the many outstanding men who lived in the County and called it home. It seems almost unbelievable that one small geographical area produced so many men of ability within a short space of time. The lives of these individuals in many instances are a history in themselves and the brief accounts which follow can give no more than a glimpse of their personalities and resume of their careers.

The records of Charles County are studded with references to the Stone family beginning with the Provincial Governor, William Stone, who was granted "Poynton Manor" as a reward for faithful service to the Proprietor. The family saw its real flowering in the generation which lived through the period of the Revolutionary War. Probably the most distinguished member of the family was Thomas Stone, the Signer of the Declaration of Independence. Thomas Stone was the youngest of the Maryland Signers, as he was born in 1743, the son of David and Elizabeth Jenifer Stone. He received a fair education at the private schools of the county, when he removed to Annapolis, where he studied law under the auspices of Thomas Johnson. He commenced practice in Frederick, and after two years he removed his practice to his native county, where he was quite successful because of his talent and industry. In 1768, just prior to his removal to Charles County, he married Margaret Brown, the youngest daughter of the elder Doctor Gustavus Brown. Sometime after this, perhaps about 1770, they built their home "Habre de Venture" at Port Tobacco. In 1774, although a very young man, he was appointed by the Provincial Convention as a member of congress, and was re-elected the following year. While a member of the Maryland Convention, on the 28th of April, 1775, he wrote the following letter to his wife:

"We have this day received a confirmation of the unhappy contest between the king's troops and the people of New England; and I am afraid it is too true. This will reduce both England and America to a state to which no friend of either ever wished to see; how it will terminate, God only knows. My heart is with you, and I wish it was in my power to see you, but many gentlemen insist that I should stay to assist in deliberation on those important affairs. I wish to do my duty, and shall be obliged to stay here longer than I expected, but I hope to see you on Sunday, if nothing new occurs.

"We have accounts that numbers of people are killed on both sides; which I am apprehensive will preclude all hopes of a reconciliation between this and the mother-country; a situation of affairs which all thinking men must shudder at . . . People here seem to feel very severely on the present occasion. I have determined to act according to the best of my judgment, rightly; but, in the important and dangerous crisis to which we are reduced, the best may err. Pray God preserve you and bless our little ones. We are like to see times which will require all our fortitude to bear up against. We must do our best, and leave the rest to Him who rules the affairs of men."

He was a member of the Maryland Senate in 1777, and his services in that body are thus described by a member who sat with him:

"He was truly a perfect man of business; he would often take the pen, and commit to paper all the necessary writings of the senate, and this he would do cheerfully, while the other members were amusing themselves with desultory conversation. He appeared to be naturally of an irritable temper, still he was mild and courteous in his general deportment, fond of society and conversation, and universally a favorite from his great good humor and intelligence. He thought and wrote much as a professional man and as a statesman, on the business before him as those characters—he had no leisure for other subjects—not that he was unequal to the task, for there were few men who could commit their thoughts to paper with more facility or greater strength of argument. There was a severe trial of skill between the senate and the house of delegates, on the subject of confiscating British property. The senate for several sessions unanimously rejected bills passed by the house of delegates for that purpose; many, very long and tart were the messages from one to the other body on this subject; the whole of which were, on the part of the senate, the work of Mr. Stone, and his close friend and equal in all respects, the venerable Charles Carroll, of Carrollton."

In the year 1784, after he had finally relinquished his seat in congress, he moved to Annapolis, where his practice became very lucrative and his professional reputation rose to very distinguished eminence. As a speaker, it was said his strength lay in argument, rather than in manner. When he began, his voice was weak, and his delivery unimpressive, but as he became warmed with his subject, his manner improved, and his reasoning was clear and powerful.

He was a man of very strong feelings and affectionate disposition; and his love for his wife, after forming the happiness of a large portion of his life, became the cause of his early death. In the year 1776, while he was in congress, Mrs. Stone visited Philadelphia with him, and as the small-pox was then prevalent in that city, it was decided to protect her from it by inoculation. She was accordingly inoculated, by the mercurial treatment, and from this time it seemed her health gradually declined. She was afflicted with rheumatism for eleven years, and finally on the 1st of June, 1787, she died in Annapolis, in her thirty-fourth year. This was a great blow to Mr. Stone. He declined all further business, both public and private, and retired to his seat near Port Tobacco, in Charles County, where he sank into a deep melancholy. Dr. Brown and Dr. Craik, his physicians, finding little amendment in his spirits after the lapse of some months, advised him to make a sea voyage. Obeying their advice, he went to Alexandria to embark for England. While waiting to sail, he died there suddenly, in his forty-fifth year, on the 5th of October, 1787.

A few days before his death, he wrote the following letter of advice to his only son, then a boy of twelve years of age, which is the dying counsel of a virtuous parent, actually in the near prospect of death.

"My dear Frederick: I am now in a weak state, about to travel, and probably shall not see you more. Let me intreat you to attend to the following advice, which I leave you as a legacy; keep and read it, and resort to it.

"In the first place, do your duty to God in spirit and in truth, always considering him as your best protector, and doing all things to please him; nothing to offend him; and be assured he is always present and knows all your thoughts and actions, and that you will prosper and be happy if you please him, and miserable and unhappy if you displease Him. Say your prayers every day, and attend divine worship at church regularly and devoutly, with a pious design of doing your duty and receiving instruction. Think more of your soul's health and the next world than of this, and never do wrong on any account. Be honest, religious, charitable and kind, guarded in your conduct, and upright in your intentions.

"Shun all giddy, loose and wicked company; they will corrupt and lead you into vice, and bring you to ruin. Seek the company of sober, virtuous and good people, who will always show you examples of rectitude of conduct and propriety of behavious—which will lead to solid happiness.

"Be always attentive to the advice of your uncles, Dr. Brown and Michael J. Stone, and do nothing of consequence without consulting them. Be respectful to your seniors, and all your friends, and kind to everybody. Seek to do all the good you can, remembering that there is no happiness equal to that which good actions afford. Be attentive and kind, and loving to your sisters, and when you grow up protect and assist them on all occasions.

"Take care not to be seduced by the professions of any person to do what your heart tells you is wrong, for on self-approbation all happiness depends.

"Attend to your educational learning, and never let your mind be idle, which is the root of all evil, but be constantly employed in virtuous pursuits or reflections.

"Let your aim in life be to attain the goodness rather than greatness among men: the former is solid, the latter all vanity, and often leads to ruin in this and the next world. This I speak from experience.

"I commend you to Heaven's protection. May God of his infinite mercy protect you and lead you to happiness in this world and the next, is the most fervent prayer of your loving father."

Thomas Stone was six feet and half an inch in height. He was a taciturn man, of strong feelings, and more remarkable for terseness of style than eloquence of diction. He left three children, amply provided for — Margaret, Mildred and Frederick.[15]

By resolution of 1834, the Governor of Maryland was authorized to have a full length portrait of Thomas Stone painted for the State House, and in 1874 the Assembly directed a portrait be painted and contributed to the collection in Independence Hall in Philadelphia.

Thomas Stone's brother, John Hoskins Stone, born in 1745, had an equally honorable career of public service. He too was trained for a legal career. In 1774, as a lawyer already of some reputation in both Charles County and in Annapolis, he was elected a member of the Committee of Correspondence, and in 1775 a member of the Association of Freemen of Maryland. When the war actually began he joined the military service and was made a captain in January 1776. By December he was promoted to Colonel. During his military service he fought in the Battles of Long Island, White Plains, Princeton and finally at Germantown where he was so severely wounded that he had to resign from the service in 1779.

He was made a member of the Council Chamber of Maryland in 1779 and was appointed to the executive council. His career of public service included acting as clerk for Robert Livingston when he was Secretary of Foreign Affairs under the Articles of Confederation. He was a member of the House of Delegates in 1786 and served on the committee which prepared instructions for delegates to the Constitutional Convention.

In 1794 he was rewarded for his long years of public service by the highest elective office in the state. As Governor, John Hoskins Stone assumed administrative responsibilities not previously regarded as part of the position. He was the first Governor to send messages to the Legislature calling attention to legislation which he felt necessary for the welfare of the state. On an appeal from George Washington, Governor Stone gave the financial aid of the state for building the government buildings in the District of Columbia. He kept the support of the State of Maryland firmly behind Washington during the criticism heaped upon the President through his second term. Governor Stone was twice re-elected. He retired to his home in Annapolis where he died in 1804.[16]

The third member of this family to follow in the path of public service was Michael Jenifer Stone, younger brother of Thomas Stone and John Hoskins Stone. He was born about 1750 and he too was educated for the legal profession. After taking a prominent part in county affairs for a number of years, he was elected a Representative to Congress from the State of Maryland and served from 1789 to 1791. While in Congress he was one of those who voted for locating the seat of government at Washington.

On his return to the county, Michael Jenifer Stone was made Judge of the Circuit Court of Charles County, a position which he held for many years and in which he served with honor and distinction.

The story of the Stone family leads into the story of their close friend, relative and neighbor, Dr. Gustavus Richard Brown of Rose Hill. The first generation of this family in Charles County was Dr. Gustavus Brown, who is known as the elder Dr. Brown to distinguish him from his son who is perhaps better known. The elder Dr. Brown was born in Scotland in 1689 and came to Maryland in May,

1708, where he established a successful practice as physician in the Nanjemoy area of Charles County. About 1714 Dr. Gustavus Brown purchased from Philemon Hemsley 300 acres southeast of Port Tobacco called "Rich Hill" and he also patented an estate named "Middleton" in the Nanjemoy area in 1734. He went to Scotland for a few years but returned to Maryland in 1734. His residence in later years is in doubt, but it probably was "Rich Hill", as he was evidently a member of Port Tobacco Parish, where he was a vestryman in 1758. He offered to give the church an organ about this same time. In addition to his duties as a physician, the elder Dr. Brown was a prominent public citizen. He was one of seven trustees to fill vacancies in the lists of school teachers in the province. He was Associate Judge of Charles County in 1723 and again in 1755 and also one of the men chosen to lay out the town of "Charlestown" at the head of Port Tobacco Creek as county seat. Dr. Brown's first wife, Frances Fowke, had eight daughters and one son. His second wife was Margaret Black Boyd, who was mother of Dr. Gustavus Richard Brown and of Margaret Brown who married Thomas Stone. The elder Dr. Brown died in 1762. He seems to have been buried at Rich Hill, for when that property passed from the hands of the family in 1806, they reserved the graveyard in which Gustavus Brown was buried.

The younger Dr. Brown, Gustavus Richard, was born October 17, 1747. He was sent to the University of Edinburgh and received his degree in medicine in 1768. He came back to Charles County, began his practice in Nanjemoy in 1769, and married Margaret Graham. Dr. Brown achieved some fame as a physician and had a widespread practice all over his section of the state and neighboring counties of Virginia.

An interesting account of Dr. Brown is given by Nicholas Cresswell, a young Englishman who had set out for Virginia in 1774 in search of a farm on which he intended to settle. For the next three years he travelled in the American colonies and kept a journal in which he told of his experiences. On June 7, 1774, he became ill with a fever and the next day arrived in Port Tobacco. At the insistance of local residents he called in Dr. Brown who diagnosed the case, and in the words of Mr. Cresswell, gave him "some slops" and put him to bed. Several days later, though feeling no better, he went out to Nanjemoy, where Dr. Brown lived at that time. The doctor gave him more "physic" and he reports he feels no better. There is no entry until June 17 when he records that he is much better and says the doctor says he is out of danger. The doctor advised him to drink a little more rum than he did before he was ill and Cresswell says he thinks the illness was caused by drinking water instead of rum. He continues to improve and on June 20 he says the doctor sent him a box of pills with directions to take two in the morning and two in the evening. Cresswell says "These are the last I intend to take". By June 23rd Mr. Cresswell records "a violent pain in his bowels, a constant thirst and a bad taste in his mouth". He continues to get worse with his throat and tongue much swollen and a continual thirst so he sends for the doctor. By Saturday, June 25, they sent an express for the doctor. When Dr. Brown arrived he examined the pills and immediately went to the bedside of the sick man. "Began to beg pardon for the mistake he said his prentice had inadvertantly committed by sending me strong mercurial pills, in the room of cooling ones. I immediately gave him as hard a blow as I could with my fist over the face and would have given him a good trimming had I been able." At which Dr. Brown frowned upon the young man, begged him to be calm and to follow his directions and said he would soon be well again. Thereupon, he prescribed doses of Brimstone and Salts which brought Mr. Cresswell some ease from the pain—though he says "I am full of pain and much swelled, spitting and slavering like a mad dog, my teeth loose, and my mouth very sore. If I happen to die I hope this will appear against the rascal." The doctor came back to inquire about Mr. Cresswell the next day but did not go in to see him and sent every day to inquire about him. By July 5 Mr. Cresswell was up and about but records that his clothes hang about him like a skeleton. He had not laid eyes on the doctor since he struck him but he decided to go and pay him for services. When he visited Dr. Brown, the doctor treated him with kindness, acknowledged Cresswell had cause of complaint, "though inadvertantly", and refused to be paid until Cresswell had fully recovered. The recovery was long and slow and included a sea voyage taken on the doctor's advice. By October the young man was again in Maryland and in good health. He records that "This morning (October 19) settled with the doctor who has charged me 14 guineas and had the impudence to tell me it is very cheap.[17]

In 1774 Dr. Brown bought the lands patented as Rose Hill near Port Tobacco as he found Nanjemoy was inconveniently located for growing practice. The handsome home which he built on this property is architecturally a fine Georgian house which compares favorably with the best that were built in this country.

During the Revolutionary War, Dr. Brown was an active patriot. In 1774 he was a member of the Committee of Correspondence and in 1776 and 1777 he served as Judge of Charles County. Throughout the war he attended troops in the area when they were ill. He and his apprentice set up a house for smallpox inoculation in 1776. Dr. Brown served as a member of the Maryland State Convention to ratify the Constitution of the United States in 1787. His interest in education prompted him to accept a term as a member of the Board of Visitors and Governors of St. John's College in 1789. He also was instrumental in 1799, in founding the Medical and Chirugical Faculty of Maryland.

Dr. Brown's chief fame today lies in the fact that he was called to the bedside of George Washington during his last illness. Though it is often said that Dr. Brown was to blame in the excessive bloodletting which hastened Washington's death, the fact is that Dr. Brown arrived at the bedside after the last bleeding.

Another interesting facet to Dr. Brown's personality is to be found in an unsigned manuscript in *Letters From or About Medical Men*, Vol. 3, Toner Collection, Library of Congress. In speaking of Dr. Brown his unknown admirer says "In skill and taste in horticulture no man equalled him, he cultivated with success, rare and beautiful plants from all quarters of the globe, medicinal, ornamental and culinary such being the exquisite beauty of his garden that it was a popular and fashionable theme throughout society."

Dr. Brown died in 1804 and is buried at Rose Hill. The epitaph that his devoted wife Margaret placed over his grave attests to the many virtues of this famous citizen of Charles County.[18]

SACRED
TO THE MEMORY OF
DOCTOR
RICHARD GUSTAVUS BROWN.
THIS TOMB-STONE ERECTED
BY HIS RELICT
MARGARET BROWN.
IN TESTIMONY
OF HER RESPECT AND AFFECTION:
AND AS A MONUMENT
OF HIS SKILL AS A PHYSICIAN,
AND HIS LEARNING AS A SCHOLAR:
OF HIS WISDOM AS A PHILOSOPHER,
HIS PATRIOTISM AS A CITIZEN,
AND HIS GENEROSITY AS A FRIEND:
OF HIS ELEGANCE AS A GENTLEMAN,
AND HIS HOSPITALITY AS A NEIGHBOR:
OF HIS KINDNESS AS A MASTER,
HIS TENDERNESS
AS A HUSBAND AND PARENT,
AND
OF HIS BENEVOLENCE AS A MAN.
HE DIED 30th SEPTEMBER 1804,
AGED 56 YEARS.

Charles County's most famous military man emerges from history as General William Smallwood, who was in command of the Maryland line during the Revolutionary War. Smallwood was born in 1732, the son of Bayne and Priscilla Heabard Smallwood. Many references give Kent County as the place of his birth but this is rather improbable as the record of Bayne Smallwood's life in Charles County seems continuous. Bayne Smallwood did own land in Kent County but no record has yet been found to prove that he actually lived there or that his son William was actually born there. Instead we find Bayne Smallwood listed as merchant and planter in Charles County, at one time presiding officer of the Court of Common Pleas, and also as a member of the House of Burgesses.

The young Smallwood was sent to England for his education. When he returned to his native county he served as a member of the Lower House of Assembly. His first military service was in the French and Indian Wars. Smallwood served as a member of the Maryland Convention in 1774 and on January 2, 1776, he was made Colonel of the Maryland Battalion and on July 10 with nine companies he joined Washington in New York. Smallwood's troops took part in the Battle of Brooklyn Heights where they covered the retreat of the Continental Army from Long Island. He fought and was wounded at the Battle of White Plains. It was for his gallantry in the Battle of White Plains that Congress appointed him Brigadier General on October 23, 1776. Smallwood and his troops also took part in the Battles of Brandywine and Germantown. At the latter place, his Maryland troops again saved the day and captured part of the enemy camp.

During the winter of 1777 and 1778 the General and his troops were stationed in the Wilmington area. We have some wonderful personal descriptions of the General from the journal kept by a young teen-age Quaker girl named Sally Wister whose family had fled into the country when the British occupied Philadelphia. Sally's refuge was not far from the General's headquarters and she refers to him on several different occasions. The first time she met him was on October 20 when she says "The General is tall, portly, well-made; a truly martial air, the behaviour and manner of a gentleman, a good understanding and a great humanity of disposition constitute the character of Smallwood."

On October 27 she writes "We had the pleasure of the General and suite at afternoon tea. He (the General, I mean) is most agreeable: so lively, so free and chats so gaily that I have quite an esteem for him."

Sally's next account dated November 1 is even more enthusiastic. "I declare this General is very, very entertaining, so good natured, so good humour'd and yet so sensible, I wonder he is not married. Are there no ladies formed to his taste?"[19]

General Smallwood resented the foreign officers who volunteered for service with the Continental Army because of the high rank given these men and the authority it accorded them. He complained in 1778 that Maryland men who should be enlisting with him in the Maryland Line were drifting to Count Pulaski who had headquarters in Baltimore.

In 1780 Smallwood took his troops south where they won new laurels in the southern campaign under General Gates. In September, 1780, Smallwood was raised in rank to Major General and on October 14, 1780, he, General Gist, officers and men of the Maryland and Delaware lines were sent a resolution of thanks for their part in the Battle of Camden. Despite General Smallwood's strenuous objections at being placed under the orders of General Steuben, he continued to serve until November 15, 1783.

On his return home, Smallwood was elected to Congress in 1785 but before he could take the seat he was chosen Governor of the State of Maryland, and served three successive one-year terms. As Governor of Maryland, General Smallwood in 1787 convened the Assembly to consider the adoption of the United States Constitution which was accepted in 1788.

In 1788 General Smallwood retired to his home in Charles County where he lived the pleasant life of a Maryland gentleman. He was active in the Masonic organization in the County, he helped to organize and served as the first president of the Maryland chapter of the Society of the Cincinnati and he was an active member of the vestry of Durham Parish. In 1791 his subscription to the vestry was estimated at 3,000 pounds of tobacco, the largest contribution in the parish.

General Smallwood died at his home "Smallwood's Retreat" on February 14, 1792, and his grave there is marked by a stone erected to his memory by the Sons of the American Revolution in 1898.[20]

A group of Charles County people calling themselves the Smallwood Foundation have recently reconstructed on its original site "Smallwood's Retreat," which had fallen into complete ruins. The house and the surrounding area have been taken over by the State of Maryland as a State Park and the house will be maintained as a museum with the land being used as a recreational area.

Another member of the Smallwood family who deserves mention is William Truman Stoddert, nephew of the General who was born in 1759. His boyhood home was "Southampton Enlarged" on Pomonkey Creek. He was left an orphan at the age of nine, inheriting the estates of his mother and his grandfather. William Smallwood was appointed executor of the estates and it seems likely that he played a large part in rearing the youngster. Young Stoddert attended Philadelphia College until 1776 when at the age of 17 he enlisted in the Continental Army. He served as major of the Brigade commanded by his uncle the General. His service in the war left him with shattered health when he returned to the county. After marrying Salley Massey, daughter of the Reverend Lee Massey, rector of Pohick Church, he settled on his estate called "Simpson" on Smith's Point.

William Truman Stoddert also was an active member of the Durham vestry and in 1791 was appointed with General Smallwood and others to repair the church and build the vestry house. He survived his uncle only one year, as he died in 1793 and was buried at "Simpson". The inventory of his estate shows he owned thirty-two slaves, seventeen at Smith's Point and fifteen at "Pomunkey Quarter".[21]

One of the most interesting men of the county at this time was Robert Hanson Harrison who was born in Charles County in 1745. He was a member of a distinguished family who received a land grant in the County as early as 1664, Through his mother Dorothy Hanson, he was a first cousin of John Hanson. The family lived at "Walnut Landing," about a mile west of Riverside in comfortable circumstances. Robert Hanson Harrison became a lawyer and established a practice at Alexandria, Virginia. His activities in Virginia brought him to the attention of George Washington and Harrison was soon Washington's trusted friend and legal adviser. Harrison, meanwhile, was working with the other people who were advocating a movement for freedom from the British. He acted as Clerk for the gentlemen of Fairfax County who drew up the famous Virginia Resolves and he was a member of the Committee of Correspondence in Alexandria. Not content with a passive role, he also joined the 3rd Virginia Regiment with the rank of lieutenant. General Washington invited him to become part of his official military family, and on November 6, 1775, Washington issued this order from his headquarters at Cambridge: "Robert Hanson Harrison, Esq. is appointed Aide-de-Camp to His Excellency the Commander-in-Chief and all orders, whether written or verbal coming from the General through Mr. Harrison are to be punctually obeyed." He was soon appointed Secretary by the General and from that day was one of Washington's most trusted associates. As a member of Washington's official family, he accompanied the General during most of the engagements of the first years of the war.

In the meantime, Harrison's father died in Charles County in 1780, so as the eldest of the family and as a lawyer, much of the supervision of family affairs now fell to Robert. He was also anxious to be at home with his two, now motherless, daughters. Upon his appointment as Chief Judge of the General Court of Maryland in March, 1781, he resigned from the General's staff.

Robert Hanson Harrison served on the bench until 1790. After the war, he served the State on many official committees and was often a visitor to General Washington at Mount Vernon. He was one of the first delegates selected to represent Maryland at the Constitutional Convention, but he did not accept for personal reasons. In the national elections following the adoption of the Constitution, Harrison received the six votes of Maryland's electors for the Vice-Presidency.

When the newly inaugurated President Washington sent nominations for the Supreme Court to the Senate, Robert Hanson Harrison was one of the names submitted. There is evidence that Washington had a greater personal interest in Harrison's nomination than any other. He personally wrote to Harrison requesting his acceptance, "Your friends and your fellow citizens, anxious for the respect of the Court to which you are appointed, will be happy to learn your acceptance and no one among them will be more so than myself." Alexander Hamilton wrote to him in the same vein, "If it is possible, my dear Harrison, give yourself to us. We want men like you. They are rare at all times."[22]

Harrison at first declined the appointment, but on further urging he made an attempt to go to New York. He fell ill in Bladensburg and had to return home. This time his refusal was final, based on the grounds of his ill health. It was a well founded refusal as he died at his home in Charles County on April 2, 1790.

The Harrison family is another of those family groups which contributed much to the County, for Robert's brother,

William Harrison, was a member of Congress from Maryland from 1785 to 1787, and another brother, Walter Hanson Harrison, was elected rector of Durham Parish in 1779.[23]

John Hanson was born in 1721 at Mulberry Grove, the home of his father Assemblyman Samuel Hanson in Charles County. Though records of his youth are indefinite and meagre, it is established that John Hanson pursued academic studies probably at home under private tutors and also in the Maryland schools of the period. John Hanson is one of the few persons active in this county and eventually in the State and the Nation who is of Swedish rather than of English nationality.

In 1743 he married Jane Contee of Prince George's County, and for awhile he and his wife lived at the home place and then acquired some land of their own. They had a number of children, but only two survived until their father's old age. In 1757 when John Hanson was 36 years old, he became a member of the Maryland House of Delegates and he served in that capacity until the family moved to Frederick County in 1773. He had been active in pre-Revolutionary activities in Charles County where had had assumed leadership in the movement against the Stamp Act and supported the Non-importation Agreement.

When he moved from Charles County to Frederick, he took an equally active role in the affairs of that county, serving with honor in both State and national affairs. Finally his career culminated in the honor of being elected "President of the United States in Congress Assembled."

He died at the home of a relative in Oxon Hill, Prince George's County, in 1783.

The State of Maryland, in 1898, ordered a statue of John Hanson to be placed in Statuary Hall in the United States Capitol. It is one of the two statues allotted to the State of Maryland.

Portrait attributed to John Hessilius, Courtesy of Mr. John Hanson Mitchell

DANIEL OF ST. THOMAS JENIFER, a signer of the Constitution of the United States for the State of Maryland.

The Retreat, home of Daniel of St. Thomas Jenifer, near Port Tobacco, Maryland.

Portrait of Charles Wilson Peale. National Park Service Photo
JOHN HANSON, President of the United States in Congress Assembled.

Courtesy of Yale University Art Gallery

Detail of the painting "CAPTURE OF THE HESSIANS AT TRENTON" John Trumbull showing Robert Hanson Harrison at the left George Washington at the right.

Daniel of St. Thomas Jenifer was born in Charles County in 1723. His father was Doctor Daniel Jenifer and his mother was a sister of John Hanson. As a young man, Daniel St. Thomas Jenifer was justice of the peace of his home county and later of the western circuit of the Province. In 1760 he served on the commission appointed to settle the boundary dispute with Pennsylvania and Delaware. He became a member of the Provincial Court in 1766 and from 1773 until the opening of the Revolutionary War he had a seat on the Governor's Council. In the years before the Revolution, Jenifer had faithfully served the proprietary interests. Under the last two proprietors he held office as the Proprietor's Agent and Receiver General in charge of Proprietary revenues. However, when the break came, he sided with the Revolutionists, almost all of whom had been his former political enemies in the proprietary quarrel.

Having made his decision, Daniel of St. Thomas Jenifer worked as untiringly for the cause of independence as he had worked for the Proprietary interests. As soon as he took a stand for independence in 1775, he was chosen President of the Maryland Council of Safety and he showed great activity in securing aid for the Revolutionary cause. When the State government was set up in 1777 he was made President of the State Senate.

The next year he was elected to the Continental Congress where he served from 1778-1782. Jenifer's service record shows that he was nationalistic in political philosophy and favored a permanent Union of the States. His experience with public finances led him to take a stand against the business of issuing paper money and he wished Congress to be given power to tax. Beginning 1782, Daniel of St. Thomas Jenifer was Intendant of Maryland revenues and financial agent of the State. He was on the commission to settle question of navigation of the Chesapeake and Potomac.

In 1787 he went to the Constitutional Convention and he signed the Constitution of the United States for the State of Maryland. Jenifer was a man of considerable means and he lived a rather jolly bachelorhood, exchanging visits with George Washington who seems to have been rather attached to him. Indeed he seems to have been a general favorite for, according to a contemporary, he was always in a good humor and never failed to be pleasing company. He died in Annapolis in 1790. The place of his burial is unknown.

Benjamin Stoddert was born in Charles County in 1751. He was a grandson of James Stoddert who had emigrated from Scotland in 1650 and his father was Thomas Stoddert who is found listed as a lieutenant in the militia during the French and Indian War. His mother was Sarah Marshall Stoddert, a daughter of Thomas Marshall of Marshall Hall.

The Revolutionary War began just as young Benjamin was finishing his apprenticeship as a merchant and he joined the Continental Army with the rank of Captain. He resigned from the service in 1779 and was elected Secretary to the Board of War, a post he held until 1781.

In 1781 Benjamin Stoddert married Rebecca Lowndes of Bladensburg. They went to live in Georgetown where he established a flourishing mercantile business in the town. Stoddert became known to George Washington through business contacts and soon Washington was depending on Mr. Stoddert's sagacity and business sense in the political moves necessary to establish the seat of government in Washington, D. C.

John Adams appointed Benjamin Stoddert as Secretary of the Navy in 1798. It was a position newly established in the Cabinet and Stoddert proved to be a fortunate choice at a critical time. Because the Navy was pitifully weak at that time, Stoddert built it up to fifty ships with 6,000 men in service in the two years that he was Secretary.

During his administration as Secretary of the Navy, the bill for the government of the Marine Corps was drafted; the Naval Hospital at Newport was constructed and Navy yards were established at Washington, D. C.; Gosport, Virginia; Portsmouth, New Hampshire; Charleston, Massachusetts; Philadelphia and Brooklyn. This work was virtually completed by the end of his term of office in 1801.

The political turmoil of the next few years seriously affected the economic life of the country and the last twelve years of Stoddert's life were filled with debt and sorrow. He died, heavily in debt, in Georgetown in 1813.

The Reverend Hatch Dent was born in Trinity Parish in Charles County. During the Revolutionary War he served as an officer in the Continental Army. He married Judith Poston in 1778. Dent was ordained a Minister of the Episcopal Church by Bishop Seabury in 1785 and immediately became minister of his home parish of Trinity in Charles County. In 1797 he also was given charge of William and Mary Parish.

In addition to his ministerial duties, the Reverend Mr. Dent also opened a private boys' school and in 1796 he became the first principal of Charlotte Hall School. His home place seems to have been "Dent's Inheritance". He died in Charles County in 1800.

Another Episcopal clergyman mentioned in the records is Benjamin Contee who was an officer in the Maryland Line in 1776. He served as delegate to Congress from 1787 to 1788 and from 1789 to 1791. Benjamin Contee was also Chief Judge of Charles County Orphans Court for a number of years.

James Craik was born in Scotland and educated as a surgeon in the British Army. As a young man he emigrated to Virginia where he served with the colonial forces of Virginia during the French and Indian War. He came to the attention of George Washington who made him Chief Medical Officer of the Virginia militia when Washington was himself Commander-in-Chief of the Virginia troops.

Craik bought land in Charles County in 1763 and built the handsome home "LaGrange" about this time. He married Mariamne Ewell of Prince William County, Virginia.

In 1770 Dr. Craik and George Washington went by horseback into the west to locate the lands granted by the crown to the men of the Virginia Militia who fought in the French and Indian War.

After the outbreak of the Revolutionary War, Dr. Craik joined the Medical Department of the Continental Army, and in 1777 became Assistant Director-General of that Department. In 1780 he was selected as one of the chief hospital physicians and in 1781 Congress appointed him Chief Physician and Surgeon of the Army.

After the war, Dr. Craik moved to Alexandria to be nearer his great friend George Washington. When trouble seemed eminent with France in 1798 and George Washington accepted again the position as Commander-in-Chief of the Army, he did so with the proviso that Dr. Craik should be commissioned director-general in the Medical Department.

Dr. Craik's last service to his friend was his presence during his final illness as the attending physician. In his will, George Washington left Dr. Craik his tambour secretary and circular chair.

Dr. Craik died in Alexandria in 1814 after living to a cheerful, healthy old age.

We should not fall into the mistake of thinking that all the citizens of Charles County of this period were exemplary characters. To balance the scales on the negative side, we find General James Wilkinson, traitor to his country, who was born in Benedict in 1757.

Wilkinson joined Washington's army at Cambridge after he completed studies for the medical profession. In service he became a good friend of Benedict Arnold and Aaron Burr. Wilkinson won his rank of Brevet Brigadier-General by concealing actual facts relating to the Battle of Saratoga. He became involved in the Conway Cabal, a conspiracy to depose Washington as Commander-in-Chief of the Army and then one evening gave the plot away in a drinking bout. When the Cabal was discovered he resigned his brevet commission but retained his rank as colonel.

At the end of the war, Wilkinson emigrated to Kentucky where he immediately became involved in a Spanish conspiracy designed to break the United States in two and remove any potential threat to the Spanish Empire. It has even been established that for his assistance in breeding dissension he was granted an annual pension by the Spanish government.

When his plans did not succeed, Wilkinson again rejoined the Army and after taking part in some of the Indian Campaigns he ended in supreme command of the Army in 1796. In 1805 he was appointed Governor of Louisiana. Here he became involved in Aaron Burr's conspiracy to erect a Southwestern Empire. When he saw Burr's plans were doomed to failure, Wilkinson reported them to the U. S. Government. In the trial which followed, Burr implicated Wilkinson in the conspiracy and he was court-martialed but acquitted for lack of evidence.

After the War of 1812, Wilkinson moved to Mexico and died there in 1825.

As might be expected, not everyone in the County was in favor of the cause of Independence. These people were as sincere in their conviction of the inadvisability of separation from England as the ones who were convinced that it was the only logical step. The center of the Tory sentiment in Charles County was a family which was prominent in the history of the County from the middle of the seventeenth century. From that early date, members of the family had been loyal supporters of the Crown and the Proprietor and they held many positions of responsibility in the Province.

Philip Lee who settled at "Lee's Purchase" in Charles County, was a son of Col. Richard Lee, the emigrant, founder of the great Virginia family. Philip Lee was appointed Naval Officer of the "North Potowmeck District".

One of his activities was the sale of imported slaves for a group of merchants in Bristol. In 1741 Captain Ovey of the ship "George" off Cedar Point wrote to the Naval Officer entering his ship and its slave cargo.

Philip Lee's oldest son, who was known as Squire Richard Lee, was educated in England. He was admitted to Middle Temple as a member of the bar on May 13, 1719. When he returned to the colony of Maryland, he also served as Naval Officer for the Potomac River. Squire Lee was President of the Governor's Council of Maryland for many years. During the Revolutionary War he remained an ardent Loyalist despite the Revolutionary activities of his Virginia cousins, Richard Henry Lee and "Light Horse" Harry Lee. Because of his loyalist sentiments, Squire Lee's property was treble taxed by the State.

Squire Lee lived at what must have been one of the really great estates of the county, named "Blenheim". "Blenheim" was located in the southern part of the county somewhere in the Newburg area not too far from the ferry crossing into Virginia. It seems to have been one of the favorite stopping places for people who were traveling that route through Maryland to Virginia. In 1779 Richard Henry Lee at his home Chantilly in Virginia, wrote to Henry Laurense of South Carolina: "There are three houses on your way from Philadelphia here, the masters of which are my friends and where yourself, your people and horses will be hospitably entertained. Mr. J. Giles (Susquehannah ferry); Mr. S. West (Upper Marlboro) and the Honorable Richard Lee, Esquire near Hoes Ferry."

We get another account of Squire Lee's hospitality from Philip Vickers Fithian, the young Princeton-educated, theological student who went to Nomini Hall in Westmoreland County, Virginia, to be tutor for the children of Robert Carter III. In April 1774, when on his way back to Princeton for a visit, he records in his diary: "Rode thence [from tavern at the ferry on the Maryland shore] three miles to Squire Lees who has the Naval Office here—Spent the evening with young Mr. Lee, Miss Lee, Miss Booth and Miss Washington—Toasts—I gave Miss Nancy Galloway—Between the Ferry and Mr. Lee's we passed through four gates."

A fascinating description of Blenheim and Squire Lee is found in Sister Mary Xavier Queen's little book *Grandma's Stories and Anecdotes of Ye Olden Times*. "The old mansion was a square building two stories high with an attic. The roof, for more than half its length and breadth was arranged for a fish pond and it was said that the old squire actually supplied his table with trout caught by himself in that overhead fishery, no one else was ever allowed to fish there . . . All about the roof was a railing to prevent accident to those who loved to ascend for the magnificent view there presented. When the Old Squire desired to be the perfect Englishman, he invited his visitors and guests to a view of the surrounding country through his 'first class spy glass' as he termed it. At the south end of the roof a small tower was erected to protect the instrument which was kept mounted except in bad weather, then there was a ceremony of calling two or three stalwart darkeys to aid in lowering a movable covering for the 'dear telescope'."

"Squire Lee delighted in fox hunting and his hounds were generally pronounced the best in the country. When he heard them praised his usual comment was 'English blood in them'. He kept a set of handsome barges for visiting his relatives in Virginia. Occasionally he gave magnificent entertainments all on the English plan and in the English style.

"When the writer last visited Blenheim, only the lower rooms were fit for habitation and they were occupied by mulattoes. One of the noted relics of the place at that time was a coach, said to be imported, with a bright yellow body and upper parts of black leather; the coachman's seat was much lower than the seats within. But Blenheim was razed to the ground by the Unionists during the Civil War".

Philip Thomas Lee, the second son of Squire Richard, was born at Blenheim in 1738. He too studied in England as he attended Eton College from 1753 to 1756. He was admitted to the London Bar in 1764. When he returned to America he lived at Blenheim with his father and in 1771 was appointed a member of the Governor's Council of which his father was President. Philip Thomas Lee also affirmed his loyalty to England, attending a Loyalist meeting at Annapolis May 30, 1774. He died at Blenheim in 1778 reportedly of a broken heart because of divided loyalties brought on by the Revolutionary War. English records indicate that he had two daughters living in England in 1783 who received loyalist pensions.[24]

The confirmed loyalist sentiments of the family seemed to have continued into the next generation as the D. C. Circuit Court Report for the November 1814 term lists a Richard H. Lee indicted for treason. He was accused of selling melons to the British, of showing them the channel of the Potomac River and informing to the enemy. He was not convicted.

CHAPTER III—MATURITY

THE NINETEENTH AND TWENTIETH CENTURIES

With the end of the Revolutionary War and the establishment of a stable government for the nation and for the state, life began to settle down to a more normal routine. In 1798 the Assembly authorized four election districts for Charles County, and the next year a Commission was appointed to make the division. The continued growth of the County is reflected in the description which appears in a little book by Joseph Scott entitled *"A Geographical Description of the States of Maryland and Delaware* which was published in Philadelphia in 1807. The list of towns of the County begins with Port Tobacco which then contained fifty houses, a large and elegant Episcopal Church (partly out of repair) a warehouse for the inspection of tobacco, a courthouse and a jail. Also listed are Allenfresh, Nanjemoy, Hilltop, Bennedict and Newport.

Despite the fact that Mr. Scott listed a jail as one of the buildings in Port Tobacco prior to 1807, it must have been in bad condition as in 1811 a levy was placed on the County for building a "gaol" on the public ground in Charles Town.

But the County was not able to relax for any length of time as national affairs again became of primary importance with resumption of the war against the British in 1812. In some ways this conflict had a more direct effect on the people of Charles County than the Revolutionary War as the area became one of the theaters in which fighting actually took place. For much of the War the British had kept a fleet in the Chesapeake Bay, the Patuxent and the Potomac Rivers. Sister Mary Xavier Queen reports in her book that almost every house along the lower Potomac was plundered. "Everything was lugged off that the men could carry. The feather beds, pillows were taken to windows and doors and ripped open. The poultry was shot, fruit and vegetables carried off and every outrage that could be perpetrated marked their passage through the neighborhood. The women, children, servants, horses, etc. had been sent to the interior, and silver and other valuables were secreted."

In the summer of 1814, the British fleet was active in the area of the Patuxent River. On the 15th of June, a small British fleet of 12 boats containing 180 marines and 30 of the British black colonial corps proceeded up the river to Benedict. Here the men disembarked and without a struggle drove into the woods a number of militia men, who left behind them a part of their muskets and camp equipage, as well as a 6-pounder field piece. After spiking the latter and destroying a store containing tobacco, the British returned to their boats except for five or six men, who probably had strayed too far into the woods.

On the 29th of July, Rear Admiral Cockburn proceeded with boats and marines up the Wicomico River. He landed at Chaptico where he confiscated a considerable quantity of tobacco, and visited several houses in different parts of the country (probably going into the Charles County area); the owners of which, living quietly with their families, seemed to consider themselves and the neighborhood to be at his disposal. The Admiral caused them no inconvenience other than demanding supplies of cattle and stock for the use of his forces, and for these supplies they were liberally paid.

In the meantime, the commanders of the British forces had their eye on Washington, the Capital City, which they determined to capture for the psychological effect it would have on the government. The following letter was sent to Vice Admiral, the Honorable Sir Alexander Cochrane, by Rear Admiral Cockburn from his flagship anchored off Jerome Point in the Chesapeake Bay on July 17, 1814:

"Sir

"In answer to that part of your secret letter of the 1st instant which regards the landing and commencing of operations of the English Army which you inform me is to be so soon expected in this country, and on which points you desire me to communicate my opinion, I feel no hesitation in stating to you that I consider the town of Benedict in the Patuxent to offer us advantages for this purposes beyond any other spot within the United States. It is, I am informed, only 44 or 45 miles from Washington and there is a high road between the two places which tho' hilly, is good, it passes through Piscataway near (er) to Fort Washington than four miles, which fortification is sixteen miles below the City of Washington and is the only one the Army would have to pass. I therefore most firmly believe that within 48 hours after the arrival in the Patuxent of such a force as you expect, the City of Washington might be possessed without difficulty or opposition of any kind. As you will observe by my public letter of this day, the ships of the fleet could cover a landing at Benedict, the safety of the ships and the smoothness of the water in the river would render us entirely independent of the weather in all our projected movements; an object of considerable importance when we recollect how fast the season is advancing to that period when the weather becomes so unsteady on all this coast. The Army on its arrival would be sure of good quarters in the Town of Benedict, and a rich country around it to afford the necessary immediate supplies, and as many horses as might be wanted to transport cannon etc. which advantages might certainly now be obtained without meeting with the slightest opposition, or requiring any sacrifice from us what ever, and as I have quitted the Patuxent River (on this account) do not intend again to visit it until you arrive with the Army, or I hear further from you, I trust and believe everything will remain till then in the neighborhood of that River exactly as I have now left it—The facility and rapidity, after its being first discovered, with which an Army by landing at Benedict might possess itself of the Capitol, always so great a blow to the government of a country, as well on account of the resources as of the documents and records the invading Army is almost sure to obtain thereby, must strongly, I should think, urge the propriety of the plan, and the more particularly as the other places you have mentioned will be more likely to fall after the occupation of Washington than that City would be after their capture . . ."[1]

Accordingly on Cockburn's advice, when Rear Admiral Malcolm arrived with the British troops and joined Vice Admiral Cochrane off the mouth of the Potomac, the whole fleet proceeded to the Patuxent. Part of the ships then disembarked the troops, about 4,000 in number on the 19th and 20th of August at Benedict; the rest under Rear Admiral Cockburn proceeded up the Patuxent to attack the American fleet under Commodore Barney and to supply the advancing troops with provisions and if necessary afford protection to the Army as it proceeded up the bank of the river towards Washington.[2]

Charles County men fought at the Battle of Bladensburg defending the City of Washington from the approaching enemy. The following have been identified among the troops who took part: John Acton, Thomas Burgess, Alexander Dent, George W. Davis, Roger Dunnington, William Franklin, Horatio M. McDaniel and Richard Owen.[3]

Despite the efforts of the American troops, the British captured the city and burned it. An eye witness account says that the flames of the burning offices and buildings could be distinctly seen in the county. This seems entirely possible as the lights of present day Washington may be seen as a glow in the sky from the county today.

Discouraged by a torrential hurricane rain, the British left Washington on the 25th of August, and proceeded at a leisurely pace back to Benedict, carrying their wounded and supplies with them. On the 29th in the evening, they reached Benedict without a single musket having been fired. They re-embarked the following day. The James' *History*

Courtesy Maryland State Roads Commission—Photo by M. E. Warren

THE POTOMAC RIVER BRIDGE, built from Maryland to Virginia near Newburg, Maryland.

Courtesy of Constance Stuart Larrabee, Chestertown, Maryland

ROSE HILL, handsome Georgian home built by Dr. Gustavus Richard Brown, near Port Tobacco, Maryland.

View of the Patuxent River at Benedict, Maryland.

DURHAM CHURCH, Nanjemoy Hundred Episcopal Church built in 1732.

Photo by Mildred Capron

TERCENTENARY YEAR 1958

describes the march back to Benedict saying: "No complaints, that we can discover, having been made against the British during their retreat across the country."

The end of the war of 1812 brought a period of peace and expansion in the County. In 1815 a supplementary act of the legislature provided for the erection of a new court house in Charles Town commonly called Port Tobacco to cost $15,000. The new building was ready for use September, 1821. This is the court house that is generally associated with Port Tobacco, as it is the only one of which there is any type of pictorial representation and also, it is the one remembered by the oldest generation of present day Charles Countians. The sugar bowl of the silver service for the battleship "Maryland" shows a view of the wing of the court house with Christ Church and the prison seen in the background.

In the meantime, in 1820, public sentiment had succeeded in having the name Charles Town changed officially to Port Tobacco.

A map of Maryland in 1818 appearing in Gavey's *General Atlas* shows the towns of Port Tobacco, Bryantown, Benedict and Newport. By 1831 the town of Nanjemoy is also marked. A map of 1833 includes Hill Top and Allen's Fresh. About this same time, many of the maps show a town called Pleasant Hill which was on the main road between Port Tobacco and Piscataway. It seems to have been a town of considerable size and probably was located at the edge of Mattawoman Swamp where it was crossed in leaving the County to go north.

All in all, the period right after the war of 1812 was one of peace and a time of quiet community life, so it is easy to imagine the surprise of the people in the Nanjemoy area on February 10, 1825, when a piece of iron came hurtling through the air to land on the plantation of Col. William D. Harrison, "a surveyor of this port". The local people thought it had been fired from a quarry on the Virginia side or from a packet lying in the Potomac. In fact, a movement was started to man boats to take vengeance on the captain and crew of the boat. But calmer heads prevailed; the missile was proven to be a meteorite. Most of it was sent to the Geology Department of Yale University and the rest went to Vienna, Austria.[4]

The first half of the century saw the establishment of several of the Catholic churches in Charles County. Father David, who came to America in 1792 in response to a plea from Archbishop Carroll, was sent by him to lower Maryland to take charge of three congregations known as Upper and Lower Zachaiah and Mattawoman Parishes. Lower Zachaiah Parish was composed of a group of Catholics around the chapel which had been built on Col. Boarman's place many years before. Lack of spiritual leadership in the latter part of the 18th century had made the parishioners lax in the practice of their religion, but Father David's pastorate soon renewed their fervor. The actual parish records of St. Mary's Church, Bryantown, as the Lower Zachaiah Parish became known, start from Father Robert Anjier's second term in 1816. Records showed at that time 51 parish members, a chapel and a house at the chapel. In 1838, the Piscataway Parish was entirely separated from Bryantown. It included the Mattawoman congregation which became known as St. Peter's Parish. The present Bryantown church was built in 1848 under Father Courtney. He also established a Young Ladies Academy for the parish during his pastorate, *The Port Tobacco Times* for January 20, 1848, carrying an announcement of St. Mary's Female Institute, Bryantown. In 1861 Bryantown Parish was taken over by secular priests and has been administered by them since that date.

The dedication of the Church called St. Peters which was built at Reeves' on Upper Zachaiah took place on August 15, 1860.

The Pomfret Chapel which had been built in the eighteenth century, was torn down in 1835 because it was no longer safe for public use. A new church was started on approximately the same site in 1837, but it was not completed until 1849. The dedication of the present church of St. Joseph's at Pomfret then took place on September 1, 1850.

The influence of Charles County on Catholicism on a nationwide basis can better be appreciated when we realize that it was in this first quarter of the nineteenth century that Mt. Carmel achieved a firm foundation at Port Tobacco, assuring the Carmelite nuns of the success of their venture and paving the way for establishing future Carmels in other parts of this country.

Father Leonard Neale was coadjutor Bishop of Baltimore from the year 1800, acting with Archbishop John Carroll in guiding the affairs of the infant church in America. Bishop Neale was one of the founders and ardent supporters of Georgetown College, and he served for a time as President of the college. After the death of Archbishop Carroll in 1815, Bishop Neale was elevated to Archbishop of Baltimore, but he lived only two years longer as he died in Baltimore in 1817, at the age of 71.

We also find, in this period, references to Father William Matthews who was born in Charles County in 1770. Father Matthews studied for the priesthood in Baltimore and was ordained by Bishop Carroll in 1800. He was the first native born American to be ordained a priest in this country. Father Matthews served for a time as a professor and as President of Georgetown College and continued his distinguished career as pastor of St. Patrick's Church in Washington. He was active in founding the Washington Seminary which in later years became Gonzaga High School in Washington. Later Father Matthews was appointed vicar apostolic and administrator of Philadelphia.

Also worthy of mention are two women of the county who had gone with their families to Kentucky early in the 19th century. Catherine Spalding was one of the founders of the religious order of the Sisters of Charity of Nazareth, Kentucky, and she served for many years as the Mother Superior of the Order. One of its co-founders was Theresa

Carrico also of Charles County. The strength and vigor of the new Order, continuing even until today, attest to the soundness with which its foundation had been laid.

The Episcopal Church continued to be a strong religious influence in the County throughout the 19th century. Christ Church at Port Tobacco is mentioned in almost every reference found to the town of Port Tobacco from the middle of the 18th century and throughout the nineteenth century. The first half of the latter century was divided between two ministers—the one, the Reverend John Weems, who served from 1787 until he died in 1821. In 1822, the Reverend Lemuel Wilmer took over the parish and ministered to it until 1869. He was a man of strong personality and firm convictions and he remained a loyal supporter of the Union throughout the Civil War in a parish that was almost solidly Confederate in sympathy.

The description of Port Tobacco of 1807 speaks of the elegant Episcopal Church as being partly out of repair. Evidently it continued to deteriorate, because in 1816 the State Legislature authorized five lotteries to benefit religious causes. Among them was a lottery of $20,000 for the Parish of Port Tobacco in Charles County and from its proceeds, the church was put into repair. The lottery was a favorite method of raising funds in the early 19th century—so much so that legislative approval was required to keep the activities somewhat under control. Lotteries became so numerous that they eventually defeated their own purposes and the passage of this group in 1816 marked the last lottery franchises for religious purposes granted by the legislature.[5]

An event of the most far-reaching consequence to education in Charles County took place early in the nineteenth century. Maurice James McDonough of Pomfret who died on January 9, 1804, left his estate for the education of the poor children of what is called "McDonough District." The story of Maurice McDonough is one of the most interesting and inspiring to be found in the whole of Charles County history. Tradition says that he was a peddler who walked the length and the breadth of the area he served with a pack on his back selling miscellaneous small goods to his customers in the western section of the County. He was living in the Pomfret area as early as 1750 and in 1786 he bought from Bennett H. Clements 136 acres of land known as "St. Matthews" lying on the west side of the road between Port Tobacco and Piscataway. He is listed among those who took the Oath of Allegiance to the State of Maryland in 1778.

In McDonough's will, dated December 28, 1803, and probated February 14, 1804, he left to his wife, Elizabeth, during her life, all his property. He named her executrix and willed that she pay £5 current money each year of her life to "Pomfret Chappel". On her death, Richard Barnes, Benjamin Contee and Richard Ferguson, his executors, were directed to sell all his land and invest the money "with all convenient speed" in public funds or bank notes and that "monies arising thereby to be subject to the order of the Orphans Court to and for no other purpose than that the said Court will cause to be educated and maintained, in such manner as the Court may think meet, as many poor orphans, or poor children of indigent parents, as possible from the dividends or interest." The children had to live in "McDonough District" which he defines as "beginning at the lower end of Cedar Point; along by the Port Tobacco Church, up to the place where Charles Coombs now lives, thence to the public fording place of Mattawoman on the public road from Port Tobacco to Piscataway, then by Richard Barnes' old mill and then to the lower end of Cedar Point." He carefully stipulated how the trustees were to be selected and perpetuated. The initial investment amounted to about $2,000.

When McDonough died, there were no public schools in the county and the trustees thought that it was his intention to provide a primary education to the children in the area in which he worked. However, very shortly after his death public schools maintained by the county began to be established and by the time the trustees found it feasible to carry out his wishes they decided to make a high school available to as many as possible. By 1902 the $2,000 invested according to McDonough's instructions had grown to $50,000 with an income of $2,200 a year so they purchased the Lintner School building at La Plata, and with an annual state appropriation of $5,000 added to the original fund, they opened McDonough Institute in 1903. Classes went from kindergarten to the tenth grade and offered an academic course, commercial course, agriculture and teacher training. It had boarding accommodations and provided scholarships for those who otherwise could not afford to attend.

McDonough Institute was the only high school in the county until 1924, and it is estimated that about 2,000 children of Charles County received all or part of their education there. Since the establishment of public high schools, the McDonough money has been allocated by the Trustees for use for tuition scholarships for college or business education for children in the McDonough District. Certain it is that few of the citizens of Charles County left for themselves a more enduring monument than Maurice McDonough and he deserves to be listed with the military heroes and national statesmen of whom the county is justly proud.

But to return to the 19th century, a meeting was held in January, 1846, to set up standards for primary schools. The Court decided that the school term should consist of 220 days a year and the school day was set at 6 hours. The salaries for teachers were low and sometimes they were provided by private contributions. Nevertheless, by 1860, the *Port Tobacco Times* records 32 school houses in the County and 32 teachers, pointing to the fact that all 32 were one room schools. In that year, there were 5 new school houses of which three replaced old ones. The number of pupils is put at 866. Tax for the support of schools amounted to $7,500 and the salary for each teacher was $300.

The paper also contains notices of various private schools in the County, listing in 1848 Cottage Hall Seminary for young ladies and also St. Mary's Female Institute at Bryantown. In April, 1854, appears an announcement of St. Thomas Parish school which charged $100 for tuition and board and for day students, $20.00 tuition or $2.00 a month.

The first newspaper to be published in the County was a temperance paper called the *State Register*, edited by Legran I. Luckett. The first issue of the *State Register* was published at Port Tobacco on May 16, 1842.

The first issue of the *Port Tobacco Times* was published and printed by Elijah Wells, Jr., in 1844, and from that date on it becomes the most important record available on Charles County history. It is especially valuable as a source for material on the opinions of the people of the County during the critical period of the Civil War.

The *Port Tobacco Times* carries the complete news of the first Agricultural Fair of the Charles County Agricultural Society which was held October 29, 30 and 31 at Port Tobacco in 1848. The farmers exhibited their stock, crops, vegetables and fruit and the housewives entered their butter, bread, soap, quilts. By resolution of the Committee only members of the Society were allowed to compete for the premiums except in the Ladies Classes and dealers exhibiting Agricultural Implements. In this latter category, a Mr. Charles H. Drury of Baltimore exhibited a horsepower thrasher and other farm equipment.

The *Port Tobacco Times* for November 16, 1848, carries the list of premiums awarded at the fair. They gave prizes for livestock in amounts from $3.00 to $7.00; horses, mules, cattle, sheep, hogs, tobacco ($5.00 for the best hogshead) corn, wheat, potatoes, vegetables and fruit. Daniel Jenifer, Jr., won $7.00 for the best yoke of oxen. The ladies were awarded prizes for bread, butter, home made soap, home spun cloth, home made quilts and home made counterpanes. One of the prizes for quilting was awarded to Miss Olivia Floyd of Rose Hill. The premiums were mostly in silver plate from the establishment of Mr. Samuel Kirk of Baltimore City. Winners of premiums included Richard B. Posey, John Hamilton, Henry A. Neale, Col. William Thompson, Dr. Frances R. Wills, William Stone. The principal address at the fair was made by the Honorable John Grant Chapman who was a member of the United States House of Representatives from this district. His speech was printed in booklet form by Elijah Wells, Jr., and today is a collector's item, as it is one of the rare publications that has a Port Tobacco imprint.

As was common in a society which was dependent upon horses for transportation, and farm power, horse racing was one of the principal recreations of the gentlemen. The *Port Tobacco Times* gives notice of a race course started by Francis Thompson and Company, six miles from Port Tobacco at Middleton. They advertised 3 days of racing in October 1845, featuring horses from Baltimore, Virginia, North Carolina and Maryland as well as the immediate vicinity. Admissions to the races were based on mode of transportation to the track charging $.75 for a 4-wheel carriage, $.50 for a 2-wheel vehicle, $.25 for a man and horse. Those on foot paid only $.12½.

Races were also advertised in Bryantown for October 26, 27, 28, 1854.

The paper for 1857 also advertised tournaments, a type of entertainment which has survived in Southern Maryland to the present day. The tournament, based on the tournaments of the days of chivalry and brought to the new world by the English colonists, placed in competition, gentlemen astride their favorite horses trying to spear increasingly smaller rings with their lances, for the privilege of selecting the Queen of Love and Beauty.

A rather good map of Maryland for the year 1852 shows the following towns in Charles County: Trappe, Hill Top, Port Tobacco, Chapman Town, Bryantown, Benedict, Popes Creek, Allen's Fresh, and Newport.

John Livingston's Law Register for 1852 names and locates the following members of the bar in the County:

Allen's Fresh—William D. Merrick (retired)

Bryantown—John J. Hughes

Harris Lot—Peter W. Crain (on the Bench)
John T. Stoddert (Retired)   Z. H. Turner

Port Tobacco—Richard Barnes (on the Bench) William C. Barnes, George Brent, John G. Chapman (Retired), Gerard W. Crain, James Ferguson, George P. Jenkins (Retired), George W. Matthews, John W. Mitchell, Walter Mitchell (Retired), Robert S. Reeder, Frederick Stone, William B. Stone (Retired) and Nicholas Stonestreet.

Several of the men listed above deserve more than passing mention. It is possible that John Grant Chapman who was born at "Glen Albion" in Charles County in 1798 was considered in his own time the foremost Charles Countian of the first half of the century. His first teacher was the Reverend John Weems, Episcopal minister at Port Tobacco. Poor health made his education intermittent, but he studied law and was a practicing attorney in Port Tobacco by 1819. He was elected to the Maryland Legislature in 1824 and served until 1830, part of the time as Speaker of the House. In 1831, he was elected to the Maryland Senate serving three years as President of the Senate, being elected unanimously. He retired from the Senate in 1836 but was again elected to the House. From 1845 to 1849 he was a member of the United States House of Representatives. He was President of the State Constitutional Convention in 1851 and in 1852, he presided at the Whig Presidential Convention held in Baltimore. John Grant Chapman died in 1856 at Waverly. He was buried at St. John's and was many years later reinterred at La Plata.

Another Charles countian of this period achieved a reputation which was wider than the geographical limitations of his native county. Daniel Jenifer II was born in Charles County in 1791. He was educated to law and soon rose to a position of influence which resulted in his becoming a local judge and later in his election to the State Legislature as a Whig. He served as a member of the United States Congress from 1831 to 1833 and from 1835 to 1841.

As Member of Congress Jenifer fought a duel in 1836 with Jesse A. Bynum, Congressman from North Carolina. The duel grew out of a political quarrel and it has the distinction of being the last duel fought at the old dueling grounds at Bladensburg. Six shots were exchanged without injury to either party so the affair was amicably settled.

President William Henry Harrison appointed Daniel Jenifer U. S. Minister to Austria in 1841 and he served until 1845. While he was abroad he did a lot of work on the tobacco trade, a question in which he was greatly interested. He had served as Presiding Officer at the Tobacco Convention held in Washington in May, 1840, and again in December 1840 to discuss various aspects of the export trade.

Daniel Jenifer's home was in the lower part of Charles County where he built a handsome frame house he called "Charleston". He was an intimate life long friend of Henry Clay who visited him there frequently. Jenifer retired to "Charleston" and died there in 1855.

Robert Sennett Reeder was born in 1815 in Charles County, the son of Thomas Harrison Reeder, physician of eminence, and Elizabeth Sennett. He received his elementary education at a neighborhood school, and in 1831 attended Kenyon College in Ohio. When he finished school, Reeder taught for a few years, part of this time at Charlotte Hall School.

He was admitted to the bar in 1841 on the motion of his dear friend, John Grant Chapman. In 1843, he was elected to the Maryland Legislature and he also served many years as states attorney of Charles County, being elected in 1851 under the reformed constitution of Maryland. Mr. Reeder was a temperance advocate and he held to the rather strange theory that no act should be passed as a law without the unanimous approval of all members of both houses of the legislature.

About this same time an event of some importance took place at the county seat. The *Port Tobacco Times* for March 9, 1851 announces that for the first time water is being conveyed to Port Tobacco in pipes. The town continued to grow, and in 1858 the *Times* announced a bill to incorporate the village of Port Tobacco. Evidently prices were high in the little town despite the numerous stores which advertised in the paper, as a Baltimore visitor complained that he had to pay 35 cents for a hair cut which would only cost a quarter in Baltimore; and a Port Tobacco housewife records that she had to send to Alexandria for paint to re-do her chairs as it was so high at home.

Despite the metropolitan aspect of the town as it appears through the columns of the paper, we are reminded of its more primitive aspects by a notice the bailiff inserted in the paper on May 6, 1858, advising owners of property they had to have "privies and premises cleaned and limed on or before May 20" or suffer a $5.00 fine.

Communication between Charles County and the outside world was not easy. Geographically the County, with St. Mary's County and Calvert County, occupies a peninsula between the Potomac River and the outside world with the only land outlet to the north. During the first two centuries of the County's existence, travel was most difficult. Horses and sail boats were slow and a trip of any distance required many long, weary hours of travel. No appreciable change came until well into the 19th century.

The invention of the steamboat opened an entirely new era of more rapid transportation for the whole country and especially for Charles County with its vast expanses of deep water.

By 1817 steamboats appeared in these waters. Coming from Baltimore the first boats operated up the Patuxent and undoubtedly made Benedict a port of call. No record could be found of the names of any of the first vessels until 1845, when the "Planter" is mentioned.

History records the first steam vessels as being crude, no more than wooden barges with the boiler and engine mounted in them. The fuel used was wood and the mortality from fire was very high.

In 1854 the Weems Line reorganized and operated a number of boats along the bay, the Patuxent, Potomac and Rappahannock Rivers. Among the vessels which plied these waters were the afore-mentioned "Planter" as well as the "George Weems", the "Theodore Weems", the "Mary Washington," the "Matilda," and the "Winona." All these vessels were side wheelers.

How exciting it must have been for the planters along our majestic streams, to watch for the approach of these river boats. They symbolized a new comfortable and more modern approach for personal transportation to cities of the State. They furnished a means of reasonably priced transfer of the manufactured goods to the farms and the raw products of these farms to the city markets.

The United States mail service traversed only parts of the county and then only at infrequent intervals.

In 1839 one route from Washington touched Piscataway, Pleasant Hill (first stop in Charles) Port Tobacco, Allen's Fresh, Newport and thence into St. Mary's County via Chaptico and Ridge.

The Port Tobacco Times in 1845 announced mail arriving from Washington Mondays and Thursdays between three and four P. M. and leaving Wednesdays and Saturdays between seven and eight A. M.

Another mail line and public transportation advertised in 1848 issue in this manner:

"Leave Washington Monday and Thursday 6 A.M. returning the following day. Leaving Newport in time to be at Port Tobacco at 8 A.M. Arriving in Washington before the cars leave for Baltimore. Thus enabling persons from Newport and Port Tobacco going to Baltimore to get there the same day they leave home. Fare to Port Tobacco $2.00, Newport $2.50".

The first reference to daily mail service was in 1855. Another daily service mail stage is noted in 1868 between Glymont and Port Tobacco. This stage left Glymont on the arrival of the mail steamer from the District of Columbia at 8 A.M. It arrived at Port Tobacco at 11:30 A.M., and left at 12:30 to meet the steamer at Glymont on its return from Aquia Creek. Fare on the stage was $1.50.

Another route of travel to the Capital from Port Tobacco was by way of the Bumpy Oak Road to Marshall Hall to board the steamer there.

While all these improvements were taking place in transportation of goods and products to and from counties and markets how did the people reach the terminal wharves and rail stations?

Fortunately most areas of the county were blessed with excellent deposits of gravel and with this material very passable summer time roads could be built. Sometimes in the winter long stretches would become quagmires, because of the mud beneath.

The first county roads were built and maintained by tax money or help in kind. County tax monies were used to employ road superintendents and furnish some equipment. Farmers, their tenants and hired hands supplied the labor.

On October 12, 1854, the *Port Tobacco Times* printed this notice, "To Whom it may Concern—All persons who wish to have good roads in the Fourth Election District of Charles County are requested to be punctual in sending their hands when called on. So often they refuse as some gentlemen have done and be the first to complain.

"I pledge myself to devote my whole attention to the roads and early attendance of hands will be required and no man doing a days work at home before sending him on the roads for the future. I shall send all hands back that do not come at 8 o'clock A. M. which is the regular hour."

Signed—J. H. H."

Undoubtedly he and other road superintendents were handicapped in building and maintaining the road system with such an uncertain labor supply.

Mud and chuck holes were not the only handicap to travel in the early roads, because this notice appeared in the same newspaper in 1869:

"Person having fences encroaching upon the Public Roads in this County are hereby requested to remove them, else it becomes the duty of the Supervisors to do so.

Signed H. C. Page, Supt."

About the middle of the century we find the first Methodist Churches being built in this circuit which included Charles County. A minister was then sent to each church so that his family could be with him rather than alone for a month at a time while he rode his circuit. About this time Mr. Carpenter gave a piece of land to be used for a church which he wished named Bethel. At first the meeting place was a small plank building on one side of the lot which was used until Bethel Church was built in 1859. As the congregation grew it was necessary to build a new church in 1892 which seated about 250 or 300 people. Then in 1880 ground was given for another Methodist Church in La Plata by Mr. Thomas Chapman. The Bethel Congregation and the La Plata Congregation have today become the United Methodist Church which is erecting a large church in La Plata.

The altar and pews used in the basement church at La Plata were handmade for Bethel Church by two members of the congregation who were named Penn and were direct descendants of William Penn of Pennsylvania.

Through this whole period which is now being considered, the social and economic life of the county was basically dependent on the institution of slavery. For this reason Charles County was faced with all the problems which were an inherent part of a system which allowed human beings to be owned by other human beings as mere property. Most slave owners treated their human property kindly and took good care of them, if not for humanitarian reasons, at least because of the monetary investment they represented. But the treatment of the slaves was a private matter, entirely up to the owner or his overseer and even in such a small community as Charles County, the same abuses occured which condemned the system universally.

Early in the 19th century there lived in Charles County a negro slave named Josiah Henson. His early life was one of such hardship that he finally escaped to Canada in 1830, where he became a Methodist minister. Harriet Beecher Stowe used the story of Josiah Henson's slave life as the basis for her character of Uncle Tom in the famous book "Uncle Tom's Cabin", which was such a powerful influence in bringing an end to slavery in the United States.

Early in the 1850's Charles County was beginning to feel the first undercurrents of the Civil War. The proximity of the county to the border of the slave states, and the fact that it was traversed by many as a route between North and South made it an especially sensitive area. The tobacco economy of the county was based on slavery so the landed people of the county doubly resented the pressures that were being brought to bear to abolish the institution. The Negroes themselves, next door to freedom, were infected by the general unrest to such an extent that in 1856 it was necessary to begin nightly partrols of the county with officers appointed by the Justices of the Peace.

The election of 1860 was accompanied by heated arguments and even hotter tempers. In common with most of the south, the people of Charles County were predominantly supporters of the Democratic Party and they looked upon it as the party behind whose candidate all the conservative element of the country might unite with success. The Constitutional Union Party was still too new and too heterogeneous for people to be quite sure of its political philosophy. But all were united in feeling that the election of a Republican President would be a national calamity. The consternation with which the results of the election of 1860, when it was found that the Republican candidate, Abraham Lincoln, had won, can be easily imagined.

The *Port Tobacco Times* for December 20 and December 27, 1860, gives an account which shows quite clearly the sentiments of the people.

A meeting was held at Middletown on the 18th of December for the purpose of consulting and agreeing on some plan of action in reference to those in the district who voted for Lincoln and Hamlin in the recent election. Colonel Frances Thompson presided over the meeting, and Eugene Digges was appointed Secretary. The following resolutions were adopted by the Meeting:

"Whereas we believe that the law of self-preservation is the first and strongest of nature and further believing that the propagation of the 'irrepressible conflict' doctrine in our midst is prejudicial alike to our interests, hostile and fatal in its consequences to our institutions and disgraceful to our honor as a community. Therefore be it

"*Resolved* That we deeply censure—those—who cast their votes for Lincoln and Hamlin

"*Resolved* That although we greatly regret that several of our native fellow-countrymen have been betrayed into such an expression of sentiment as renders them justly liable to our indignation, nevertheless, as an earnest of our moderation, we are willing to overlook their indiscretions for the present with brighter hopes and better expectattions from them for the future.

"*Resolved* That while we are disposed to act leniently and deal gently with our fellow countrymen, we are determined to remove from our midst Nathan Burnham whose longer presence amongst us is most highly objectionable. His own vote for Lincoln and the influence which he has exercised point to him as a Black Republican emissary, and renders his presence intolerable.

"*Resolved* That we give Natham Burnham until the 1st day of January 1861 to leave the county and that the Chairman of this meeting be and is fully authorized to appoint a committee of four to see that the object of these resolutions are duly executed and whose further duty it shall be, should the said Nathan Burnham refuse to leave as above stated, to expel him *vi et armis* from our county."

The Committee appointed to carry out the resolutions was composed of William J. Middleton, Benjamin W. Garner, William A. Mudd.

The State itself was in a turmoil as it seemed the time had come for a decision as to its future course of action, be it on the side of the North or on the side of the South. In an effort to reach an agreement and in view of Governor Hick's vacillation, the people of the State decided to send delegates to a convention in Baltimore to ascertain the position which the citizens of the State wished the State to maintain in the crisis.

In Charles County a broadside dated January 25, 1861, and entitled "Charles County Convention" stated that the three delegates elected to represent that county in a state convention should have the power to vote on any measure regarding Maryland's relations with the Federal Government provided the action of the convention was later submitted to the vote of the people. The use of coercion by the Federal Government on seceding states was opposed and it was the considered opinion of the members of the Charles County Convention that there was "a close association of interests between Maryland and the other border States."

On March 12, the State Conference Convention met and again expressed their feeling that through the influence of Maryland and the other border slave states, the extremists of the South might be persuaded to be more moderate and the fanatics of the North compelled to be more just. They appointed a committee from the State including Walter Mitchell of Charles County to wait on the Virginia Convention then in session and urge that body to recommend a border state convention. But their efforts came too late as before anything could be accomplished, actual hostilities had broken out.

It wasn't long before the war became an actuality to the people of Charles County. Their predominantly Southern sympathies being well known, they soon found themselves treated as residents of occupied territory. On June 20, 1861, one hundred Federal Troops landed at Chapel Point and went to the residence of Captain Samuel Cox at "Rich Hill" near Bel Alton and demanded immediate delivery of state arms which he had no choice but to surrender.

The *Port Tobacco Times* of October 24, 1861, offers evidence that the people of Charles County had not lost their sense of humor despite the situation with which they were confronted. A black headline on the back page of the paper announces in large letters **"The Enemy Approaches."** Having caught the eye of the reader, it goes on in smaller print "The Bed Bug Season is now at hand and every family and owner of a bed should at once provide themselves with a bottle of 'Bed Bug Poison.' It never fails as prepared, wholesale and retail by Apothecaries' Hall, Port Tobacco, Md., Corner fronting the Court House."

The truth of the matter was that "the enemy" actually was approaching, as on October 31, the Fifth Regiment of General Sickles' Brigade passed through Port Tobacco and encamped at Mulberry Grove. The whole of this brigade and a brigade of General Hooker's, numbering ten to twelve thousand troops, were sent into the county, mostly between Mattawoman and Budd's Ferry for the purpose of preventing the threatened crossing of the Confederates into Maryland. Batteries were erected by the Federal Troops at Budd's Ferry near the mouth of the Chicamuxen Creek in Charles County, and General Hooker's corps was stationed here during the whole of the winter to protect them. There is a manuscript military map of the western section of Charles County drawn by one of General Hooker's men, in the Map Division of the Library of Congress, entitled "Surveys and Reconnaissances in the Vicinity of Budd's Ferry, Charles County, Maryland by R. S. Williamson, Capt. Topographical Engineers." The map is especially interesting as it gives the names of the people who lived in the houses along the roads from Port Tobacco leading west. The Catholic Church at Hill Top is also indicated on the map.

The newspaper at this time records almost weekly, arrests of County citizens who were being taken to Washington for questioning about their activities and feeling finally ran so high that it was necessary to assign a guard to Port Tobacco to keep the peace between the citizens and the soldiers. An editorial in the *Port Tobacco Times,* on Dec. 19, 1861 summarizes the complaint:

"OUR SITUATION

"The State of Maryland has cast her vote for the Union and Government by the largest majority ever known to this State . . . Charles County then stands before the Government and the world this day a loyal county. Charles County has ever been loyal; we challenge a disloyal act to be laid at her door—and yet what is her condition? As a loyal county and State, obedient to the recognized law, faithful to the Constitution, the citizens of this State have a right, and undisputed right to protection in their person and property. Twenty thousand Federal troops are stationed upon the soil of Charles County, their camps extending from Mattawoman Creek to Liverpool Point. These troops are here 'For our protection,' we are told; 'to protect us from the Rebels,' and yet, in fact, we are exposed to more danger, to more losses and damage or at least as much as if these very Rebels were here. Our farmers are deprived of their provender to such extent that their cattle must die. Our citizens are deprived of homes almost; and fences, farms, and fields fall prey to the ruthless hands of those very friends who come here to protect us.

"Our negroes,—ah, this is the point,—our negroes—are taken from us time and again, with no remuneration and the threats of violence if we seek to recover them."

General L. C. Baker in his book on *The History of the Secret Service*, includes a letter he wrote to Secretary of State Seward, on November 27, 1861, in which he says, "On my arrival at Port Tobacco, the headquarters of Colonel Graham's regiment, I found the inhabitants complaining bitterly at their alleged ill-treatment and depredations committed under his command. In justice to Colonel Graham, however, I found on inquiring that the inhabitants had been the first aggressors. There are residing at this place but four or five union men, the balance either being sympathizers with secessionists or open and avowed aiders and abettors of treason. The postmaster at this place is secretly doing all in his power to further the interests of the Confederacy. Eight miles from the above named locality is a small town known as Allen's Fresh. There are but two union men at this place. I found in the Post Office here five letters addressed to fictitious names, on opening them I discovered that they contained sealed letters addressed to well-known secessionists in Virginia. The Post Master was one of those who assisted and contributed to organize and equip Confederate soldiers in Virginia. At the Newport Post Office, some two miles from Allen's Fresh, I found a package of 34 letters post-marked 'Newport P.O., Maryland' all ready to be forwarded to different localities in the North. On examining the letters, I found they were all written in Virginia and had all been dropped into the office by one person."

Mr. Thomas A. Jones, who lived at Popes Creek sheds some light on this question of communications with Virginia. He says that Popes Creek was the favorite spot for crossing the river to Virginia, as it was both easily accessible from the North and also the people in the neighborhood were known to be in sympathy with the South. Jones lived on the high bluff directly south of Popes Creek at this time, and he says he took people across the river every night and sometimes made several trips in one night. On one occasion that he mentions specifically, he carried 10 or 12 men and women in one boatload; so the number of people passing illegally into the South was obviously large. He was arrested for these activities in September 1861, and spent six months in the Old Capitol prison in Washington.

Shortly after Jones returned home in the spring of 1862, he was approached with the request that he consent to act as Chief Signal Agent north of the Potomac for the Confederacy. He accepted the responsibility with some misgivings upon the condition that he be given entire control of the ferry and of all the other Maryland agents. It was difficult and dangerous work because of the Federal gunboats on the river, their armed patrol on shore, and a detachment of troops quartered at Popes Creek, another on the farm of Major Roderick Watson right next to the Jones farm. Jones had noticed that it was difficult to see a small boat on the river just about sunset because of the sun shining on the water as it set in the west plus the long shadows cast by the cliffs on the Maryland shore. The shore patrol did not go on duty until sunset so a boat would come from the Virginia shore just before sunset; leave mail in the fork of a dead tree on the river bank on the Maryland side, picking up the packet left there to take back to Virginia. Then Jones would go down later and pick it up. If activities on the Maryland shore were such that it was not safe for a boat to cross, a black signal was hung in the window at Major Watson's house by his daughter.

The mail received from Virginia was then taken to Post Offices in different places by other agents selected by Mr. Jones. Jones mentions by name Dr. Stoughton W. Dent, M.D., and his brother-in-law Thomas H. Harbin as being two of his agents. Dr. Dent made almost daily visits to Popes Creek in the guise of professional calls, and he took out with him the mail hidden in his long overcoat, his high boots or, in the summer time, in a long linen duster amply supplied with pockets. He would take the mail to Port Tobacco or to Bryantown or sometimes as far as Charlotte Hall.

Mr. Jones served as Chief Signal Officer for the duration of the War, and he boasts that in all that time not one letter or paper was ever lost.[6]

Many of the Charles County boys had already crossed the lines to serve in the Confederate Army. They felt it was the only way they could express their feelings about the official position the State had taken in the conflict. Most of them went to Richmond and joined the Maryland commands that were being organized there. One of the batteries formed in July, 1861, was the First Maryland Artillery which contained a whole group of Charles County men. The First Lieutenant was William Fendlay Dement who was born in Cedar Point Neck in 1806. Dement had attended Georgetown University and Mt. St. Mary's College at Emmitsburg and then returned home to farm. He was one of the men to help organize the First Maryland Confederate Artillery. After the Seven Day Battle for Richmond between Lee and McClellan, he was promoted to Captain, then to Major, and placed under Stonewall Jackson in the Valley of Virginia. He and his battery participated in the Battles of Seven Pines, the Second Manassas, Cedar Run, Manchester, the capture of Harper's Ferry, Sharpsburg, Gettysburg, Cold Harbor and Appomattox. Dement was wounded twice but returned to his farm near Pomfret after the war where he lived until his death in 1907.

Major Dement was considered one of the best Artillery Officers in the Confederate Army and he had a whole group of Charles County men serving under him including Dr. John T. Digges, William F. Compton, James A. Dorsett,

Charles Riddle, William F. Bowling, L. M. Southerland, and P. A. L. Contee.

Not all the Charles County men served in this battery as we also find individuals like Basil Spalding who ran away from school and enlisted in the Confederate Cavalry in 1862 when he was just a boy of 17. He served to the end of the War in Mosby's Raiders. After the war, Mr. Spalding lived at Green Park near Pomfret until his death in 1929.

Perhaps the most famous of all Charles Countians to serve in the Confederate cause was Admiral Raphael Semmes. Semmes was born at Efton Hills near Nanjemoy in Charles County in 1790. He was appointed a midshipman in the United States Navy 1826. While waiting for his orders, he studied law and was admitted to the bar. He was promoted to Lieutenant in 1837 and served with distinction in the Mexican War. In recognition of his services in the Mexican War, a resolution was passed by the General Assembly of Maryland that thanks and congratulations of the Legislature were tendered to him for his gallant conduct during the war with Mexico and they recommended him to the favorable consideration of the Executive of the National Government for promotion.

In 1861, Semmes resigned from the United States Navy and immediately entered the Confederate Navy. He was put in command of the noted Confederate raider "The Alabama" which, in a cruise of three years, did more damage to Union shipping than any single ship in the Confederate Navy. The "Alabama," most formidable of the Confederate Privateers, destroyed an estimated eight to ten million dollars worth of United States property.

After the War, Admiral Semmes settled in Mobile, Alabama, where he practiced law and devoted himself to literary pursuits until his death in 1877.

The feelings of the people in the County in regard to the Union side may be seen in their response to President Lincoln's call for volunteers. In 1862, there was one volunteer furnished from Charles County. As the draft authorized by Congress apportioned 382 soldiers to be furnished by the County, and as most of the eligible young men had gone south, the burden fell heavily on those who remained. Some of the problem was solved by the practice of purchasing substitutes at prices ranging from $300 to $700.

In view of the overwhelming sentiments of the majority of the citizens of the county, tribute must be paid to those who remained loyal to the Union. Such a man was the Episcopal Minister at Port Tobacco, the Reverend Lemuel Wilmer, pastor of Christ Church. His stand by his convictions must have been especially difficult because of difference of opinion with most of his congregation.

One of the most interesting figures of this period was Miss Olivia Floyd who lived at Rose Hill. Miss Olivia had been a cripple since childhood due to a broken back which had never been properly set. Together with her sister Mary and brother Robert Semmes, she inherited Rose Hill from her uncle Ignatius Semmes in 1843. Miss Olivia was an agent and a messenger for the Confederacy during the Civil War. Her brother Robert was fighting with General Stuart's Cavalry in the Confederate Army and, after his death from battle wounds in 1863, Miss Olivia became an even more ardent worker for the cause. She used a wooden boat model made by her brother as a place of concealment for money and papers.

In the winter of 1864 a handful of Confederate troops made a successful raid on St. Alban's, Vermont and escaped with their lives, their horses and the money they had captured into Canada. Here they were promptly arrested by Canadian authorities and Union officials sought their extradition to put them on trial on the grounds that they were spies. Their very lives depended on the group being able to establish the fact that they were duly commissioned officers of the Confederate Army acting on official orders.[7] A message was started south requesting the commissions of the men. It passed from hand to hand, from Southern sympathizer to sympathizer, all the way from Canada to Maryland until it finally reached Miss Olivia who was the last link of the chain of communications into confederate territory.

Miss Olivia had no more than received the message when she heard that the Union troops were coming to search the house. There was a pair of brass andirons in the parlor and she put the papers in the hollow brass ball at the top. When the Union soldiers arrived they searched the house and then came into the parlor and sat by the fire with their feet propped on those very andirons without suspecting a thing. When the soldiers left Miss Olivia put the note in her hair and carried it to the signal station at Popes Creek where it was sent to Richmond, with the result that the soldiers on trial in Canada received copies of their commissions in time to save them.

Long years after the war was over Miss Olivia was invited to attend the Confederate Reunion held in Louisville as a guest of Col. Bennett H. Young, the commanding officer of the raiders. With the assistance of Mr. Adrian Posey she went to the reunion and was treated as one of the honored guests. Miss Olivia is said to have sent Col. Young the andirons and the ship model which had played such an important part in her activities during the war.[8]

Another facet in the picture of Charles County during the Civil War is the fact that the Seventh Regiment Infantry, United States Colored Troops, Maryland Volunteers, which was composed of colored men from Maryland, had their regimental camp at Benedict, Maryland. The troops spent the winter of 1863 at Camp Stanton, Benedict, in drilling and preparing for active field duty. The location of the camp turned out to be an unhealthy one, and many of the volunteers died during the winter season. The regiment was activated in 1864 and it fought in all the subsequent major campaigns of the Army of the Potomac with many casualties.

The people of Charles County were faced with the end of the war in 1865, and in view of their open and avowed sympathies, they found themselves supporters of a lost cause both socially and economically. They had scarcely time to face this fact when they were plunged without warning into one of the most dramatic episodes in the history of the County.

The chain of events started at Ford's Theater in Washington on April 14 when President Abraham Lincoln was shot by John Wilkes Booth.

When Booth made his escape from the rear of the theater, it was his intention to make his way to the Potomac River guided by another one of the conspirators, David E. Herold, who professed to be familiar with the roads through Southern Maryland. They hoped to cross the river in a boat which had been placed by the plotters in Port Tobacco Creek some months before when their first plan was abduction rather than assassination. It is likely that the boat was one that had been purchased from Richard M. Smoot by one of the conspirators, an unattractive man named George A. Atzeroth, who lived at Port Tobacco and carried on his trade as a housepainter.

Booth and Herold joined forces at the Eleventh Street Bridge and took the road south to Surrattsville where they stopped at the Surratt home to pick up the guns and ammunition which had been put there as one of the arrangements of the old abduction plot. They did not stop long, but by this time, Booth's leg, which he had broken leaping from the President's box, had become so painful that he was in urgent need of medical help.

Accordingly, they altered their route to make a stop at the home of Dr. Samuel A. Mudd who lived in the northeastern section of Charles County between the present town of Waldorf and that of Gallant Green. Dr. Mudd was a well-known physician in the area having practiced medicine there since his graduation from medical school in 1856, and Booth had met Dr. Mudd in November of 1864 when he

THE LINCOLN CONSPIRATORS

David E. Herold, who accompanied Booth on his flight through Charles County.

George A. Atzerodt, house painter and carriage maker of Port Tobacco, one of the conspirators.

John Wilkes Booth, the assassin of President Abraham Lincoln.

Courtesy National Park Service

CHARLES COUNTIANS INVOLVED IN BOOTH'S FLIGHT THROUGH
CHARLES COUNTY

Dr. Samuel A. Mudd, who set Booth's broken leg.

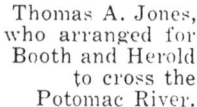

Courtesy National Park Service

Thomas A. Jones, who arranged for Booth and Herold to cross the Potomac River.

OBITUARY.

A virtuous, brave, generous, noble-souled man has fallen. Another victim is added to the list of the gallant dead, sacrificed upon the altar of their country's freedom. Mother, sisters, relatives, friends—an entire community—mourn the death of ROBERT S. FLOYD, late of Charles county, Md. He died on the 3d of April, 1863, at the residence of Dr. Cooper, in Fauquier county, Va., of wounds received at the battle of Kelly's Ford, on the 17th of March, in the 34th year of his age.

The subject of this notice was surrounded by all that could render life desirable. He had ample opportunities of indulging a refined and cultivated taste, and was contented and happy in the company of his devoted mother and sister, which he preferred to the flashing wit or the light vivacity of gay society. It was his peculiar delight to cultivate the home affections, beautifying and adorning all around by his superior taste and skill. But in obedience to the dictates of what he conscientiously believed to be duty, he left mother, sister, friends and the home of his boyhood, which he delighted so much to adorn, and around which lingered a thousand fond and happy associations, to seek amid the clash of arms in defence of his adopted country those rights and that freedom of action denied him in his native State.

About the 1st of June, 1861, he left Maryland in company with a number of kindred spirits and enlisted in General Stuart's Cavalry, and was a devoted follower of that intrepid leader up to the time he received the fatal wound. The period for which the company enlisted of which he was a member, expired about a year since. Influenced by the considerations which first induced him to become a soldier, he immediately re-enlisted, and was elected to an office of high responsibility, the duties of which he discharged to the entire satisfaction of his superior officers.

Though the purpose of this notice is in no respect to enter into the private character of the deceased, it would be unjust to his memory if it was not stated, that high moral and religious principle, an affectionate disposition, an instinctive sentiment of delicacy, propriety and consideration for the feelings of others, and a retiring modesty and simplicity of deportment, as much distinguished and endeared him in the social relations of life, as his military attainments elevated him in the estimation of his superior officers and his comrades. He furnished, indeed, a bright example of the soldier, the scholar, the gentleman and the Christian.

Though deprived of the melancholy satisfaction of ministering to his wants in his suffering hours, and of being with their hero son and brother in his last moments, the fond mother and sisters have the happy consolation of learning that he was attended by kind stranger friends, and, above all, of knowing that he had always lived as lives the innocent, and that his

Spirit now soars above
*   *   *

OBITUARY FOR ROBERT FLOYD, brother of Miss Olivia Floyd, who died of wounds received in fighting in the Confederate Army during the Civil War.

Photograph courtesy of Mrs. Matthew Henson

MATTHEW HENSON, Negro Arctic Explorer who was with Admiral Robert E. Peary when he reached the North Pole, April 6, 1909.

spent a few days in the Bryantown area for the avowed purpose of buying a horse. The injured man and his companion arrived at Dr. Mudd's home about 4 A. M. on April 15. Booth was wearing a disguise, and they introduced themselves to the Doctor under the assumed names of Tyler and Tyson. They told Dr. Mudd that the injury happened when the man's horse had fallen and hurt him. Dr. Mudd set the broken leg without question and gave the men a bedroom for the night. Booth kept to his room the next day until after Dr. Mudd left the house to visit some patients near Bryantown. While Dr. Mudd was gone, Herold assisted Booth downstairs and, despite remonstrances of Mrs. Mudd who knew that the Doctor felt the injured man was not fit to travel, the two of them mounted their horses and started south through Zekiah Swamp. They lost their way on the paths which criss-cross the swamp and rode aimlessly until they ran into a Negro named Oswald Swann who agreed to guide them to "Rich Hill," the home of Col. Samuel Cox near Bel Alton, whose southern sympathies were well known. Colonel Cox directed the fugitives to a pine thicket about a mile west of the house and advised them to stay there until arrangements could be made to get them across the river.

The next man to enter the story is Thomas A. Jones. Col. Cox sent for Jones on Sunday morning to ask for his assistance in getting the men across the river. He directed Jones to the thicket in which the men were hidden, and Jones went to see Booth and Herold to promise his assistance. He returned to the thicket on Monday with food and newspapers and begged the men to be patient.

In the meantime, the whole countryside was aroused to such an extent that it was unthinkable to take the men out of hiding and across the river. As soon as it was discovered that Booth and Herold had headed south, the area was swarming with Federal troops and detectives. When Dr. Mudd told about visitors of that Saturday morning, Booth was identified, but the two men had dropped completely from sight since they left Dr. Mudd's house. Assuming that the fugitives were in hiding in the swamp, the troops determined to comb the area around Chapmantown, Bethtown and Allen's Fresh. The military forces consisted of 700 men of the 8th Illinois Cavalry, 600 men of the 22nd Colored Troops and 100 men of the 16th New York. They swept the swamps by detachments, dismounted, with the cavalry guarding the clearings. The soldiers formed a cordon around the swamp and one group swept the swamps longitudinally while the others pushed straight across. They then covered the whole countryside, scouring from Cobb's Neck up and from Allen's Fresh down.[9] Jones says they visited every house in Southern Maryland. It seems amazing that it was actually possible to keep the assassin hidden in the county for a full week without discovery under such vigilance.

Mr. Jones went to Port Tobacco on Tuesday to listen to the public gossip and see if he could learn anything from the people gathered at the county seat. When he stopped for a drink at the bar room of the Brawner Hotel, Captain Williams, one of the detectives, advised him that he would give a $100,000 reward for information leading to Booth's capture.

Jones continued to visit the two men in the thicket daily taking them food and newspapers. On Friday, a week from the assassination, Jones was in Allen's Fresh, when a rumor that Booth was seen in St. Mary's County sent all the soldiers hurrying in that direction. As night drew on, it got cloudy and foggy, so Jones decided the time had come to act. At dark he went to the hiding place and led Booth and Herold to a boat he had hidden at Dent's Meadow about a mile north of Pope's Creek on the river. Part of the trip was over the main road, and the whole journey was full of hazards. At Dent's Meadow, Jones gave Booth and Herold the boat and started them across the river with a compass to guide them. A spring flood tide carried the boat up to the Nanjemoy shore that night so Booth and Herold hid on the shore that day and on Saturday night, crossed the river into Virginia.

Both Thomas Jones and Samuel Cox were arrested within a few days. They were first taken to the old brick tavern at Bryantown where they were held under guard and then they were moved to Carroll prison in Washington. But no real evidence existed against either man, and the government was unable to build up any worthwhile case against them. Jones was held for six weeks and then released, and a week later Cox was also liberated.[10]

Poor Dr. Mudd was not so fortunate. It was easy to establish that he had actually set Booth's leg as the boot he cut from the broken leg was found in Mudd's house when it was searched. He had to stand trial with the worst of the conspirators and he was sentenced to imprisonment at Fort Jefferson on Dry Tortugas Island. Feelings ran so high in the north after the assassination that reason was obliterated. The people were hungry for victims to punish for the death of the President, and that fact that Dr. Mudd had done no more than fulfill his obligation as a doctor, was brushed aside. It is certain that he had no actual role in the conspiracy, but he was left in prison until 1869. All those four years, Mrs. Mudd and the Doctor's friends in Charles County worked for his release. The doctor himself, though bitter at the injustice done to him, helped the prison doctor, the staff of guards, and his fellow prisoners through a yellow fever epidemic which broke out on the island.

Dr. Mudd was released and pardoned as one of President's Johnson's last official acts. He returned to the county but his health was broken by his long imprisonment and he died in 1883.[11]

As an aftermath of the escape of John Wilkes Booth, early in May of 1865 from six to eight thousand United States troops were garrisoned in Prince George's, Charles and St. Mary's Counties. They were quartered mostly at or near Chapel Point with headquarters at Port Tobacco. On the 1st of May, the following circular was issued:

"Headquarters, Military District of Patuxent
Port Tobacco, Md., May 1st, 1865

"Circular:

"A considerable portion of the inhabitants of this military district having heretofore rendered themselves notorious for their hostility to the government, many of them engaging in blockade running, supplying the enemy with goods, and in some cases with munitions of war, affording an asylum for the worst criminals, and more recently, giving the murderer of the President of the United States an uninterrupted passage through parts of three counties, feeding him and his confederate, and concealing their presence, it is necessary that this infamy should be blotted out, and a new condition of things be inaugurated. The following regulations are therefore made:

"1. No person will be allowed to engage in any occupation, trade or profession without taking an unconditional oath of allegiance, which oath will state that it is taken voluntarily, without mental reservation, and acknowledging the right to require, and authority to administer the same. Taking the oath will not be deemed conclusive evidence of loyalty; and, as none but loyal persons will be permitted to carry on any business, the oath must be accompanied by consistent conduct and loyal acts.

"II. No person will be allowed to wear any rebel uniforms, or to display or have in his possession any rebel flags, or insignia of rank; nor to utter any disloyal sentiments, or question by word or deed, the rightful authority of the government of the United States.

"III. All officers, soldiers and citizens who have been in rebel service, and have not taken the oath of allegiance; all persons who have been engaged in running the blockade, aiding the enemy, concealing or aiding in the flight of Booth and his confederates, or who have failed to give such information as they possessed of his intentions, his place of concealment, or of his orders and abettors, will be arrested and sent to these headquarters.

"IV. All truly loyal persons who sympathize with the government are requested to furnish such information as they possess, and otherwise to cooperate in this effort to discover the guilty and vindicate the supremacy of the law and they are assured that the fullest protection will be afforded them.

"V. Military commanders in this district are charged with the duty of enforcing this order, and will excercise the utmost vigilance to discover and arrest all guilty parties.
"By command of
"H. H. Wells, Colonel Commanding
"Official: A. V. Teeple, Lieut. and A. A. A. G."

Brigadier General Bartlett was placed in command of the department of the Patuxent a few days later and he ordered the following oath of Allegiance: "I.................................., of Charles County, Maryland, do solemnly swear that I will bear true faith, allegiance and loyalty to the Government of the United States; That I will support and defend its Constitution, laws and supremacy against all enemies, whether domestic or foreign; any ordinance, resolution or law of any State Convention or Legislature to the contrary notwithstanding. Further, that I will not in any wise give aid or comfort to, or hold communications with any enemy of the government, or any person who sustains or supports the so-called Confederate States; but will abstain from all business dealing or communications with such persons. And I do this freely, without any mental reservation or evasion whatsoever, with full purpose and resolution to observe the same. I also fully acknowledge the right of the government to require this oath, the authority of the officer to administer it, and its binding force on me."

The following places were designated as military stations where the oath of allegiance was to be administered: Port Tobacco, Milstead's, Nanjemoy, Pleasant Hill, Pomonkey, Bryantown, Beantown, Benedict, Newtown, Allen's Fresh, Newport and Swann Point.[12]

With the end of the Civil War, the history of Charles County becomes but a mirror in miniature of the history of the whole south. The structure of society was disorganized to say the least by the emancipation of the Negro. The economic foundation of the county had been based on the institution of slavery, and when it was abolished, credit collapsed, the future became uncertain and all was gloom and despair. The land was still there but there was no one to work it, and a system of taxation instituted by the "Carpet-bag" government threatened even the tenure of the land. It was at this time that the people of the county became engulfed in a defeatist attitute which really handicapped progress in the county until well into the 20th century.

Perhaps the most obvious result of the war was certain changes in the political system in the county, which exist even to the present time. Before the war, in common with most of the south, Charles County voted overwhelming Whig and then, with the death of the Whig party, the vote could be counted for the Democrats. Then, with the passage of the Fifteenth Amendment, giving the Negroes the right to vote, there came an abrupt switch in the political balance. In 1868, the General Sessions of the Legislature authorized redistricting Charles County into nine election districts, as follows: (1) Port Tobacco, (2) Hill Top, (3) Nanjemoy, (4) Allen's Fresh, (5) Harris Lot, (6) Middletown, (7) Pomonkey, (8) Bryantown, (9) Patuxent City and, for the first time in 1870, registration lists showed a colored majority in the county. While the number of registered Negroes expressed as a percentage of the total colored population, was considerably smaller than the percentage for the white population, they became the deciding factor in elections. The Republican campaign of 1870 was largely the work of Dr. W. R. Wilmer, a son of the Reverend Lemuel Wilmer, and he campaigned so vigorously that single-handed he won a majority for the Republican candidate for Congress.

He then started to work toward capturing the county government in 1871, but he was handicapped by the lack of party members qualified to hold public office. A party whose candidate for Governor in 1867 polled only 7 votes in the county was obviously at a disadvantage in making up a complete slate for county offices. So Dr. Wilmer decided the solution was to recruit among the Democrats. He found it not too difficult to gain recruits because the Democratic party, owing to the virtual one party system which had existed so long before the war, was split by factions. Besides, he was obviously representing a victorious party and in a position to make tempting offers. He was not able to make much progress in 1871, but by 1873 a full fusion ticket composed of Republicans and "Independent Democrats" was presented to the voters. The leader of the "Independent Democrats" was Dr. George Dyer Mudd who ran on the ticket for state senate. Surprisingly enough, many of the "Independent Democrats" were Confederate veterans who perhaps returned home from the war and found the party in the hands of those who stayed behind and so were interested in joining a new party, even the party of Radical Reconstruction.

The Fusion ticket won every office, and the pattern was set which has prevailed to the present day. From that election on, the term Independent Democrat was dropped and anyone running on the Republican ticket was called a Republican. The party leaders remained a small group however, depending on the Negro vote for their victories and recruiting candidates for office among the Democrats.

Despite their difficulties on the county basis, Democrats of Charles County continued to take full part in state politics. For the years immediately after the war, Barnes Compton was the most prominent Democrat on the local scene. He served in the State Senate in 1867 and 1869, and was President of the Senate both times. He was elected to Congress in 1884 and served almost continuously until 1893. Compton moved to Prince George's County in 1880 and county leadership fell to a small group including F. M. Cox who was editor of the *Port Tobacco Times.*

While all this jockeying for political power was in progress, the county itself was changing. The most significant changes were brought by the coming of the railroad to the area. As early as 1854, the *Port Tobacco Times* records the first agitation for a railroad into Charles County with a group proposing a connection with the Baltimore and Potomac Railroad. Plans had to be abandoned during the war period, but were revived immediately thereafter, and by 1872 a line was built by the Baltimore and Potomac Railroad from Bowie, Maryland, to Popes Creek in Charles County with the idea that at some future date the railroad would cross the river at this point and join one of the main lines on the Virginia side.

The charter of the Baltimore and Potomac not only included the permission to construct this main line but it also allowed the building of branch lines not to exceed twenty miles in length. It was the privilege granted by the Charter which led to the Baltimore and Potomac Railroad being purchased by the Pennsylvania Railroad. The Pennsylvania Railroad's charter did not give the road access to Washington, D. C. but an extension to that city was considered as most advantageous. Upon acquiring the Baltimore and Potomac Railroad they took advantage of the provision for building branch lines and constructed one from Bowie into the Capital City. For this same reason, the main line of the Pennsylvania Railroad which ends at Popes Creek must remain in operation to assure continued access to Washington.

The *Port Tobacco Times* for Friday, January 3, 1873, announced that a regular daily train of cars for passengers began running on Wednesday morning last from Cox's Station to Bowie. The train was scheduled to leave Bowie at 9:45 A. M. and arrive at Popes Creek at 1:00 P. M. It then left Popes Creek at 1:15 P. M. and arrived at Bowie at 4:30 P. M.

New little towns sprang up in the county wherever the train made regularly scheduled stops.

The town of La Plata, which was destined to become the most important, was the result of a scheduled stop called La Plata Station. The February 21, 1873, issue of the paper announced that the railroad company was erecting at La Plata station, a warehouse and passenger room under one roof. The building was to be 36 by 18 feet in size and the platform along the front was 77 feet long and 8 feet wide. An editorial in March says, "La Plata is one of the stations on our railroad and will no doubt prove an excellent place for business. Mr. T. R. Farrall will occupy a store when finished. La Plata is 3½ miles from Port Tobacco and 2 miles from Salem Station by railroad."

The beginning of the town of La Plata and the railroad station of that name were on land which belonged to the Chapman family on a farm called "La Plata". When the town was laid out, the Chapmans donated all the land required to make streets in the town. The La Plata Post Office was established officially on November 28, 1873, with Robert F. Chapman as Postmaster.

Being favorably situated the town grew quickly. By 1876, it was one of the main stations in Charles County, indicated on the *Railroad Map of Maryland, Delaware and the District of Columbia,* published by Gray.

The name of the new town is a puzzler as it does not seem to have any relationship to the Spanish words 'La Plata' meaning 'the silver.' The most logical explanation seems to be that the Chapman farm, because of its terrain was originally called "Le Plateau", which is the French designation for a large, flat area. Little by little, the natives of Charles County corrupted the spelling and the pronounciation until it became the La Plata with the long ā sound which we have today. The fashion of giving French names to places in this country dates back to the 18th century as evidenced by the names of "La Grange" and "Habre de Venture" in Charles County, and others too numerous to mention scattered throughout the thirteen colonies.

La Plata was not the only railroad town to spring up in Charles County. In 1873 the name of the Post Office at Duffield was changed to White Plains and the location was moved two miles east to the railroad station.

Waldorf was another station on the line, and it appears as a town and Post Office on a map put out by the Post Office Department before 1880.

Another railroad also exists in the County. It was surveyed in 1868 and was known as the Southern Maryland Railroad. It was to extend from the Pennsylvania at Brandywine in Prince George's County, across the eastern side of Charles, through Hughesville, and to terminate at Point Lookout in St. Mary's County. It was never completed beyond Mechanicsville. After many years of financial reverses the property and rights of ways were acquired by the United States Navy at the time of the building of the Naval Air Station in St. Mary's County and the line was completed to that place.

Both the river steamers and their landing places were subject to disasters. The *Maryland Independent* of September 20, 1876 records the following:

"We learn that a portion of the Wharf at Glymont was washed away during the prevalence of the storm on Sunday last. A lot of tobacco belonging to Mr. Benjamin D. Tubman which was stored therein, awaiting shipment was damaged to a considerable extent."

"The Wharves at Pye's Landing, Sandy Point, Smith's Point, Liverpool Point and Chapel Point have all been washed away or seriously damaged. At Chapel Point the warehouse on the wharf is left, but the entire flooring of the wharf leading thereto is gone. A small shed that covered the boiler of the mill at that point was beat down by the storm. At Port Tobacco Warehouse a large lot of lumber and shingles that had lately been landed there was floated off and scattered in every direction, a quantity of coal recently landed was also scattered about."

The "Theodore Weems" burned in 1899 and was rebuilt at St. Mary's City. The rebuilt vessel burned again in 1907 and was rebuilt off Holland Point near Benedict.

In later years the Maryland, Delaware and Virginia Steamboat Company became a competitor of the Weems Line and purchased all their boats. This company, actually a subsidiary of the Pennsylvania Railroad, controlled in total thirty-five river steamboats plying the Bay and the rivers of Maryland and Virginia.

The only one of these vessels still afloat is the "Dorchester" which plied the Potomac from 1920 to 1932. The "Dorchester" now named the "Robert E. Lee" is at present an excursion steamer out of the port of Washington, D. C.

Reminders of the glorious days of steamboat transportation are still evident in the stark, rotted piling along the waterfront of the Potomac and its tidal inlets.

In Mattawoman the remains of Grinders Wharf is evident, but of Proctors Wharf in that Creek nothing remains. Among other prominent landing places were Posey's Wharf on the Chiccamuxen, Chapel Point and Brentland on the Port Tobacco, and along the Potomac, Glymont, Liverpool, Riverside, Popes Creek, Lower Cedar Point and Lancaster (Rock Point).

The only remaining usable wharves along the whole river frontage which can accommodate boats of any size are those at Marshall Hall, Indian Head and Rock Point.

With the coming of the railroad to the county, and with the decline of water transportation, Port Tobacco began to decline. The Port Tobacco river had silted up from soil erosion until it became increasingly difficult to get boats any nearer the town than the landing at Chapel Point. The thought of moving the county seat must have occurred to more than one, and we pick up the first whisper of the coming controversy in a small comment which appeared in the *Port Tobacco Times* as early as 1873. In the issue of August 8 is found the statement "About 130 years ago or thereabouts Port Tobacco was very near being utterly extinguished by removal of the County Seat to Chapel Point and nothing but the then powerful influence of the Scotch merchants of the former place prevented it."

That was but the opening statement of a violent controversy which was to rage for many years and split both political parties into violently partisan factions. On the Democratic side, one faction headed by J. Samuel Turner, Clerk of the Circuit Court, favored the move to La Plata; while the second group, headed by Mr. Cox, held out for Port Tobacco. The Turner group founded a new newspaper in La Plata in 1893 named the *Crescent* which publicized their views on the controversy.

The Republicans split into two groups also, which were led by two young attorneys who had in time replaced Dr. Wilmer and Dr. Mudd as leaders of the party. One was Sydney E. Mudd, a nephew of Dr. Mudd who had already been elected to a term in the Maryland House of Delegates and had also served part of a term in the United States House of Representatives after successfully contesting the 1888 election of Barnes Compton. The other faction was headed by State Senator Adrian Posey, owner of the *Maryland Independent* which was established in 1872, who led the La Plata men in the Republican Party.

The election of 1893 was fought on the basis of Port Tobacco versus La Plata rather than on purely party lines and the divisions it brought into the parties were bitter and lasting, especially among the Democrats.

The controversy over the location of the county seat reached a climax when the Court House at Port Tobacco burned on August 3, 1892. The cause of the fire was undetermined, but fortunately all the county records had been removed from the building before the fire. The question of the new location of the Court House was determined by a race in June, 1895, between La Plata and Chapel Point in which La Plata won.

Construction began on the Court House in La Plata immediately, and it was dedicated in 1896. The architect of the building was Joseph C. Johnson, and the contractor was James Haislip. They worked under the supervision of a building committee composed of Dr. James J. Smoot, William Wolfe, J. Hubert Roberts, John H. Mitchell, John W. Waring, Adrian Posey and George W. Gray.

At the time the new Court House was built, old Christ Church at Port Tobacco was taken down and removed to La Plata stone by stone, to be erected there in exactly the same position in relation to the new Court House that it had occupied in Port Tobacco to the old Court House. And, with the removal of the Court House and the church, the village of Port Tobacco rapidly sank into the ghost town that it is today.

After the election of 1895, the leadership of the Democratic Party passed into the hands of the younger generation. It was led by two young attorneys, Walter J. Mitchell and W. Mitchell Digges, who not only worked to regain some control of County government, but also aligned Charles County with the "Progressives" of the Democratic Party in state elections. The voice of this group after 1898 was the *Times-Crescent,* a merger of the old *Port Tobacco Times* purchased from Mr. Cox and the La Plata *Crescent.* Under the editorship of Walter J. Mitchell it became the mouthpiece of the Democratic Party and has remained in that capacity until the present time. Other party leaders prominent in the early 20th century who might be mentioned, are Mr. P. R. Wills and Dr. Louis Carlyle Carrico.

The Republican Party continued to be the majority party in county elections under the leadership of Sydney E. Mudd, Sydney E. Mudd, Jr., Adrian Posey, various members of the Bowling family of Bryantown and La Plata, and other hard working party members, some of whom are still active today.

It might be interesting to note that Mr. Adrian Posey also founded the first bank in Charles County, the Southern Maryland National Bank which was established in La Plata in 1906.

An important step in helping Charles County to lift itself from the mental and economic depression which followed the Civil War was the establishment of a Naval Station at Mattawoman Neck in 1890. The 880 acres of land were purchased from land which was originally a grant to Captain Thomas Cornwallis in 1636 of a 5,000 acre tract, even then called Mattawoman Neck. The Naval Proving Ground at Annapolis was a long and hazardous journey by water from the Naval Gun Factory in Washington, so the Proving Ground was moved to Mattawoman Neck in 1890, only a short distance down the Potomac River and the first ordnance was tested at the station in 1891. The Naval Powder Factory was constructed on the same land in 1898 with the first powder coming off the line in June, 1900. Right from the beginning, the factory employed Charles County farmers and the additional income brought into the county by the industrial work was an important contribution to the welfare of the county. In the early years, bad roads necessitated the use of the river to transport both the supplies to the Factory and the finished product from the Factory. The operation expanded steadily in the years before World War I. In 1901, an additional ten thousand fifty acres of land was purchased on Stump Neck. The acid plants were built in 1904 and 1907, and the Explosive "D" plant, built in 1915, made powder used in torpedoes. A railroad connection with the Pennsylvania Railroad was made with a 14½ mile spur line built to White Plains in 1917 to facilitate the increased production demanded by World War I. The government built 100 houses for personnel in 1918 and a Post Office and a school were constructed on the village green.

The Proving Ground was moved to Dahlgren, Virginia, in 1921, as the larger guns and improved ammunition demanded more range for their testing. In 1940 jet propulsion research was started which led to the development of the "bazooka", revolutionary weapon of World War II, and in 1949, production started in a pilot plant for rocket propellants.

Right up to the present day, the economic security which the Naval Powder Factory affords the County makes it the most important industrial operation in the County.

In 1909, the widening horizons of the outside world again touched the history of Charles County. On April 6, Edwin Peary arrived at the North Pole after a long and hazardous journey. With him when he reached the Pole were four Eskimos, 40 dogs and his chosen companion, a colored man named Matthew Henson.

Matthew Henson had been born near Nanjemoy in Charles County a few years after the end of the Civil War. At the age of 12 he shipped out of Baltimore on a Clipper Ship "The Katie Hines" whose master Captain Childs took an interest in the boy and gave him a good education. When he was just a young man Matthew Henson met Robert E. Peary and he accompanied the explorer on all of his trips to the Arctic in his attempts to reach the North Pole.

In his recent book about Matthew Henson entitled "Dark Companion", Bradley Robinson includes many tributes paid to Henson by the other men on the Polar Expedition. Commander Donald B. McMillan quotes Admiral Peary in assigning each man to his task on the attempt to reach the Pole, "Henson is not to return. I can't get along without him." McMillan characterizes Henson as quiet, efficient, modest, always at his assigned job and continues "a carpenter, he built sledges; a mechanic, he made alcohol stoves; an expert dog driver, he taught us to handle our dogs. Highly respected by the Eskimos, he was easily the most popular man on board ship." Other members of the expedition also testified to the fact that Henson was held in high admiration and affection by his fellow explorers. They said that Peary referred to Henson as the best traveler he had known and the most indispensable man.

Shortly before the turn of the century the history of air transportation touched briefly on Charles County. In 1896 when Samuel P. Langley, then Secretary of the Smithsonian Institution began testing his experimental heavier-than-air flying machine, the unpiloted plane landed in Charles County, after having flown the Potomac River. This was the first flight of a heavier-than-air craft that had ever taken place. Langley then started work on a machine which would accommodate a pilot but a launching ship was necessary to get the plane airborne. In the summer of 1903, the launching ship was anchored off Liverpool Point. Unfortunately the launching apparatus proved faulty and before Langley could make the necessary corrections, the Wright Brothers had made their flight at Kitty Hawk, so Charles County does not go down in history as the birthplace of the air age.

Today the county has one private airport near Pomonkey which is used by private planes and commercial planes engaged in crop dusting and spraying for insect control on the tobacco which grown in the county.

We cannot leave the history of the county without touching briefly on one development of the 20th century which greatly influenced life in the area. The first electrical transmission into Charles County was over a line built to Waldorf and La Plata late in the 1920's. The power for this line came from the Potomac Electric Company's line near Clinton. It reached only a few people in the county and the cost of electricity was proportionately high.

On February 5, 1936, an Electric Cooperative for Charles County was organized at Welcome under the guidance of the Rural Electrification Administration. This Co-op combined with one in the process of formation in St. Mary's County. With loans from the R.E.A. the Southern Maryland Electric Cooperative lines were energized in July, 1938, in the area west, south and east of La Plata and via Budd's Creek into St. Mary's County. Later extensions were also made into southern Prince George's County.

In 1945 the Co-op purchased the lines of the Eastern Shore Public Service which provided electricity to Waldorf and La Plata and also to a part of Calvert County. The 2600 miles of line and the approximately 20,000 customers now serviced makes the Southern Maryland Electric Cooperative one of the biggest in the nation.

The waters which touch so much of the land area have contributed their share of food supplies and income to Charles County since the early days of its settlement. Today approximately one quarter of a million dollars a year come into the county from fish, oysters and crabs with most of the activity centering at Benedict on the Patuxent River and at Rock Point, Popes Creek and Riverside on the Potomac River.

It is exceedingly difficult to pick out of the story of the present day the events and activities which should be recorded in a history of this kind. We have tried to select a few which illustrate the progress of the county and those which have had the most far-reaching effect on its citizens. The other things of importance such as the establishment of consolidated schools in the county, the building of the hospital, the coming of the motion picture theater, the Charles County Public Library, the wide representation of religious denominations, are all so much a part of the picture of progress repeated all over the State and even over the country that they are to be expected. Today, Charles County, having reached the mature age of 300 years, can take it place along-side any place in the country in regard to facilities and services available to its residents.

The most far reaching event of the present century was the construction of the Potomac River Bridge to Virginia late in the 1930's. The bridge was built on the very route of one of the 18th century ferries, going from a point between Pope's Creek and Lower Cedar Point to the Virginia shore at Dahlgren. For the first time Charles County became part of a through U.S. Highway and the whole area was opened up to rapid commercial development. Route 301 going from the county line at the north to the bridge at the south is a quick route from Baltimore to Richmond, avoiding the city of Washington and it is very heavily traveled. The length of the road through the county is built up almost continuously with motels, restaurants and service stations.

The Bridge has finally opened up Charles County to the outside world and has opened the outside world to those who live in the county and has ended for all time the isolation of the area. It means a definite change in the old way of life in which the people had so long been sufficient unto themselves because of this very lack of access.

The County today is in a period of transition. Improved transportation has made the area readily accessible to Metropolitan Washington so that much of the present and future development points to its eventual conversion to a suburban residential community. Despite this fact there is much in the leisurely pattern of living in the County today which is a direct inheritance from the past and it is to be hoped that it will be cherished in the future. If the people who come into the County preserve this pleasant life, they will find it a rewarding experience and a bulwark against the troublous times in which we live.

AGRICULTURE

The past three hundred years have seen little or no change in principal source of income in Charles County. Tobacco was then as it now the backbone of the economy. There has been significant change in production methods and uses.

Surprisingly, the early colonists were faced with some of the same problems facing producers in this modern age; particularly in the field of marketing. The problem of depressing surpluses of today was just as real in the earliest days.

In 1666, the General Assembly debated the idea of passing a law planned to bring about a "Cessation of growing tobacco".

The "weed" was the only crop suitable for export. The earlier colonist grew it to the exclusion of food and feed crops. It was the legal tender for the payment of debts, fines and the purchase of supplies. They produced more than the available ships could carry abroad and to other colonies. Surpluses accumulated, prices dropped.

The Assembly was now divided into the upper and lower house. The former composed of a group selected by the Lord Proprietor stood for his rights and interests. The latter elected by the freemen stood for the rights and interests of the people. So in the discussion of the Cessation Act it was not surprising to find a disagreement.

The Lower House presented these arguments against cessation:

1. It would increase the quantity of tobacco, because it would encourage other colonies to grow it.
2. It would "disencourage" the merchants from sending their ships to the colony. Thus deprive them of their necessities these ships would carry into the colony.

3. Seamen would not come in because of the loss of freight outward bound.
4. Freemen would move to other colonies where they could make use of their labors without restraint. This depopulation would weaken the colony and render it prey to their savage enemies.
5. The quantity was not depressing the price, but the want of ship due to the war and pestilence in the Mother Country.

The Upper House replied to these reasons and ordered the Lower House to consider them and to debate an Act for Encouragement of Trade and an act for the advance of more stable commodities than tobacco.

Needless to say they disagreed and attempted to disprove the reasons given against cessation. Agreement was reached provided care be taken and provision made for the satisfaction of debts and the neighboring colony of Virginia complied with cessation also.

It remained for Lord Baltimore, who had the final word, to prohibit the enforcement of this act. He held that it provoked dangerous discontent, and was to the disadvantage of the poorer small growers, who were most in number.

Many other laws were passed from time to time to regulate tobacco production and marketing; among them, regulation of the size of the hogshead, preventing the sale of ground leaves and second crop, duties on export, (except to England, Ireland and Virginia).

Also provision for government operated warehouse, employment of government inspector. All undoubtedly aimed at improving the crop and the economic well being of the producer. One is conscious again and again of the same problems over the three hundred years.

But what about this "weed", "the gold of the Province" that has played such an important part in our lives? From whence did it come? What developments have taken place over the years?

Nicotiana Rustica, tobacco grown by the Indians.

Photographs from
U. S. Dept. of
Agriculture

Nicotiana Tabacum, medium broadleaf Maryland tobacco now produced in Charles County.

Photographs from Maryland Tobacco Growers Association

SCENES FROM THE STATE TOBACCO WAREHOUSE IN BALTIMORE
(Upper) The sample is pulled from the hogshead.
(Lower) The State seal is applied to guarantee the packing.

Photographs by W. B. Posey

METHODS OF TRANSPORTING TOBACCO

(Upper) Flatbed wagon pulled by mules carrying two hogsheads of tobacco.

(Lower) Modern transportation of tobacco.

Photographs by W. B. Posey

METHODS OF TRANSPORTING TOBACCO

(Upper) The rolling hogshead pulled by a team of oxen or slaves—the earliest and most primitive type of transportation.

(Lower) The single hogshead pulled on a two wheeled ox cart—the next stage of development.

The first settlers in what is now Charles County found the Indians growing it. Columbus in 1492 found the natives of the West Indies cultivating tobacco, and the Spaniards found it also in Mexico in 1531. But there were differences in the varieties grown in each area of the new world.

Undoubtedly, the variety grown by the Indians in this area was *Nicotiana Rustica*. This produced small rough leaf of poor aroma and flavor. Colonists coming to Virginia brought in other varieties from the West Indies mainly *Nicotiana tabacum* and found it more desirable than *rustica*.

From this developed two distinct sorts in general use, one known as *Orinoca* and the other *Sweet Scented*. By natural crossing and selection numerous sub-varieties or strains of each of these were recognized. Usually these were given the names of prominent growers who developed them.

Orinoca was described as having a short pointed leaf and a strong flavor while *Sweet Scented* had a rounder leaf with five veins and mid rib and was mild in flavor.

The name *Orinoca* still survives and is applied in general to the tobaccos grown in lower Virginia and the Carolinas, but the name *Sweet Scented* has long disappeared. However, from its description it must be the forerunner of the present Maryland type, although it is not now outstandingly sweet scented.

In the Virginia colony in 1618 twenty million pounds of tobacco was exported at a price of 55 cents. In 1627 this had increased to five hundred thousand. In fact, although the foreign markets rapidly expanded, production increased at an even greater rate with the Maryland Colony in production. In 1639 the total exports from the two colonies was a million and a half pounds and the price had declined to six cents per pound. At the outbreak of the Revolutionary War exports of tobacco had increased to about one hundred million pounds, nearly all of which was produced in Maryland and Virginia.

All the counties in Maryland produced some tobacco, but

as the years rolled by the heavier lands of Western and Northern Maryland could not grow it of the wanted aroma and burning qualities and they changed to grain, grass and livestock. As the cities grew in population the Eastern Shore with similar land to Southern Maryland changed to truck and fruit crops. Now only the five counties in Southern Maryland, of which Charles is one, produce tobacco.

When cured the Maryland leaf is of an extra ordinarily light dry and chaffy character, low in nicotine, light reddish brown in color and relatively thin. It has a rather weak aroma and possesses excellent burning quality.

Charles County now produces about nine million pounds of tobacco in an average years which returns a gross income of between four and five millions of dollars.

However interesting the chronicle of tobacco may be, that of other farming operations is likewise of importance.

Charles County like all the colony was for the first two hundred years predominately agricultural. So the attitudes of the small farmer characterized the people as a whole. Frontier isolation tended to make people narrow, but primitive conditions made them resourceful, self-reliant, practical, hard working.

They knew almost nothing about farming in this new land. So at first they almost starved in spite of the abundance of the wilderness. Not until they learned new ways from the Indians did they make a success of the new life. They did have some advantage of the almost thirty years of experience of the Virginia Colony.

Jefferson wrote "those who till the soil are the chosen people of God". Land ownership was the key to individual success of the colonists. There were several ways for them to acquire this coveted possession: as manorial grants from the Lord Proprietor; (such grants were to his personal friends or to those who had rendered some great personal service to the colony); by head right, a system of awarding fifty acres of land to each settler and to each person a colonist would bring into the colony.

Agricultural implements were crude and scarce. Labor was also at a premium since four out of five of the freemen were independent farmers. This led to systems of inducing new labor to come to the new world. Many sold themselves as voluntary indentured servants in order to get to Maryland.

Servants were a most prized possession and they were a possession, because they were indentured to their master for a period of years, and he had money invested in their passage to the colony. The term servant not only indicated household help, but any man or woman who was an artisan, an apprentice or a farm worker. Cost of passage was about six pounds sterling. The period of indenture depended upon the skill, ability and value of the servant. Indentured servants were sometimes persons of good class who were under a written contract, stating the terms of their employment. This contract was written in duplicate, on one piece of parchment or paper and the copies were indented by irregular cuts or notches where the paper was cut apart, so they matched when the two contracts were laid together. One copy was kept by the master and one by the servant. Hence in case of any dispute the copies could be produced by each party in order to see if they were identical. From this practice came the name indentured servant. A period of five years was the usual indenture for a person without a trade. After this indenture of five to seven years they were freemen and could take up land. Others came as involuntary indentured servants of from seven to ten years, usually paupers, vagrants, debtors or petty criminals condemned and transported to the colony. The faithful performance of their indenture gave them a right as freemen. The indenture system was discontinued about 1700 and following it came the increased importation of slaves from Africa.

The first colonists grew their crops in clearings they found which were made by the Indians, and then cleared more land by axe and fire. Indian corn was the major food crop, because it had so many uses. The European grains, wheat, rye, barley, oats, buckwheat and peas followed. Livestock was scarce, all animals had to be imported and in the earliest days only the rich could own them. As the livestock increased native grasses were inadequate and this led to the importation of timothy, blue grass and clover for forage.

Farm tools were crude and scarce. Those mentioned most in lists of imports, will and inventories were: hoes, scythes, axes, reaping hooks and shovels.

Livestock was all important in the early period. Cattle and hogs are frequently mentioned and in many instances there is mention of wages and debts paid with cattle.

In his will Ignatius Causine of Causine's Manor, near Bel Alton, left a steer to the minister as he states "as being a Christian and deserving the prayers of the church." It is likely that the first cattle and hogs were imported from Virginia.

It was not unusual for masters to trade servants. As is the case of transaction between James Neale of Wollaston Manor and Wm. Marshall, Neale had an indentured woman who was wanted by Marshall. Capt. Neale was willing to sell because he had another who could take her place so he informed Marshall the servant he wished to buy had good qualities and also had her faults. She was a good cook, could make butter, but she was also a whore and a thief. He advised Marshall that if he could break her of these bad habits she would make a good servant. There is no record that the deal was consummated.

It was not uncommon for destitute widows to indenture their children. Mrs. Anne Gess of Charles County bound her 3 year old son to Henry Adams, a county commissioner, and her daughter-in-law too as a maid servant to Thomas Baker, another commissioner. There is no explanation as to whether she could legally indenture a daughter-in-law, but perhaps this may be considered a mother-in-law's revenge.

There were laws regulating the treatment of servants

as well as those concerning the behavior of servants toward their masters.

In Charles County Charles Turner was accused of mistreating a boy servant, John Ward, and he was brought before the County Commissioners. In the indenture Turner had agreed to feed and clothe Ward and teach him the carpenter's trade, but Ward had little or no clothing and was in a sick and emaciated condition. There is no record of the decision in this case.

On the other side of the picture Wm. Marshall, a member of the Board of Commissioners, presented to his fellow members three servants, Matthew Brown and a boy and girl, who had run away. Servant Matthew Brown seemed to have been the ring leader, so he was stripped to the waist, taken to the whipping post and given twenty-seven lashes on the back. The boy was given nine lashes and the girl seven.

Fences to impound livestock were unknown. They ran at large in the woods. The early Charles Countians fenced the crops from the livestock, using the plentiful supply of wood. This led to each livestock owner having his own earmark for the livestock.

These marks were registered with the County Commissioners. The first of such registrations recorded in Charles County Court records of June 4, 1658 strangely enough by a woman "Mis Jane Cockshoote entereth her marke of hogs and cattle Viz Croft one the right eyre and too slits in the crope, and over keeld one the left eare". On the same day one John Goldsmith also registered his mark as follows: "The right eare croft and slit and the lefteare half moone taken out under and over".

Livestock running at large presented some problems. Early Charles Countians depended upon upland game to increase their food supply. Hog stealing which appears in the records often meant the killing of ear-marked hogs running at large in the forest. This sport was indulged in not only by the servant class but the planters as well. Food supplies were so important the Assembly was forced to pass severe laws recognizing hog killing or stealing as a crime and as a cause for action for damages against the offender. A reward also went to the informer.

The act of 1649 provided for the payment of twice the value of the animal to the owner, of two hundred pounds of tobacco to the informer and a fine of three hundred pounds of tobacco to the Lord Proprietary. The act of 1662 for the second offense added the penalty of a letter "H" branded in the shoulder of the culprit. Even more severe was the the act of 1666. This provided for the first offense triple damages and the culprit was to spend four hours a day in the pillory before the Provincial Court and have both ears cropped, for the second offense treble damages and an "H" branded on his forehead. But for the third offense he was to be adjudged a felon, with benefit of clergy, which of course meant the death penalty.

In proceedings of the court held in Charles County in September 4, 1660 appears the first case of hog stealing, "Whereas the Courte was informed that Gyles Gouer was Suspeckted for stealing of hoggs, his Mate Richard True was sworne and examined in open Courte who sayeth That when he went up to Nanjemy he Helpt Gyles Gouer to frame his house, and as he was at worke Gyles and his mate Thomas Pryer came to this defent and asked him if he would concent to kill hoggs with them and this defent replyed noe he would not steall any hoggs he hooped to come honnestlyer by them, and further he saith not.

"It is therefore ordered that the sherife take the said Gyles Gouer into his custody and keepe him until he put in suffiistient secriretly for his good abareinge" [Probably abearance meaning good behavior].

Noted in an early session of the Charles County Court was a case of James Lee owner who accused Wm. Allen, John Muir, John Boyden and John Cabell of stealing and killing his hogs, contrary to the laws of the Province. The four men admitted to having killed the hogs and Allen offered to replace them. Lee would not agree to the offer saying "he was unwilling to accept a pig in a poke" (a pig he had not seen) although the defense produced a note signed by Lee authorizing Allen and Cabell to kill any of his hogs in Lewis' Neck. Each of the four men was required by the court to pay to Lee double the value of each hog, two hundred pounds of tobacco to Lee for informing on them and 300 pounds of tobacco to the Lord Proprietor and also court costs. This was rather expensive hog meat.

In the same session of the Court Thomas Standbridge was accused of stealing and killing hogs belonging to Daniel Johnson. He was found guilty and paid the same fine as the others.

By 1680 horses became so plentiful, they ran wild. Some colonists were granted license to hunt them and finally a law was passed preventing the importation of any more horses.

Wolves and predatory animals harassed the planters' stock so colonists were advised for their own protection, to keep dogs. In one case in the Charles County Court, James Fox alleged he had gone to the house of Arthur Turner and was bitten in the leg by a bitch. As a result he was too lame to make a crop and he hauled Turner into Court to pay for the loss of the crop and the cost of the cure for the bite. Turner claimed Fox had carelessly trod on the dog so the court dismissed the case.

So the first forty two years of Charles County was a struggle for the settlers to become established, to learn to survive in a new world. They practiced a primitive type of agriculture, farming small tracts wrested from the wilderness. Their dependence was not solely from the farm. They were also hunters, trappers, fishermen and builders. In the woods was an abundance of game and predatory animals, in the waters fish and oysters for the taking, and everywhere berries, nuts, wild cherries, crabapples. The struggle for survival made the colonists hardy, resourceful and self reliant.

An abundance of land and a scarcity of labor led to the importation of slaves. The Indian would not be enslaved, in fact, it was prohibited by the Lord Proprietary. So by the dawn of the eighteenth century the county was a ready market for Negro slaves. The result was the accumulation of more land and the beginning of the plantation system. Thus, the eighteenth century became the golden era for agriculture. With cheap labor and cheap land, tobacco could be produced in large quantities. Though the price might be low it was a paying crop. The plantation owners imported cattle and horses for power and made needed improvements in farming tools. Bottoms for shipping became more plentiful to carry the agricultural products to the markets.

Plantation owners began to experiment with other than staple crops, to provide new sources of income. These included cotton and silk. The government offered bounties for silk production with the mandatory planting of mulberry trees for food for the silk worms.

The first seventy five years of the eighteenth century witnessed the building of many of our fine plantation homes including West Hatton, Hard Bargain, Araby, Rose Hill, La Grange, Habre de Venture and many others.

Also during this lush era many young sons of the planters were sent abroad to obtain an education which was not possible here.

With plentiful money and handsome homes the planters imported or ordered made by the artisans in this and other colonies, fine furniture, silverware and all the other things to make living more comfortable and more gracious. The Mother Country demanded more and more of the new wealth of the colonies. Duties on products shipped abroad and heavy taxes on imports became so burdensome the colonies revolted.

With the war of revolution, as in all wars, prices on food products sky-rocketed for a time and with the return of the soldiers after victory came the agricultural depression.

But Charles County farmers could still produce tobacco at a profit with their slave labor.

The increased population, building of roads and canals, invention of the steam boat and later the building of railroads all helped make tobacco production profitable.

The effect of the war between the states was devastating on farming during the latter part of the nineteenth century, making it the darkest period agriculture has ever experienced. Charles County farmers were compelled to dispose of some of their land. Many plantation houses fell into decay and land formerly used for crop production reverted to forests.

Twentieth century agriculture can be briefly stated. Tobacco remains the cash crop of Charles County to the present day. However, there are some factors which should be mentioned; these include improvements on machinery, in soils and in know-how. All these contribute to products much better than our colonial forebears could produce.

The change in usage of Maryland tobacco is also important. From the establishment of the country up to World War I, there was little or no change in the market for our tobacco. It was exported as an unmanufactured product. World War I changed this. Domestic manufacturers found it could be used and was a desirable component of the cigarette. The introduction of American made cigarettes to the allied forces in Europe increased the demand for Maryland tobacco. So from the beginning of the outbreak of war Charles County farmers as well as those in all the Maryland growing area met the challenge by increased acreage. Surprisingly the yield per acre remained stable. Exports in the unmanufactured state dropped to about six million pounds and remained so until the termination of the Korean conflict.

At present growers are experiencing another reversal of usage of their product. The amazing popularity of filter cigarettes has lowered the domestic use of Maryland tobacco which does not have a strong enough flavor or aroma for this kind of a smoke. So just in the past decade exports are on the increase and domestic use is decreasing.

The principal foreign user of Maryland tobacco is Switzerland, which manufactures a so-called "all Maryland" cigarette that is in great demand. As Swiss manufacturers buy only the best grades, they pay the highest prices.

Along with the changes in demand for Maryland tobacco, there has occurred an evolution in the marketing processes. From the earliest days of the County to 1938 all Maryland tobacco was packed in hogsheads for the market. The packing was done on the farm or by country buyers who purchased from the farmers. The packed tobacco was then sent to colonial or state operated warehouses. At the warehouses samples were drawn from the hogsheads and the tobacco offered for sale to the buyers. A small proportion of the crop is still sold in this manner at the state operated warehouse in Baltimore. Maryland tobacco is the only crop in the United States which is still using the hogshead method of sale.

In 1938, this ancient sales method was changed. All other tobacco types had long ago been offered in the loose leaf auction sales floors. In that year the first loose leaf auction market was opened at Hughesville in Charles County. Within a few years four other auction floors were in operation in Southern Maryland. Currently about ninty-five percent of the total poundage produced is sold over these auction floors and the balance moves through the hogshead market in Baltimore.

During all the three hundred years of agricultural production in Charles County tobacco has remained the principal money crop with variations in production occurring only in times of adversity when tobacco was bringing low prices. The past half century has brought production of some canning crops, chiefly tomatoes, which became popular in the agricultural decline of the first decade of the century. The most significant change was brought by the depression of the 1930's when there was a decided trend toward the production of livestock, mainly beef cattle.

The story of production in the county would not be complete without some mention of the forest in our economy. Today about seventy percent of the total land area is in forests. The humid coastal plains of which Charles County is a part provide ideal conditions for the production of timber. Virginia pine and gum take over depleted and abandoned farm lands. Tulip poplar grows luxuriantly on the richer, moister soils. The oaks are abundant on the better highlands. Along the lowlands, loblolly pine grows well. For many years farmers have had a ready and lucrative market for the Virginia pine and gum as pulpwood for the manufacturing of paper products. The market for tulip poplar and some of the gum is in veneer manufacturing. The oaks and loblolly as well as other species have a ready market for building materials. Three quarters of a million dollars come into the county, mostly to the farm owners, each year for the products of their forests. In fact it ranks second to tobacco in the farm income of Charles County.

IN CONCLUSION

The main narrative of this History of Charles County ends with the 19th century. It is the considered opinion of the authors that the history of our own day is too close to us to afford the proper perspective and for this reason our references to the 20th century have been confined to facts rather than personalities.

It seems certain that because of the wealth of material on the subject which has been uncovered and organized with less than a year's research that much more will come to light as the opportunity for further research presents itself. Perhaps this can someday be covered in another publication.

Throughout the whole history of Charles County there are many interesting side lights which we did not have time to follow as our interest prompted. Many of these things, which are only mentioned in this book, could be expanded into a book on one subject alone. The story of the old homes of Charles County is an example of the kind of subject we would like to have pursued farther. There is also a great deal of material on the people of Charles County in every century which intrigued us.

In the last analysis, our problem became one of selection and we tried to select that which would be most useful to all in a general history such as this is intended to be. To those of you who may wish that some of this other information could also have been included, we can only agree with you and promise that as the opportunity presents itself we will try to see that it reaches publication in some form or other.

The last year's work has increased our love and respect for Charles County and the people who have lived within its bounds.

NOTES AND REFERENCES

Chapter I

1. *Narrative of a Voyage to Maryland by Father Andrew White, S.J.*, edited by Rev. E. A. Dalrymple. Baltimore, 1874. p. 31 ff.
2. Smith, Captain John, *The General Historie of Virginia*. London, 17th century.
3. *Narrative of a Voyage*, etc. pp. 37-40.
4. Bryan, Oliver N., "Antiquities of Charles County, Maryland." *Smithsonian Institution Annual Report*. Washington, 1874.
5. Graham, W. J., *The Indians of Port Tobacco River, Maryland and Their Burial Places*. Washington, 1935.
6. *Narrative of a Voyage*, etc. p. 82.
7. Graham, p. 9.
8. Gilbert, William Harlan, Jr., "The Wesorts of Southern Maryland, An Outcasted Group", *Journal of the Washington Academy of Sciences*. XXXV, (August 15, 1945), No. 8.
9. Berkley, Henry J., "The Proprietary Manors and Hundreds of St. Mary's, Old Charles, Calvert, New Charles and Prince George's County", *Maryland Historical Magazine*, XXIX, (1934), 243.
10. *Archives of Maryland*, Vol. XLI, p. 87.
11. Mathews, Edward B., *The Counties of Maryland, Their Origin, Boundaries and Election District*. Baltimore, 1907, p. 476.
12. *Archives of Maryland*, Vol. XLI, p. 89.
13. *Archives of Maryland*, Vol. I, p. 382 ff.
14. *Archives of Maryland*, Vol. LIII, p. 102-104.
15. *Archives of Maryland*, Vol. LIII, p. 111.
16. Hill, Harry W., *Maryland's Colonial Charm Portrayed in Silver*. Baltimore, 1938, p. 199 ff.
17. *Archives of Maryland*, Vol. LIII, p. 159.
18. *Archives of Maryland*, Vol. VIII, p. 24.
19. *Charles County Records*, Liber A, p. 277.
20. Allen, Ethan, *The History of Maryland*. Philadelphia, 1866, p. 46.
21. Scisco, Louis Dow, "Evolution of the Colonial Mitilia in Maryland", *Maryland Historical Magazine*, XXXV, (June, 1940), 166-177.

22. Keith, Arthur T., "Two Forgotten Heroes", *Maryland Historical Magazine*, XIX, (December, 1924), 339.
23. Newman, Harry Wright, *Seignory in Early Maryland*. Washington, 1949.
24. Berkley, Henry J., "Extinct Towns of the Chesapeake Bay Region", *Maryland Historical Magazine*, XIX (No. 2), 125-134.
25. Scharf, J. Thomas, *History of Maryland*. Baltimore, 1879, Vol. I, p. 410.
26. *Archives of Maryland*, Vol. VII, p. 611.
27. Scharf, p. 411, footnote.
28. *Land Office Records*, Liber A, Folio 275.
29. Scharf, p. 364.
30. McIlvain, Rev. J. Wm. "Early Presbyterianism in Maryland", *Johns Hopkins University Studies in History and Political Science*. Vol. VIII, (1890), pp. 1-13.

Chapter II

1. Wheeler, Joseph Towne, "The Layman's Libraries and the Provincial Library", *Maryland Historical Magazine*, XXXV, (March, 1940), 66.
2. Jones, Hugh, *The Present State of Virginia from Whence is Inferred a Short View of Maryland and North Carolina*. Chapel Hill, N. C., 1956, reprint.
3. "Colonial Militia", *Maryland Historical Magazine*, VI, (March, 1911), 54.
4. "Correspondence of Governor Horatio Sharpe", *Maryland Historical Magazine*, XII (No. 4), 371.
5. Scharf, p. 104.
6. Scharf, p. 193.
7. Queen, Sister Mary Xavier, *Grandma's Stories and Anecdotes of Ye Olden Times*. Boston, 1899.
8. The John Hanson, Jr. and Walter Hanson Papers in the Maryland Historical Society, Baltimore, Maryland.
9. Rowland, Kate Mason, *The Life of George Mason, 1725-1792*. New York, 1892, Vol. I.
10. Crowl, Philip A., *Maryland During and After the Revolution, A Political and Economic Study*. Baltimore, 1943, p. 73.
11. *Maryland Calendar of Wills*, Vol. V, p. 146.

12. Kelley, Lawrence J., S.J., *A Carmelite Shrine In Maryland*. Washington, 1950.
13. "Trinity Parish", *Maryland Historical Magazine*, I (No. 4), 325.
14. Bayard, Ferdinand M., *Travels of a Frenchman in Maryland and Virginia in 1791*. Williamsburg, Va., 1950.
15. Sanderson, John, *Biographies of the Signers of the Declaration of Independence*. Philadelphia, 1822.
16. Buchholz, Heinrich Ewald, *Governors of Maryland from the Revolution to the Year 1908*. Baltimore, 1908, Chap. VII.
17. *Journal of Nicholas Cresswell*. New York, 1924.
18. Howard, John Tilden, "The Doctors Gustavus Brown, Father and Son of Charles County, Maryland", *Annals of Medical History*, IX, 1937.
19. Myers, Albert Cook, *Sally Wister's Journal*. Philadelphia, 1902.
20. Buchholz, Chap. IV.
21. Myers, p. 85.
22. Perlman, Philip B., "Some Maryland Lawyers in Supreme Court History", *Maryland Historical Magazine*, XLIII, (No. 3), 181.
23. Ness, George T., "A Lost Man of Maryland", *Maryland Historical Magazine*, XXXV, (No. 4), 315-336.
24. Jones, E. Alfred, *American Members of the Inns of Court*. London, 1924.

Chapter III

1. Cockburn Papers, Division of Manuscripts, Library of Congress.
2. James, William, *Naval History of Great Britain from the Declaration of War by France, 1793 to the Accession of George IV*. London, 1837.
3. Thomas, Roger, "Southern Maryland", *The Old Line State, a History of Maryland*, ed. by Morris L. Radoff, Baltimore, 1956.
4. *National Academy of Sciences Memoirs*, 13, 1915.
5. Ezell, John S., "The Church Took a Chance", *Maryland Historical Magazine*, XLIII, (December, 1948), 276.
6. Jones, Thomas A., *J. Wilkes Booth, An Account of His Sojourn in Southern Maryland after the Assassination of Abraham Lincoln His Passage Across the Potomac and his Death in Virginia*. Chicago, 1893.
7. Sass, Herbert Ravenel, "An Affair at St. Alban's", *The Saturday Evening Post*, March 27, 1948.

8. Story told by Miss Floyd to Mrs. William Carlyle Turner, "Keechland", Popes Creek, Maryland.
9. Baker, General L. C., *History of the United States Secret Service*. Philadelphia, 1867.
10. Jones, *op. cit.*
11. Mudd, Nettie, *Life of Dr. Samuel A. Mudd, Containing his letters from Fort Jefferson, Dry Tortugas Island, Where He was Imprisoned Four Years for Alleged Complicity in the Assassination of Abraham Lincoln*. 2nd ed., Georgia, 1955.
12. Scharf, pp. 656-657.

Appendix No. 1

Old Charles County—often confused with the present Charles County. The Maryland Archives, October 3, 1650 defines Old Charles County as follows "South side Patuxent beginning at Susquehannah Point extending itself from thence into the middle of the woods towards St. Maries southward, and from thence westward along the middle of the woods betwixt the Potomeck and Patuxent River as far as Mattaponia toward the head of the Patuxent River, and from thence againe eastward along the river side to said Susquehannah Point" Robert Brooke was named commander of the county. The Governor and Council issued the proclamation establishing the county and the order was made void by the Governor's order July 3, 1654.

Maryland Archives, Vol. 3, pp 259-260

To determine old Charles County on a present day map it would be as follows:

"South side of Patuxent River beginning at Susquehannah Point." Susquehannah Point is Cedar Point on the modern map and on the site of Patuxent Naval Air Station.

"Extending itself from thence into the middle of the woods toward St. Maries Southward." This would bring the line to about one mile south of Hermansville on State Route No. 2.

"And from thence westward along the middle of the woods betwixt the Potomeck and Patuxent River as far as Mattaponia toward the head of the Patuxent River," The line then would extend really north westward passing near Great Mills, Morganza, Waldorf, Brandywine and Cheltenham. If the word Mattaponia means the Creek by that name the line would end near the present village of Cheltenham. If it indicates the grant of land, it would extend a few miles further north passing near Croom. The Mattaponia grant being on the Patuxent River east of Croom.

"And from thence again eastward along the river side to said Susquenhannah Point," Probably means on the east side of the Patuxent River back to starting point. This was done to include the river in the county in order that the commander would have control over the river as his grant of land and house. De La Brooke Manor is located on same in St. Mary's County off State Route 6 below New Market.

Old Charles County therefore included parts of St. Mary's and Calvert and what is now Charles and Prince Georges. It was not defined as a unit of government, but rather as a defense unit under Brooke, who had the authority to recruit men for military service.

As the Patuxent River furnished the warlike Susquehannock Indians a means of access into the Colony, old Charles County was likely set up as a defense measure.

Appendix No. 2

CHARLES COUNTIANS OF PROMINENCE

PROPRIETARY GOVERNORS

    1649-1651   William Stone
    1652-1654   William Stone
    1657-1660   Josias Fendall
    June 1657 to February 1658   Dr. Luke Barber
    Latter appointed by Fendall to serve during his absence

SIGNER OF DECLARATION OF INDEPENDENCE

    1776   Thomas Stone

SURGEON GENERAL CONTINENTAL ARMY

    1777   Dr. James Craik

SECRETARY TO GENERAL GEORGE WASHINGTON

    1777-1781   Robert Hanson Harrison

NOMINATED AS ASSOCIATE JUSTICE OF SUPREME COURT

    1789-1790   Robert Hanson Harrison

GENERAL CONTINENTAL ARMY

    1777   William Smallwood

DELEGATES TO CONTINENTAL CONGRESSES

    1775-1785   Thomas Stone
    1778-1782   Daniel of St. Thomas Jenifer
    1780-1783   John Hanson

PRESIDENT OF THE COUNCIL OF SAFETY

    1775-1777   Daniel of St. Thomas Jenifer

MEMBERS OF PROVINCIAL CONVENTION WHICH FRAMED THE FIRST STATE CONSTITUTION IN 1776

    Robert T. Hooe, John Dent, Thomas Semmes, John Parnham

MEMBERS OF THE GOVERNORS COUNCIL

    1780-1782   John Hoskins Stone
    1782-1783   Benjamin C. Stoddert
    1784-1785   John Hoskins Stone

PRESIDENT OF THE UNITED STATES IN CONGRESS ASSEMBLED
1781 John Hanson

SIGNER OF THE ARTICLES OF CONFEDERATION
1781 John Hanson

SIGNER OF THE CONSTITUTION OF THE UNITED STATES
1787 Daniel of St. Thomas Jenifer

MEMBERS OF THE STATE CONVENTION RATIFYING THE CONSTITUTION OF THE UNITED STATES
1788 Zephaniah Turner, Gustavus R. Brown, Michael J. Stone, John Parnham

GOVERNORS OF MARYLAND
1785-1788 William Smallwood
1794-1797 John Hoskins Stone

MEMBERS OF THE U. S. HOUSE OF REPRESENTATIVES
1789-1791 Benjamin Contee
1794-1795 Michael Jenifer Stone
1793-1801 George Dent
1796-1801 William Craik
1833-1835 John Truman Stoddert
1845-1849 John G. Chapman
1863-1865 Benjamin Gwinn Harris
1867-1871 Frederick Stone
1881-1883 Andrew C. Chapman
1885-1899 - 1891-1895 Barnes Compton
1889, 1890 - 1897-1899 - 1901-1909 Sydney E. Mudd, Sr.
1915-1924 Sydney E. Mudd, Jr. — Died 1924

MEMBERS OF THE U. S. SENATE
1817 Alexander C. Hanson
1838-1845 William D. Merrick

CABINET MEMBER SECRETARY OF NAVY
1798-1801 Benjamin Stoddert
Also Secretary of War 1800

SECOND ARCHBISHOP OF BALTIMORE
1815-1817 Leonard Neale

PRESIDENTS OF THE MARYLAND SENATE
1777-1780 Daniel of St. Thomas Jenifer
1791   William Smallwood
1792   George Dent
1835-1836 John G. Chapman
1868-1870 Barnes Compton
1931-1934 Walter Jenifer Mitchell

SPEAKERS MARYLAND HOUSE OF DELEGATES
1789-1790 George Dent
1798-1814 Henry H. Chapman
1816-1817 Nicholas Stonestreet
1827-1844 John G. Chapman
1896-1897 Sydney E. Mudd, Sr.

JUDGES, MARYLAND COURT OF APPEALS
1844-1845 William B. Stone
1867   Peter Wood Crain
1867-1881 George Brent
1881-1890 Frederick Stone
1923-1934 W. Mitchell Digges
1934-1941 Walter J. Mitchell

ATTORNEY GENERAL OF MARYLAND
1851 Robert J. Brent

ADMIRAL OF NAVY OF CONFEDERATE STATES
1861 Raphael Semmes

TREASURER OF MARYLAND
1874 Barnes Compton

ADJUTANT GENERAL OF MARYLAND
1896 L. Allison Wilmer

COMPANION OF ADMIRAL ROBERT E. PEARY IN DISCOVERY OF NORTH POLE
April 6, 1909 Matthew Henson

References—*Maryland Manual, Encyclopedia Americana, Catholic Encyclopedia;* Courtesy Charles County Public Library; Congressional Biographies, Courtesy of Senator J. Glenn Beall.

BIBLIOGRAPHY

Books

Allen, Ethan, *The History of Maryland.* Philadelphia: 1866.

Baker, General L. C., *History of the United States Secret Service.* Philadelphia: 1867.

Bayard, Ferdinand M., *Travels of a Frenchman in Maryland and Virginia with a description of Philadelphia and Baltimore in 1791.* Edited by Ben C. McCary. Williamsburg, Virginia: 1950.

Buchholz, Heinrich Ewald, *Governors of Maryland from the Revolution to the Year 1908.* Baltimore: 1908.

Carmel, Its History, Spirit and Saints. Compiled by the Discalced Carmelites of Boston and Santa Clara. Boston: 1927.

Crowl, Philip A., *Maryland During and After the Revolution, A Political and Economic Study.* Baltimore : 1943.

Culver, Frances Barnum, *Blooded Horses of Colonial Days.* Baltimore: 1922.

Daley, John M., *Georgetown University, Origin and Early Years.* Washington, D. C.: 1957.

Davis, George Lyn-Lachlan, *The Day-Star of American Freedom or the Birth and Early Growth of Toleration in the Province of Maryland.* New York, 1855.

Graham, William J., *The Indians of Port Tobacco River, Maryland and Their Burial Places.* 1935.

History and Roster of Maryland Volunteers, War of 1861-65. 2 vols. Compiled. The General Assembly of Maryland. 1899.

Hill, Comm. Harry W., U.S.N., *Maryland's Colonial Charm Portrayed in Silver.* Baltimore: 1938.

Ingraham, Edward D., *Sketch of the Events which Preceded the Capture of Washington by the British, 1814.* Philadelphia: 1849.

Jones, E. Alfred, *American Members of the Inns of Court*. London: 1924.

Jones, Hugh, *The Present State of Virginia from Which is Inferred a Short View of Maryland and North Carolina*. Reprint. University of North Carolina: 1956.

Jones, Thomas A., *J. Wilkes Booth, An Account of His Sojourn in Southern Maryland After the Assassination of Abraham Lincoln, His Passage Across the Potomac and His Death in Virginia*. Chicago: 1893.

Kelley, Laurence J., S.J., *A Carmelite Shrine in Maryland*. Washington: 1950.

Lee, Cazenove G., Jr., *Lee Chronicle*. New York: 1957.

Livingston, John, *Law Register for 1852*. New York: 1852. *Portraits of Eminent Americans Now Living*. New York: 1854.

McGrath, F. Sims, *Pillars of Maryland*. Richmond: 1950.

Mathews, Edward B., *The Counties of Maryland, Their Origin, Boundaries, and Election Districts*. Baltimore: 1907.

The Life of Dr. Samuel A. Mudd Containing his Letters from Fort Jefferson, Dry Tortugas Island Where He was Imprisoned Four Years for Alleged Complicity in the Assassination of Abraham Lincoln. Edited by Nettie Mudd. New York and Washington: 1906. Georgia: 1955.

Myers, Albert Cook, *Sally Wister's Journal*. Philadelphia: 1902.

Newman, Harry Wright, *Seigniory in Early Maryland*. Published by the Descendants of the Lords of the Maryland Manors: 1949.

Queen, Sister Mary Xavier, *Grandma's Stories and Anecdotes of Ye Olden Times*. Boston: 1899.

Radoff, Morris Leon, ed. *The Old Line State, A History of Maryland*. Baltimore: 1956.

Robinson, Bradley, *Dark Companion*. New York: 1947.

Rowland, Kate Mason, *The Life of George Mason, 1725-1792*, New York: 1892.

Scharf, J. Thomas, *A History of Maryland*, Vols. I to III. Baltimore: 1879.

Scott, Joseph, *A Geographical Description of the States of Maryland and Delaware.* Philadelphia: 1807.

Skirven, Percy G., *The First Parishes of the Province of Maryland.* Baltimore: 1923.

Smoot, Richard Mitchell, *The Unwritten History of the Assassination of Abraham Lincoln.* Baltimore: 1904.

Smyth, J. F. D., *A Tour in the United States of America.* London: 1784.

Stanton, Samuel Ward, *Steam Navigation on the Carolina Sounds and in the Chesapeake in 1892.* Edited by the Steamship Historical Society. Salem, Mass.: 1947.

Side Wheel Steamers of the Chesapeake Bay, 1880-1947. Compiled by John A. Haen. Glendale: 1947.

Steiner, Bernard C., *Maryland Under the Commonwealth.* Series XXIX, No. 1 of the *Johns Hopkins University Studies in Historical and Political Science.* Baltimore: 1911.

White, Father Andrew, S.J., *Narrative of a Voyage to Maryland.* Edited by Rev. E. A. Dalrymple, S.T.D. Baltimore: 1874.

Public Documents

Archives of Maryland. Especially Vol. LIII, Proceedings of the County Court of Charles County, 1658-1666, and Vol. LX, Proceedings of the County Court of Charles County, 1666-1674.

List of Signers in Charles County of Oath of Allegiance to Maryland in 1778. Charles County Records, Liber X, No. 3, 1775-1778, fols. 641-651.

Reports

Smithsonian Institution Annual Report, 1874. Bryan, Oliver N., "Antiquities of Charles County, Maryland." Washington.

National Academy of Sciences Memoirs. Vol. 13. 1915.

Pamphlets

Discourse of Rev. Edward I. Devitt, S.J. of Georgetown College. August 15, 1898. Centennial Celebration of St. Ignatius Church, St. Thomas Manor, Charles County, Maryland. Washington: 1898.

Unpublished Material

John and Walter Hanson Papers, Maryland Historical Society, Baltimore, Maryland

Thomas and Walter Stone Papers, Library of Congress, Washington, D. C.

Account Book of Henry H. Chapman, 1794. Maryland Historical Society, Baltimore, Maryland

Michael Jenifer Stone Papers. Maryland Historical Society, Baltimore, Maryland.

Articles

Gilbert, William Harlen, Jr., "The Wesorts of Southern Maryland: An Outcasted Group," *Journal of the Washington Academy of Sciences*, XXXV, 1945, No. 8.

Howard, John Tilden, M.D., "The Doctors Gustavus Brown, Father and Son of Charles County, Maryland", *Annals of Medical History*, IX, 1937.

McIlvain, Rev. J. William, "Early Presbyterianism in Maryland", *Johns Hopkins University Studies in History and Political Science*, VIII, 1890.

Maryland Historical Magazine. Published by the Maryland Historical Society, 201 W. Monument Street, Baltimore 1, Maryland. Articles as follows:

Barry, Rev. J. Neilson, "Trinity Parish, Charles County, Maryland", Vol. I, No. 4, December 1906

"Colonial Militia" 1740, 1748, Vol. VI, No. 1, March 1911

Johnston, Christopher, "Neale Family of Charles County", Vol. VII, No. 2, June 1912

"Correspondence of Governor Horatio Sharpe", Vol. XII, No. 4, December 1917

Steiner, Bernard C., "Some Unpublished Manuscripts from Fulham Palace Relating to Provincial Maryland" Vol. XII, No. 2, June 1917

"Men of Maryland Specially Honored by the State or the United States", Col. Charles Chaille-Long, Comp., and supplemented by Louis H. Dielman, ed., Vol. XII, No. 3, Sept. 1917 and Vol. XIII, No. 1, March 1918

Berkeley, Henry J., "Extinct River Towns of the Chesapeake Bay Region", Vol. XIX, No. 2, June 1924

Culver, Francis B., "The Ancestry of Rev. Hatch Dent", Vol. XIX No. 2, June 1924

Keith, Arthur L., "General William Smallwood", Vol. XIX, No. 3, Sept. 1924

Keith, Arthur L., "Two Forgotten Heroes", Vol. XIX, No. 4, Dec. 1924

"The Beginnings of Charles County", Vol. XXI, No. 3, Sept. 1926

"Colonial Records of Charles County", Vol. XXI, No. 3, Sept. 1926

Keith, Arthur L., "Smallwood Family of Charles County", Vol. XXII, No. 2, June 1927

"Port Tobacco Parish—List of Ministers from 1692", Vol. XXII, No. 3, Sept. 1927

Keith, Arthur L., "The Berry Family of Charles County", Vol. XXIII, No. 1, March 1928

Scisco, Louis Dow, "People of Early Charles County", Vol. XXIII, No. 4, September 1934

Berkeley, Henry J., "The Proprietary Manors and Hundreds of St. Mary's, Old Charles, Calvert, New Charles and Prince George's Counties", Vol. XXIX, No. 4, September 1934

Wheeler, Joseph Towne, "The Laymen's Libraries and the Provincial Library", Vol. XXXV, No. 1, March 1940

Scisco, Louis Dow, "Evolution of Colonial Militia in Maryland", Vol. XXXV, No. 2, June 1940

Ness, George T., "A Lost Man of Maryland", Vol. XXXV, No. 4, Dec. 1940

"Vignettes of Maryland History", Vol. XL, No. 1, March 1945

Robey, Ethel Roby, "Port Tobacco, Lost Town of Maryland", Vol. XL, No. 4, Dec. 1945

"Portraits in the Maryland Historical Society", Vol. XLI, No. 1, March 1946

Perlman, Philip B., "Some Maryland Lawyers in Supreme Court History", Vol. XLIII, No. 3, September 1948

Ezell, John S., "The Church Took a Chance", Vol. XLIII, No. 4, December 1948

Rightmyer, Rev. Nelson Waite, "The Character of the Anglican Clergy in Maryland", Vol. XLIV, No. 4, December 1949

Beitzel, Edwin, "Newton Hundred", Vol. LI, No. 2, June 1956

"Boundaries of Prince George's County Prior to 1695", Vol. LI, No. 3, Sept. 1956

Hayden, Ethel Roby, "The Lees of Blenheim", Vol. XXXVII, No. 2, June 1942.

Bibliography

Agriculture

Archives of Maryland, Vol. I   Proceedings and Acts of the Assembly of Maryland 1637-1664.

Archives of Maryland, Vol. II   Proceedings and Acts of the Assembly of Maryland 1666-1676.

Archives of Maryland, Vol. LIII   Proceedings of Court of Charles County 1658-1666.

Archives of Maryland, Vol. XLIX   Proceedings of the Provincial Court 1663-1666.

Year Book of Agriculture 1936. U. S. Department of Agriculture

Year Book of Agriculture 1940, U. S. Department of Agriculture

Farmers in a Changing World, U. S. Department of Agriculture

TERCENTENARY YEAR 1958

Appendix No. 3

Charles County

Record of the heads of families, number of free white males 16 years of age and over and under 16 years, free white females and slaves, from the first census of the United States taken in 1790.

NAME OF HEAD OF FAMILY.	Free white males of 16 years and upward, including heads of families.	Free white males under 16 years.	Free white females, including heads of families.	All other free persons.	Slaves.	NAME OF HEAD OF FAMILY.	Free white males of 16 years and upward, including heads of families.	Free white males under 16 years.	Free white females, including heads of families.	All other free persons.	Slaves.
Adams, George	3		2		3	Allen, James	1		4		1
Acton, James	3		3			Allen, William	2		2		5
Adams, Adam, Free Negro				2		Adams, Rhody	2	3	1		3
Adams, Henrietta	1		5		7	Adams, Charles	1		2		3
Allen, Zecheariah	2	2	3		6	Allen, William	1	1	5		
Adams, Ignatius	3	1	3		7	Adams, William	2	1	3		12
Adams, Richard	2	1	2		11	Armstrong, Robert	1		1		
Adams, Benja	1		1			Adams, George	1	1	6		
Adams, Samuel	1	1			4	Adams, Richard, Senior	1	5	1		
Athey, Charles	1	2	3			Bryan, Stripling	1		2		1
Adams, Leonard	3		1		1	Burch, Jonathan	1	2	2		14
Arvin, Thomas Junr	1	4	4			Briscoe, William	1		5		20
Armes, Stacey		1	3			Barber, Cornelius (Newport:)					
Adams, Ann (Mulatto)				7		Perugin Callhill, Overseer	1				13
Anderson, William	1	2	3			Boarman, Ralph	2	1	5		39
Acton, Osborne R.	1	1	2		2	Berry, Thomas	1	1	3		3
Arvin, Thomas, Senior	2	1	3		1	Barnes, Humphrey, of					
Arvin, Edward	1	3	3			Richmond	1				1
Arvin, Joshua	1	4	4		1	Boswell, Ignatus	1	3	1		3
Askin, Elizabeth			1		7	Barnes, Henry	4	1	2		18
Acton, Henry, of John	1	3	4			Bowie, John	1	1	1		4
Acton, John	2		1		5	Boswell, Walter	2	1	4		4
Acton, John, Junior	1	2	6			Boswell, George	1		2		6
Adams, James (Overseer for						Boswell, Joseph	1		3		2
Samuel Edelen)	1		2		11	Boswell, Sarah			2		6
Athey, Hazea	1	3	2			Boswell, Edward	2	3	4		
Atchinson, John	2		3			Blair, Matthew (Merchant)	4				1
Ash, Charles	1		5			Brawner, John C.	1		2		3
Ash, William	1	1	2			Brawner, Henry	1	2	4		4
Atchinson, Joshua	2	1	1			Brent, Chandler	2	3	3		29
Adams, John	2	4	4		11	Brent, Ann			1		5
Adams, John R.	1		1		12	Butler, John	2	3	4		
Anderson, Jonathan	1	1	3		9	Barnes, Matthew	3	1	5		2
Anderson, Joseph	1		2		4	Bradley, John	1		1		
Anderson, Benjamin	1		2			Boswell Sarah (Widow of					
Alexander, James	2		1		1	William)	1		5		10
Allbrittain, William	1	2	4		1	Boswell, Edward W.	1		1		3
Adams, John, Junior	1		2		2	Bullman, Thomas	1	1	5		
Adams, Joseph (Nanjemoy)	1	2	5		2	Bush, John	3		2		7
Adams, Zepha	1	3	3			Boswell, Elijah	2	1	8		5
Anderson, James	2		2			Boswell, Josias	1	4	2		4
Allen, Joseph	1	4	3			Bell, Basill			1		13
Allbrittain, Charles	1	1	4		1	Burgess, Thomas	1		3		3
Adams, Ann (Mulatto)				6		Brawner, Benjamin	1	1	6		6
Amory, Samuel	1	4	1		14	Boswell John, of Matthew	2	2	4		9
Allen, Francis					4	Burrows, John	1		9		
Allen, George	1	2	4			Burrows, Samuel			1		
Allen, William (of James)	1	3	1		5	Brent, Robert	1	3	7		29
Anderson, Hendley (Mulatto)				1		Boswell, Milley	1	2	4		

180   CHARLES COUNTY, MARYLAND

NAME OF HEAD OF FAMILY.	Free white males of 16 years and upward, including heads of families.	Free white males under 16 years.	Free white females, including heads of families.	All other free persons.	Slaves.	NAME OF HEAD OF FAMILY.	Free white males of 16 years and upward, including heads of families.	Free white males under 16 years.	Free white females, including heads of families.	All other free persons.	Slaves.
Brooke, John	1	2	6	..	24	Burrows, Gabriel	2	1	1	..	..
Bruce, John	1	2	2	..	16	Brown, Richard (Free Negro)	..	..	..	1	..
Bateman, Benjamin, Senior	1	1	4	..	..	Burch, Walter (of Oliver)	1	5	2	..	15
Beavin, Walter (Newport)	1	..	1	..	3	Brimhall, Jeremiah	1	..	..	..	3
Beavin, Leonard (Newport)	1	1	2	..	3	Barker, William	2	..	1	..	7
Brooke, Baker	1	..	3	..	20	Barker, William, Junior	1	1	2	..	5
Brady, Gerrard	1	1	5	..	..	Boarman, Leonard, Junior	1	..	1	..	15
Bond, Thomas	3	3	3	..	6	Boarman, John	1	3	5	..	16
Barron, Nathaniel	1	5	2	..	..	Boarman, Mary Ann	1	..	3	..	27
Brady, Owen	1	1	4	..	1	Boarman, Leonard	1	..	1	..	12
Blandford, William	3	1	7	..	6	Boarman, Mary (Widow of George)	2	..	3	..	28
Beall, Thomas	1	6	2	..	4						
Bannister, Richard	1	1	1	..	..	Boarman, Eleanor	..	..	1	..	10
Brown, Catherine	2	..	3	..	36	Burkells, William	2	..	4	..	3
Brown, Doctor Gustavus R.	5	2	4	..	37	Bryan, William (Mulatto)	..	..	..	1	..
Baggett, Ignatius	1	2	2	..	..	Boarman, Joseph	1	..	2	..	14
Bean, John	1	1	3	..	2	Burch, Richard (of Oliver)	1	4	5	..	..
Beane, Leonard	1	2	4	..	5	Burch, Justinian (of Oliver)	1	5	5	..	9
Boarman, James, of Edward	2	..	1	..	5	Butler, Jacob (Mulatto)	..	..	..	1	..
Berry, Pryor	1	2	4	..	..	Burch, Oliver	1	..	2	..	9
Berry, James	1	1	2	..	1	Burch, Henry (and a Mulatto Boy to be Free at the Age of 21 years)	1			1	
Beavin, Joseph	1	1	4	..	2						
Blandford, Richard	1	1	2	..	4			..	..	..	..
Blandford, Elizabeth	..	1	2	..	4	Butler, Josias (Mulatto)	..	..	..	5	..
Blandford, Charles	2	2	3	..	1	Boarman, Thomas J.	5	1	1	..	18
Blandford, Ann	2	..	5	..	4	Boarman, Duke	1	..	..	..	2
Beavin, Matthew	2	2	4	..	4	Boarman, John (of Thomas James)	1		2		3
Beavin, Paul (Mulatto)	..	..	..	1	..						
Boon, Nicholas	3	4	4	..	13	Boarman, Joseph	3	1	2	..	12
Boon, John	1	..	5	..	5	Bolling, Thomas	1	..	..	..	10
Boswell, Thomas	1	..	3	..	..	Bolling, John	1	1	3	..	5
Bryan, Lewis	1	2	2	..	1	Bolling, Catherine	3	..	3	..	11
Bryan, William	1	..	1	..	..	Boon, James	2	3	4	..	6
Been, Benjamin	1	..	..	..	..	Bolling, Francis	1	..	..	..	14
Brenighan, Zecharia	2	..	3	..	..	Boarman, Jane (Widow of Thomas James)	..	..	2	..	15
Berry, John	1	2	3	..	3						
Berry, Elizabeth	..	..	1	..	2	Boarman, Ralph of Thomas James	1	..	1	..	12
O'Bryan, William	1	..	2	..	..						
Berry, Samuel	1	4	3	..	2	Boarman, Henry	1	..	2	..	17
Berry, Humphrey	2	..	1	..	12	Boarman, Mary (Widow of James)	..	..	1	..	23
Berry, Joseph	2	..	5	..	..						
Berry, Benjamin	2	3	6	..	2	Butler, Rhody (Mulatto)	..	..	..	1	..
Berry, Hezeka	2	3	3	..	4	Brightwell, Richard	1	..	3	..	4
Boon, Walter	1	1	2	..	..	Bryan, Basil	1	2	3	..	..
Beale, Charles	2	2	3	..	8	Bryan, Mary Ann	1	2	2	..	1
Beale, Sarah	..	..	2	..	2	Bryan, John	2	2	5	..	..
Brent, Richard	2	2	2	..	14	Bryan, Ignatius	2	1	5	..	..
Beavin, Benjamin	1	3	4	..	7	OBryan, James	1	1	1	..	..
Beavin, Richard	3	..	1	..	10	OBryan, Josias	1	4	3	..	..
Beavin, Paul	1	..	..	..	3	Burch, Jesse (Mill Wright)	3	2	2	..	5
Beavin, James (Mulatto)	..	..	..	1	..	Brimhall, William	4	2	5	..	2
Beavin, Wheeler	2	1	4	..	1	Brightwell, Robert	1	3	3	..	..
Beavin, Richard, of Basil	3	1	2	..	3	Barron, Catherine	..	..	1	..	..
Beavin, Elizabeth (Widow of John)	..	2	3	..	..	Barron, Thomas	2	..	2	..	9
						Burch, Jonathan	2	2	2	..	15
Beavin, Susanna (Mulatto)	..	..	..	1	..	Brawner, Barton	4	3	4	..	2
Butler, Charles (Free Negro)	..	..	..	1	..	Brawner, William	1	2	3	..	13
Billingsley, John	1	..	4	..	10	Brawner, John	2	..	2	..	7
Beavin, Heza	2	2	3	..	10	Barnes, William (Junior)	1	2	1	..	..
Beavin, John	1	5	4	..	5	Barnes, William, Senior	3	4	4	..	1
Brent, Charles	2	4	5	..	21	Barnes, Godshell	2	2	1	..	1
Burch, Edward	1	2	3	..	9	Bell, Edmund G.	1	2	1	..	..
Burrows, Zephaniah	2	..	3	..	..	Bowie, Abraham	..	..	..	..	..
Branson, Leonard	1	..	2	..	..	Bowie, Mary Ann	2	1	5	..	1

TERCENTENARY YEAR 1958 181

NAME OF HEAD OF FAMILY.	Free white males of 16 years and upward, including heads of families.	Free white males under 16 years.	Free white females, including heads of families.	All other free persons.	Slaves.	NAME OF HEAD OF FAMILY.	Free white males of 16 years and upward, including heads of families.	Free white males under 16 years.	Free white females, including heads of families.	All other free persons.	Slaves.
Barnes, Catherine			2		8	Carrington, John, Senior	2		2		6
Barnes, Richard	1		4		22	Carrington, Mary	1		1		1
Bateman, James	2	1	1			Cope, John	2	1	3		2
Branson, Leonard	1	1	1		1	Clements, Beavin	1		1		
Barber, Cornelius (at his Quarter in Pickawaxen:						Clements, John, of Joseph	1	1	4		
						Craik, Adam	2				1
Johnathan Higg, Overseer)					9	Chandler, Stephen	1		3		9
Boarman, Eleanor (Pickawaxen)			2	2	11	Cawood, Benjamin	2	1	1		32
						Cox, William, Junior	2	4	5		13
Bateman, Richard	1	1	3		1	Cooksey, Hezekiah	2	2	3		7
Boarman, Edward	2	1	1		3	Chandler, Samuel	1		1		6
Burrows, Samuel (Free Negro)			1			Chapman, John, Senior	2		1		21
						Clements, Leonard (of Walter)	1	2	4		5
Bateman, John	1	1	2								
Bateman, George	2					Clark, Richard (Mulatto)				1	
Bateman, Elevin	1	1	1			Clements, Joseph	1		5		8
Bateman, Jesse	1		2			Clements, John A.	2	1	5		
Brooke, Matthew	1		4		1	Clements, Leonard, Senior	2		2		7
Bateman, Judith	1	4	3		2	Copher, Matthew	2	3	3		1
Burridge, Nenyan	1	1	4		2	Clark, Elijah	2	3	3		4
Bruce, Robert	1				3	Chapman, Hendley	2		1		7
Bateman, John, Senior	1		3		1	Cox, Hugh	2	2	4		12
Bateman, John, Junior	1		1		3	Clements, John (Swamp)	2	5	5		7
Blockstone, Samuel	3	1	4			Crismond, Joseph	3	3	6		
Bryan, William (Mulatto)				1		Copher, John	1		1		
Barjona (Free Negro)				1		Clements, Francis (of John)	3		5		
Bateman, Thomas	2		1		1	Bennett, John C.	1		3		1
Bruce, William	1	1	1		5	Cox, Samuel	1	2	5		21
Bowie, Rhody	2	1	6			Chandler, John	2	2	1		4
Brawner, Meredith	1	1	2		2	Craik, William, Esquire	1				23
Brawner, Joseph	1	4	2		2	Cox, John (of Richard)	1				
Barker, Shadrac	1	4	6			Cox, Richard, Senior	2		6		
Bruin, John	1		1		1	Clements, Edward (of William)	1	2	2		1
Brawner, John (Junior)	1	2	1								
Brown, Joseph	1	1				Crismond, Aaron	1		3		
Benson, Benjamin	1	1	1		12	Crismond, John	1		2		
Brooke, Thomas	1					Cox, John, Senior	1	5	2		
Blockstone, Joseph	1		2			Coomes, William	2		2		15
Burges, Mary		2	2			Clements, Eleanor	1		1		2
Brawner, Edward	1	4	2			Clements, Sarah			1		1
Bowie, Benjamin	1		1			Cartwright, Gustavus	2	1	5		13
Brawner, Isaac	1		2		2	Curtis, Samuel (Free Negro)				2	1
Bailer, Andrew	1	1	5		24	Causin, Gerrard B.	1	3	4		75
Burrows, Charles (at John Taylor's Quarter)	1	3	4		54	Cotterell, Burford	2	2	3		15
						Chinn, Thomas	2	3	4		3
Burchill, Charles	1	2	2		1	Compton, William, Senior	1		3		9
Bradshaw, Jeremiah	1	2	3			Collins, Samuel	3		2		1
Bowie, James	2	3	3		5	Clements, Walter	1	4	3		4
Bowie, David	1		2		1	Cain, Francis	1				
Barker, William	1	2	2			Cooper, James	1				
Barker, Elizabeth	2	2	3			Clements, Charles (of Charles)	3	1	5		
Basten, William	1	2	6								
Beck, Francis	1		4		3	Carrington, John, Junior	1		3		
Brawner, William, Junior	1	1	3		8	Clements, John F.	1		3		
Barkelay, William	1	2	3			Cook, William	1	3	3		9
Basten, Matthew	1		1			Cook, Robert	1		1		4
Baker, Jane			2			Beavin, Clement	1		2		
Crismond, John M.	2	1	1		1	Conway, John			1		
Crackells, Thomas	1		3		12	Coombes, Sarah		1	3		
Cooksey, Jesse	1	2	6		1	Courts, Charles	2	3	6		
Punch, William Clements	1		2			Cawood, Woodward	1	2	2		2
Coombs, Richard	1	1	5		7	Coombes, Joshua	1		4		
Cahoo, James	1	4	4			Clements, John, of Francis	1	1	3		16
Clements, Edward	2	1	1			Clements, Mary	2	3	3		12

182 CHARLES COUNTY, MARYLAND

NAME OF HEAD OF FAMILY.	Free white males of 16 years and upward, including heads of families.	Free white males under 16 years.	Free white females, including heads of families.	All other free persons.	Slaves.	NAME OF HEAD OF FAMILY.	Free white males of 16 years and upward, including heads of families.	Free white males under 16 years.	Free white females, including heads of families.	All other free persons.	Slaves.
Clinkscales, John	1	1	3	..	...	Carpenter, Viney	..	1	4	..	..
Carter, William, Mulatto	..	..	..	1	..	Clark, George	1	3	1	..	..
Clements, William, of Jacob	1	..	4	..	1	Clements, John (at Richard Barnes)	1	..	5	..	..
Clark, Elizabeth, Mulatto	..	..	..	5	..	Carter, Charles (Mulatto)	..	..	..	1	..
Cobey, William	1	1	2	..	..	Causin, Ann	..	3	3	..	..
Clements, Walter (Cornwallis Neck)	3	..	3	..	9	Contee, Benjamin, Esquire	1	..	5	..	48
Clements, Walter, of Walter	1	1	3	..	6	Cotterell, James	1	1	1	..	11
Chapman, Susanna	5	..	1	..	33	Cotterell, Benjamin	1	..	..	..	5
Conner, Joseph (Mulatto)	..	..	..	1	..	Courts, William	1	1	3	..	39
Clements, Charles, of Walter	1	..	..	..	..	Crain, Elizabeth	2	..	1	..	24
Cox, Francis	1	..	2	..	2	Chunn, Mary Ann	1	2	7	..	10
Conner, Michael L.	1	..	..	..	..	Connor, Dennis	1	1	1	..	..
Clements, William, Senior	3	1	5	..	3	Chunn, Levi	1	1	1	..	14
Conner, Owen	1	2	3	..	..	Call, Samuel (Free Negro)	..	..	..	1	..
Clements, Elizabeth	..	1	3	..	..	Compton, Reverend John W.	2	..	1	..	6
Chapman, Sarah, Widow of John	..	1	3	..	22	Campbell, John, Esquire	1	..	4	..	54
Clements, Bennadicter	1	4	1	..	..	Cotterell, Thomas	2	4	3	..	4
Cohooe, Elizabeth	1	1	4	..	..	Carter, Hannah (Mulatto)	..	..	..	4	..
Canter, William, Junior	3	2	1	..	7	Cope, Thomas	1	1	1	..	1
Canter, William, Senior	1	1	2	..	9	Cody, Matthew	1	1	2	..	1
Courts, George (Free Negro)	..	..	..	1	..	Cavender, Ann	..	..	1	6	..
Canter, Isaac	2	2	5	..	..	Clinkscales, Adam	2	..	4	..	2
Courts, Ann (Mulatto)	..	..	..	1	..	Coby, John	2	2	3	..	8
Chatham, James	1	4	5	..	..	Clements, John, of John, Senior	1	..	2	..	4
Cohooe, Sarah (Mulatto)	..	..	..	2	..	Carroll Samuel	1	1	3	..	..
Craycraft, Bladen	1	3	3	..	3	Cock, David & George (Free Negro)	..	..	..	3	..
Cooksey, Philip	3	1	4	..	3	Clark, William	1	4	3	..	..
Cooksey, Jonathan	1	2	5	..	1	Carpenter, John	1	1	3	..	..
Callicoe, Joseph	1	1	5	..	..	Courts, Benjamin	1	..	2	..	..
Canter, Susanna	2	1	2	..	5	Carroll, Richard	1	2	2	..	1
Canter, Joseph	1	1	1	..	6	Carpenter, William	1	1	2	..	3
Callico, Thomas	1	..	1	..	..	Chinn, Robert	1	..	..	..	..
Callico, James	3	1	4	..	..	Dodson, William	4	3	4	..	6
Cookseey, Thomas	1	1	3	..	4	Dagg, John	2	1	1	..	1
Carrol, Samuel	1	1	5	..	1	Dixon, John C.	1	..	1	..	2
Corry, Elizabeth	..	..	3	..	7	Dixson, Francis	3	1	11	..	..
Cooksey, Ledstone	1	3	3	..	..	Davis, Benjamin	2	3	2	..	8
Cooksey, Jesse	1	2	6	..	..	Dodson, Barton	1	2	6	..	1
Cooksey, Henry	3	4	2	..	15	Darnall, Benjamin	1	1	3	..	..
Collins, George (Mulatto)	..	..	..	1	..	Davis, Eleazer	1	4	3	..	6
Cooksey, John	1	1	3	..	6	Douglass, Thomas	1	2	5	..	1
Conyham, James, Mulatto	..	..	..	1	..	Day, Benjamin (Mulatto)	..	..	..	6	..
Carrick, Joseph	1	..	..	..	..	Doyne, Ann	1	..	3	..	6
Clements, Henry	1	..	..	..	6	Doyne, Joseph	1	..	..	..	..
Clark, Elizabeth	..	1	1	..	1	Dixon, John	1	..	..	..	4
Callico, Monica	..	..	1	..	..	Douglass, Benjamin, of John	2	1	2	..	11
Callico, James, of Peter	1	3	5	..	3	Dunning, John	1	..	..	..	..
Canter, Truman	1	..	1	..	..	Downs, William, Junior	1	2	1	..	4
Callico, William	1	3	6	..	..	Davis, Mary	..	1	2	..	..
Clinkscales, Adam	2	..	6	..	2	Dixon, Mary	..	..	4	..	1
Callico, Henry	2	1	2	..	1	Dement, Joseph	1	1	1	..	1
Callico, James	1	2	1	..	1	Digges, Henry	6	..	3	..	52
Canter, James	2	2	4	..	1	Dyson, Thomas A.	3	..	..	..	1
Canter, Leonard	1	1	2	..	3	Dodson, Jacob	1	1	4	..	11
Cahoo, James	1	1	6	..	..	Douglass, Jesse	1	..	1	..	1
Chunn, Zachariah	1	2	4	..	7	Doyne, Robert	1	1	2	..	14
Chunn, Lancelot	3	..	1	..	..	Dement, Charles	2	..	4	..	6
Colley, James	1	1	1	..	..	Dement, Edward, Junior	1	3	2	..	1
Carrington, Samuel	1	3	3	..	..	Dement, Edward, Senior	1	..	2	..	1
Clements, Samuel	2	4	4	..	..	Dent, Peter	3	1	2	..	5
Clements, Zachariah	1	..	1	..	..	Duley, Benjamin	2	1	3	..	..
Cato, George	2	3	2	..	4						

TERCENTENARY YEAR 1958

NAME OF HEAD OF FAMILY.	Free white males of 16 years and upward, including heads of families.	Free white males under 16 years.	Free white females, including heads of families.	All other free persons.	Slaves.	NAME OF HEAD OF FAMILY.	Free white males of 16 years and upward, including heads of families.	Free white males under 16 years.	Free white females, including heads of families.	All other free persons.	Slaves.
Dent, Henry, of George	2				10	Day, William (Mulatto)				1	
Deakins, Edward	3	3	7		6	Day, Henrietta (Mulatto)				3	
Dyer, Jeremiah	1	3	6		10	Demarr, John	1	2	5		
Dunning, Nathaniel	2				1	Demarr, Daniel	2	3	2		
Darnell, Thomas	1	2	4			Davis, Elizabeth	1		4		1
Duggins, Robert	1	1	5			Davis, Jeremiah	1	3	1		
Downs, William, Senior	3	1	5		3	Dent, Eleanor	1		3		31
Dixon, George	2	4	3		2	Douglass, Joseph	1	1	6		10
Dent, Captain John	1		1		17	Dutton, Zachariah	1	5	2		3
Dent, Marshall	1		2		21	Dorrett, William	2	1	3		3
Dixon, George, Junior	2		3		9	Diggs, Ann of John	2		2		14
Dulany, Daniel	1	1	1			Dooley, Thomas	1	2	3		1
Diment, John	1		3			Dutton, Notley	1		1		20
Downs, William, Junior	3	2	2			Dutton, Notley, Junior	1	3	1		2
De Jean, Alexander	2		1		16	Dutton, Gerrard	3		3		2
Dement, William	1	2	5		6	Dunnington, Peter	3	2	4		1
Dent, Ann	2	2	3		5	Dunnington, William, Junior	1	1	1		1
Day, Vinney (Mulatto)				4		Davis, Richard, of John	1	1	3		
De Mar, Joshua	2	2	4		3	Delozier, Thomas	2	2	5		1
De Mar, Francis	1	1	2			Dyal, William (Overseer for					
De Mar, William	1	1	2			George Mason)	2	3	4		10
Douglass, Benjamin, of						Dyal, Joseph	1	1	2		
Charles	1	5	4		4	Davis, James, of Henry	2	2	2		5
Dorrett, Aaron	1	2	4		2	Dent, Warren, Esquire	1		4		34
Duggins, Robert, Junior	1				2	Davis, Isaac	1		2		2
Dent, Captain Hezekiah	2	4	4		21	Donnison, Joseph	3				
Dent, Thomas H.	2	1	5		2	Dent, George (Nanjemoy)	2	1	9		38
Dent, Michael	1		1		5	Dunnington, Rebecca	2		5		
Dent, Joseph M.	1	2	4		2	Dunnington, Chloe			5		
Dent, William	3		5		4	Dunnington, George	2	3	6		15
Dent, Gideon	2	1	3		8	Dunnington, James	1		3		8
Dent, John Brewer	1	1	3		2	Dunnington, William, of					
Dent, Zachariah	1	3	1		3	William	1	2	3		2
Dent, Benjamin	1	2	2			Dunnington, William, Senior	1		1		10
Dent, Titus	1	2	3		3	Dunnington, Francis	1	4	3		5
Davis, Abraham (Mulatto)				7		Evans, Hezekiah	1	1	1		
Dent, Hatch, of John	1	1	3		7	Edelen, Francis, Junior	1		3		3
Dent, John, Senior	1		1		4	Edelen, Joseph	1	1	2		4
Dent, John, of John	1	1			7	Edelen, John	2	6	3		15
Davis, Eleanor			1			Evans, Thomas	1		1		1
Davis, Zachariah	2		5		12	Evans, Elisha (Overseer for					
Davis, Lyddia	1		3			John Simms)	1				20
Davis, Jesse (Carpenter)	1				1	Evans, John	1				
Darnal, Catherina, Mulatto				1		Enias, Charles	3		1		
Davis, George	1	2	3			Edelen, Basil	2	2	2		21
Dent, Henry (Newport)	1				2	Easten, Clem (Mulatto)				1	
Davis, Randall	1	1	3			Edelen, John B.	1	1	3		10
Davis, Joseph	2		2			Edelen, Jane	1		2		13
Davis, William	1		2			Edelen, Richard	2	1	3		30
Davis, Philip	1	1	2		10	Estep, Richard	1	3	2		6
Dyson, Gerrard	1	5	4		1	Estep, John	1	4	1		4
Davis, Benjamin, Senior	4		1		24	Edwards, Hezekiah	3	2	5		1
Davis, William, Junior	1	2	5		1	Edelen, James	2	2	4		4
Dent, Reverend Hatch	1	3	4		11	Edelen, Francis	1	2	4		7
Dement, Edward	1		2		1	Edelen, Oswald	1	1	2		7
Dement, John	1	4	3			Edelen, Susanna	2		3		6
Davis, Kenelm	1	1	3			Edelen, Edward	1	3	1		11
Dyson, George	2		2		8	Edwards, Sarah	1		8		3
Davis, Elizabeth	1	1	4			Easton, Samuel (Mulatto)				1	
Dyson, Bennett	3		4		18	Ellett, Thomas	1		2		
Dent, George, Esquire	1	2	5		20	Eglinton, Barnaby	1		1		
Delozier, John, of George	2	2	2			Eanis, David	2		3		
Dean, George	2		1			Ellett, Thomas	2		2		
Dolozier, John, of John	1		1		1	Evans, Hezekiah	1	1	1		

CHARLES COUNTY, MARYLAND

Name of head of family	Free white males of 16 years and upward, including heads of families	Free white males under 16 years	Free white females, including heads of families	All other free persons	Slaves
Evans, Jesse	1	2	4	..	12
Ellett, Richard	1	1	2	..	..
Elgin, Robert	1	3	4	..	8
Elgin, William, Senior	6	..	3	..	29
Elgin, Francis	2	..	1	..	4
Ferguson, Robert	3	..	..	..	4
Fernandez, Chloe	1	2	3	..	13
Franklin, Zepha., Junior	1	1	1	..	3
Featt, Jane (Free Negro)	..	..	..	1	..
Fowke, Gerrard	1	2	3	..	49
Franklin, William, Junior	1	2	7	..	2
Flurry, William	1	2	4	..	1
Fowke, Roger	1	2	2	..	13
Farrell, James	1	3	4	..	..
Franklin, Francis B.	1	1	2	..	29
Fitzgerald, Thomas	1	..	..	..	..
Freeman, Nathan	2	..	4	..	19
Flowers, David	1	1	2	..	2
Ferguson, Jonathan	1	2	4	..	..
Ford, Ann	2	2	3	..	13
Freeman, Moab	2	2	1	..	..
Freeman, James	1	1	2	..	..
Ford, John, Senior	2	..	1	..	16
Farrell, Charles	1	5	2	..	..
Frazer, Ann	..	..	1	..	..
Fendall, Mary	..	1	3	..	13
Franklin, John, Senior	1	3	2	..	..
Fenwick, James	2	4	2	..	50
Freeman, Richard	1	1	4	..	..
Ford, Ninian (Mulatto)	..	..	..	2	..
Ferguson, Sarah	..	..	3	..	3
Farrand, Elizabeth	1	2	5	..	..
Farrand, Zephaniah	1	1	1	..	1
Ferrand, Timothy	1	2	3	..	..
Franklin, William, Senior	1	..	3	..	1
Franklin, Edward	1	1	1	..	..
Franklin, Priscilla	..	1	3	..	15
Franklin, James	1	1	2	..	3
Franklin, Zephaniah	4	..	3	..	10
Franklin, William, Junior	1	1	4	..	..
Flurry, Edward	4	..	3	..	2
Flurry, John	1	3	2	..	1
Flurry, Edward, Junior	1	2	1	..	2
Franklin, Hezekiah	2	3	5	..	3
Farrell, John	3	1	1	..	..
Fowler, Ann	..	..	2	4	21
Fendall, Samuel	1	2	1	..	5
Fisher, John C.	1	3	3	..	..
Farr, John	1	..	5	..	2
Farr, William	1	..	2	..	7
Fearson, Walter	1	2	3	..	..
Fearson, Joseph	1	..	..	..	..
Friend, Daniel	1	1	5	..	..
Ford, Chandler	2	2	7	..	17
Fendall, Benjamin	1	3	3	..	26
Franklin, Noah	1	1	1	..	3
Fairfax, Sarah	2	2	4	..	1
Frawner, Cecily (Mulatto)	..	..	..	2	..
Ford, Phillis (Free Negro)	..	..	..	1	..
Flannagin, Barton	1	4	3	..	4
Fulcer, William	1	3	2	..	..
Fitzgerald, John	1	3	4	..	..
Fowler, Elizabeth	1	2	3	..	..
Flannagan, Ann	..	1	2	..	1

Name of head of family	Free white males of 16 years and upward, including heads of families	Free white males under 16 years	Free white females, including heads of families	All other free persons	Slaves
Fleming, Mary	1	2	4	..	15
Forbes, John	7	3	3	..	68
Goodrick, Mary, Junior	..	..	1	..	8
Gilpin, Thomas	1	3	2	..	..
Green, Henry	2	6	4	..	10
Green, Clare	1	..	2	..	8
Gray, Sarah	1	..	1	..	..
Garner, Charles	3	..	1	..	12
Green, Peter	2	3	5	..	7
Garner, John	2	1	5	..	6
Goodrick, Charles	1	..	..	..	6
Goodrick, Mary, Senior	..	..	1	..	2
Gray, Hannah	..	..	1	..	31
Gray, Joseph	2	3	4	..	9
Garber, Bennett	1	..	..	..	..
Green, Elizabeth	2	..	2	..	14
Griffin, William S.	1	1	2	..	..
Griffin, John	2	4	3	..	2
Gray, James	2	..	..	..	..
Gray, William	3	..	1	..	1
Goodrick, Walter	1	2	3	..	3
Green, Charles, Senior	2	..	1	..	10
Green, Giles, Senior	1	..	..	..	11
Green, Giles, Junior	4	..	2	..	11
Griffin, Lancelot	1	..	..	..	..
Griffin, Ann	1	1	5	..	5
Griffin, Sarah	..	..	2	..	5
Griffin, James	3	3	3	..	1
Green, John, of Francis	1	1	2	..	2
Glasgow, John	..	..	4	..	..
Glasgow, Thomas	1	..	2	..	1
Green, William	1	..	3	..	..
Green, Nicholas	2	..	4	..	2
Gambra, Richard	2	2	1	..	16
Green, Melchizedec	1	1	6	..	..
Gates, James	1	..	3	..	1
Gates, Leonard	1	2	4	..	..
Guy, William, Senior	2	1	4	..	4
Guy, John	1	3	6	..	2
Guy, William, Junior	2	1	1	..	1
Griffiths, Thomas	1	2	6	..	..
Gates, Joanna	..	1	3	..	..
Green, Austin	1	..	2	..	..
Grant, Elizabeth	2	1	2	..	14
Green, Elizabeth	2	..	1	..	1
Gibbons, Francis	1	4	4	..	4
Gill, Adam	1	1	3	..	..
Gates, William	1	3	2	..	..
Gittings, Thomas	1	2	1	..	..
Gardner, Ignatius	1	3	2	..	14
Gardner, Captain John	1	..	..	..	10
Gardner, Richard	2	3	3	..	14
Gibson, John	1	5	5	..	1
Griffy, Mary	..	..	2	..	..
Grindall, William	1	..	..	..	1
Gladding, Robert	1	..	1	..	11
Gill, Lydia	1	..	1	..	10
Garner, Joseph	1	..	..	..	10
Gardner, John	1	1	3	..	15
Gardner, Francis	1	..	..	..	8
Gardner, Henry	1	5	5	..	17
Gibbons, Nehemiah	1	1	2	..	2
Gardner, William	1	3	5	..	14
Gibbons, Jeremiah	1	1	3	..	10

TERCENTENARY YEAR 1958

NAME OF HEAD OF FAMILY	Free white males of 16 years and upward, including heads of families	Free white males under 16 years	Free white females, including heads of families	All other free persons	Slaves
Gibbons, Thomas	4		2		11
Gibbons, William	1				5
Guy, Francis	1	2	8		
Gates, Edward	1	1	2		
Gill, Robert	1	3	4		8
Good, Ann	1		4		
Good, Oswald	1	1	5		
Gill, John	2	1	6		
Glasgow, Allen	1	1	8		
Goodrick, Elizabeth		2	5		
Gray, George (Newport)	1	2	3		
Golding, Mary			1		
Golding, Robert	2	3	5		
Gray, Margaret		2	1		
Gray, John N.	2	2			1
Gray, Jeremiah	2	1	2		11
Gray, Williamson(Nanjemoy)	1	2	1		
Glover, Philip	2		2		4
Gwinn, Benjamin (John Clegget, Overseer)	1				15
Gwinn, Elizabeth			2		10
Joy, Joseph	3		4		1
Gibson, John, of William	1				9
Goose, James (Mulatto)				1	
Garner, Captain Hezekiah	1	2	3		11
Gray, Edward	1	2	3		1
Gray, (Sergeant), Benjamin	1				
Gardner, Jane		2	2		1
Gardner, George	2	3	1		5
Gray, George (Nanjemoy)	1		3		
Groves, John	1	2	6		
Groves, William	1	2	3		
Green, John (at Meeks Mill)	1	2			
Garland, William (Nanjemoy)	1		3		48
Gray, Andrew	2	2	4		
Gardner, Theophilus	1		1		
Griffiths, John	1		2		
Groves, Abednego	1		1		
Griffin, Richard	1	1	2		
Green, Samuel	1		2		
Griffiths, Zachariah	1	1	4		
Griffiths, John, Senior	1	2	6		1
Gilbert, Joseph	1	2	1		1
Groves, Elizabeth			2		
Griffin, John (Nanjemoy)	1		2		
Hayley, Sarah (Mulatto)				5	
Harley, Jonathan	1		1		
Hays, Vinney		1	2		1
Howard, Benjamin	2	3	3		1
Hall, Richard (Mulatto)				6	
Hamilton, Bennett	2	3	6		13
Hartagraves, George	2	1	6		13
Hunt, William	1		1		
Hamilton, Alexander	1	1	1		
Hanson, John, of John	2				
Hay, William, Senior	3	1	1		9
Hay, Thomas	1	3	1		2
Hayley, Dorothy			1		
Hanson, Walter, Junior	1	1	3		13
Hunt, Joseph	2	8	4		1
Hunt, Mishach	1		1		
Hanson, Theophilus	2	2	3		23
Higden, Francis, Senior, (Newport)	2	1	6		6
Hopewell, Thomas	3	3	2		13
Hutchinson, George	2	1	4		27
Hanson, Samuel, of William	1	1	2		9
Hawkins, Francis	1				13
Haslip, Samuel	1	3	3		8
Harrison, Thomas	1	1	2		12
Hand, George (Mulatto)				1	
Hand, John (Mulatto)				1	
Hanson, Samuel, of Walter	1	1	2		9
Hicks, Thomas	1	2	2		
Hill, Lydia		1	3		2
Huton, George	2	1	4		
Hawkins, Alexander H. S.	1	1	4		21
Holden, James	1	1	2		2
Holden, Chloe			2		4
Hawkins, Elizabeth	2		2		115
Hawkins, Smith	1	2	3		
Hanson, John, Senior	1		1		12
Hanson, Henry M.	1				7
Hawkins, Susanna			1		11
Hawkins, Jane			1		5
Hawkins, Caleb	1	1			4
Hill, Leonard	1		2		
Harboard, James	1	1	3		4
Harley, Henry (Mulatto)				5	
Hanson, Hoskins	1	3	4		32
Hungerford, Ann (Mulatto)				2	
Hamilton, Patrick	2		1		6
Hamilton, Edward	1				
Hamilton, Major Samuel	1	2	4		14
Hawkins, Catherine (Newport)	1		1		
Halkerston, William	1		1		9
Haydon, Joseph	1		3		
Huntington, John	1	1	4		
Haydon, James	1	4	4		2
Hindman, John	2				2
Hennekin, John	2	1	3		3
Huntington, William	1				
Huntington, Edward	1	1	2		
Hall, John	1	1	2		1
Hampton, Casey	1		5		
Hawkins, Ann			1	5	30
Howell, Mary Ann					3
Hamilton, Ignatius	2	6	3		
Harvin, Thomas	1	5	4		2
Hunt, James	1	2	3		2
Howell, Samuel	1	5	1		
Howell, Mary	1	2	6		3
Hagan, Jonathan					
Hunt, Jonathan	2	1	5		
Hill, Joseph	1	2	3		
Hunt, Silvester	1	1	1		
Hetchinson, James	1	6	2		
Hanson, Walter, Senior, Esquire	2		2		20
Hagan, Henry	1	2	4		48
Hatcher, John	1	2	5		1
Hason, Samuel, Senior, Esquire	1		2		26
Hutchinson, William	1				
Hall, Elizabeth	3		2		6
Hamilton, Duke	2	1	5		2
Hughs, Charles	1	3	3		

186 CHARLES COUNTY, MARYLAND

NAME OF HEAD OF FAMILY.	Free white males of 16 years and upward, including heads of families.	Free white males under 16 years.	Free white females, including heads of families.	All other free persons.	Slaves.	NAME OF HEAD OF FAMILY.	Free white males of 16 years and upward, including heads of families.	Free white males under 16 years.	Free white females, including heads of families.	All other free persons.	Slaves.
Hunter, David	1		2			Harrison, Reverend, Walter	1				21
Hicks, John (Mulatto)					1	Harrison, Joseph White	1				1
Henderson, James	2					Hamilton, Eleanor Ann	1		7		5
Hickey, Francis	2	1	3		2	Harrison, Grace			5		30
Hazard, Michael	2	3	8			Harrison, Ann	1	1	2		19
Hagan, Ralph	1		4		7	Hatcher, Ignatius	1	3	3		1
Hagan, Benjamin	4	3	5		1	Hamilton, William					
Higden, William	2	2	5			(Nanjemoy)	1		2		
Hill, Thomas	1	3	2			Hanson, Samuel, of Samuel,					
Higdon, Richard, Junior	1	1	4			Junior	1	1	1		5
Hamersley, Francis, Newport (Bennett Warthen, Overs'r)					4	Hudson, Caleb	1	1	3		4
Higdon, Leonard B	3	3	3		4	Johnson, John	1		3		
Hardman, Thomas	1					Jackson, William (Mulatto)				13	
Hill, William (Mulatto) Newport					6	James, John	2	1	2		
						Jackson, James (Mulatto)				1	
Hancock, William	1	4	7		2	Jenkins, Mary	1		2		12
Hancock, Abraham	1		3		2	Jackson, Zachariah (Mulatto)				1	
Hill, Monica		1	2			Jenefer, Doctor Daniel	2	1	3		38
Harvin, Zephaniah & Henry Parker Apprentice to the said Harvin	2	3	1			Johnson, Ann		2	1		
						Jameson, Benjamin	2				15
						Jameson, John	1	4	2		2
Holland, John	1	2	1			Jenkins, Edward	2		5		14
Hobbs, Isaac	1	1	1			Jenefer, Daniel, of Saint Thomas Jenefer, his Quarter Port Tobo Parish, Edward Herrick, Overseer					
Harvin, Allen	1	3	2		1						
Hagan, Joseph, of William	1	1	3		7		2				20
Hagan, Joseph, of John	1		1		4	Johnson, Archibald	2				12
Hagan, William, of William	1					Johnson, Walter	1	2	3		4
Harvin, Roswell	1	2	1			Johnson, Rachael		1	2		
Harvin, William	2		3			Johnson, Hezekiah	3	4	3		12
Hagan, James, of Ignatius	1	1	3		1	Jameson, Walter	2	1	4		25
Hagan, Benjamin (Newport)	1	2	4			Jenkins, George	1	1	4		16
Harrison, William (Newport)	1	2	4		10	Jackson, Samuel (Mulatto)				4	
Hunt, Elijah	2	2	2			Jackson, Barton (Mulatto)				4	
Hilton, Thomas	1					Jackson, John (Mulatto)				4	
Higgs, George	3	2	4			Jones, William (Nanjemoy)	3	4	2		
Higdon, John B	1	2	2			Jones, Richard	1		2		1
Huntington, Luke	1	3	3			Jones, James	1	1	2		1
Haslip, John, of Henry	1	3	7		1	Johnson, Joseph	1	2	2		2
Haslip, Henry	2		2		1	Johnson, Susanna			5		
Howard, Thomas G	1	2	4		1	Jones, William, Junior	1	2	3		1
Hart, Michael	1	1	2			Jackson, Susanna (Mulatto)				4	
Haslip, John, of Robert	1	2	3		3	Jackson, John B. (Mulatto)				2	
Haslip, Robert, Senior	1		1		11	Jenkins, William	1		2		
Hifield, Thomas	1					Jameston, Samuel					5
Hubbard, Edward	1	2	5		5	Jameson, Henry J	2		2		3
Hancock, Josias	1				5	Jameson, Ralph	1				7
Higgs, Jonathan	1	1			1	Jameson, Sarah	1		3		26
Hamersley, Henry	2	1	3		31	Jameson, Leonard	1		5		3
Hand, Jane (Mulatto)				6		Johnson, John, Senior	2	3	4		5
Hargus, Joseph	2		2		5	Johnson, John, Junior	1		1		1
Hungerford, Jane			4		13	Johnson, James	1		3		13
Hungerford, Thomas	3	1	3		19	Jackson, Abednego (Mulatto)				4	
Harris, Thomas (Pickawaxen)	1	4	4		24	Jameson, Henry	3				2
Hancock, Thomas	1		3		7	Johnson, Jacob (Nanjemoy)	1	1	4		
Hill, William (Mulatto) Port tobacco				8	2	Jenkins, Thomas (Cob Neck)	2	6	2		20
						Jones, Samuel	1				
Harley, Sarah	1	1	1			Jones, William	1	3	3		20
Haslip, Richard	2		6			Joy, Ann			2		6
Haywood, Samuel	2		2			Jenkins, Abednego		1	1		
Howard, John	1	1	4		3	Jones, John Court, Esquire	3		1		5
Halford, John (Free Negro)				1		Jenkins, John (Cob Neck)	2	1	3		3
Hudson, Richard	2		2		5	Jenkins, William	1	1	1		1
Hyfield, Frederick	1		1			Johnson, Wm. (Posey's Mill)	1				

TERCENTENARY YEAR 1958

NAME OF HEAD OF FAMILY	Free white males of 16 years and upward, including heads of families.	Free white males under 16 years.	Free white females, including heads of families.	All other free persons.	Slaves.
Jones, Benjamin	2	2	2		
Jenkins, William (Mulatto)				9	
Jones, Joseph	1	4	2		
Johnson, James (Millwright)	1	1	1		
Jackson, Thomas	3	3	2		4
Jenkins, Elerin	1		2		
Husk, Elizabeth	2	1	5		
Hurry, John	1	1	4		3
Hurry, William	1	2	1		
Howard, John	1	1	4		
Harris, John, Junior	2		2		
Hannon, Henry	1	2	2		
Hannon, Walter	1		2		
Kersey, Mary			2		
Kellow, Thomas	1	1	4		3
Kitchen, William	1		2		
King, William	1	2	1		1
Kennaham, John	1	6	1		1
King, John	2		3		7
Keech, George	2		1		10
King, Jane		1	5		5
Kerrick, Edward	1		1		1
Kersey, Daniel M.	1	1	1		1
Keech, George, Junior	1	1	1		4
Kidwell, Thomas	1		2		
Kennyham, Patrick	1		2		1
Kendrick, Zachariah	1	1	2		4
Kennia, Ignatius	1	3	3		4
King, Aquila	2	2	5		1
Kennia, John, Senior	1	3	4		1
Keech, Margaret			1		
Kirkpatrick, William	1		1		2
King, Rebecca	1		5		15
King, Williamson	1	1	3		7
Kennedy, William	1	1	3		5
Kennedy, Clement	2	2	4		11
Keibard, Thomas	2	2	4		5
Keibard, John	1	3			4
King, Benjamin (Nanjemoy)	1	1	2		1
Laymond, Charles S.	2	1	6		
Lindsay, William	2	2	7		
Layman, John C.	3	2	5		4
Latimer, James, Junior	2				8
Lovelace, William	2	6	1		
Latimer, Judith			2		14
Lowe, Ann		1	3		3
Luckett, Samuel, Junior	1	1	3		4
Lomax, Thomas	2	3	2		
Lamaster, William	2	1	5		
Luckett, Notley	1	5	1		1
Lewis, George	1	2	1		1
Lawson, Robert	1				48
Luckett, Benjamin			1		1
Lanham, Moses	1	1	3		1
Luckett, Joseph	3				8
Latimer, Ann	1		2		3
Laymond, Captain John	3		4		
Layman, William	1				
Lewis, Benjamin	2	4	3		2
Luckett, George	2	2	1		1
Linkin, Eleanor (Mulatto)				3	2
Lomax, Benjamin	1	6	6		
Lanhan, Sarah		1	1		
Luckett, Ignatius, of John	1		1		1
Lewis, John	1	3	3		
Labrador, John	1		2		1
Luckett, Thomas	2	1	6		11
Langley, John (Fuller)	1	4	5		
Lomax, Luke	1	4	3		
Leigh, William	1		1		12
Leigh, George, Esquire	2		3		24
Lenkin, Townly (Mulatto)				6	
Lenkin, Henly (Mulatto)				7	
Lush, William	1		1		
Love, Samuel	1	3	3		
Langley, William	2	3	3		
Langley, Joseph	2	5	3		
Lyon, John	1	3	4		5
Letcher, Leonard	2	1	4		2
Lyon, Henry	2	4	5		9
Leech, Thomas	2	2	3		1
Levi, Anthony	1	2	3		
Lyon, Leonard	1		1		10
Lyon, James	2	3	7		4
Lomax, John (Nanjemoy)	2	1	5		
Latimer, Ann (Widow of Marcus)	4	2	5		15
Laidler, Robert	1		1		13
Lovelin, Moab	1	1	3		
Lomax, Stephen	1		1		
Lancaster, John, Junior	1	3	2		13
Lancaster, Thomas	1	2	2		24
Langley, Joseph (Cob Neck)	3	2	5		11
Lancaster, Joseph	1		1		14
Lancaster, John, Senior	5		2		53
Laidler, John	1		3		9
Luckett, Thomas, of Thomas	1				1
Luckett, Margaret	1		5		13
Luckett, Samuel, of Ignatius	1	2			
Lutwyche, Thomas	1				12
Landergin, Thomas	1	1	1		1
Lazarus, Mary (Free Negro)				1	
Maddox, Cornelius	1	2	3		
Merrick, Thomas D., Esquire	2		1		6
Miller, Christopher	1		4		
McBride, John	8		1		
Matthews, Ignatius	1				15
Moore, Aaron	3				
McLaurin, Jane		1	4	2	
Miles, Walter	2	2	2		6
Maddox, Hendley	1	1	2		
Mankin, Richard T.	1	2	3		5
McCray, Philip	1		3		1
Moreland, Stephen	1	3	6		
Martin, Michael	3	1	5		9
Moreland, Richard	1		4		12
Moreland, William	3	7	2		1
Morris, William	4	2	5		6
McDaniel, Isaac	1				2
Mudd, James, Senior	2	1	1		4
Macpherson, Samuel	2				8
Munro, Thomas	1		1		1
Morris, Jacob	3		2		7
Maddox, Susanna		1	2		
McBane, William	2	3	6		2
Mudd, John, Junior, of James	1		1		
Manning, William	3		1		4
McDaniel, Zachariah	3	1	4		17
Manning, Deborah	1	1	2		6

188 CHARLES COUNTY, MARYLAND

NAME OF HEAD OF FAMILY.	Free white males of 16 years and upward, including heads of families.	Free white males under 16 years.	Free white females, including heads of families.	All other free persons.	Slaves.
Mayhall, John (Mulatto)				1	
Morrison, William	1		5		1
Mitchell, Samuel	1	2			1
Mayhall, Robert (Mulatto)				9	
Meekhum, Samuel	1		3		4
Millar, Alexander	1	1	2		
Mitchell, Bennett	1	5	5		23
Mitchell, Rachael	1		1		11
Maddox, Elizabeth		1	3		1
Muncaster, James	1	4	4		13
Millstead, Matthew	3	6	3		
Macpherson, Walter, Junior	2	1	2		8
Maddox, Hendley, of Ben...	2	6	4		2
Mudd, Smith	1	2	5		3
Miles, William	2	3	6		
Murray, Philip A	2	3	3		
Macpherson, John	1		5		16
Macpherson, Captain William	1	3	6		22
Martin, Thomas	2	1	3		6
Mudd, Joshua	2	3	2		12
Murray, William	2	1	1		
Miller, John	1		2		8
Moran, Luke		1	2		
Money, Isaac	1	2	5		3
Marshall, Samuel	1		1		12
Martin, Zachariah	2		2		10
Martin, Leigh	1	3	1		1
Monk, Jane (Mulatto)				4	
Manry, Ignatius	1	3	4		2
MacDaniel, Charles	2		1		1
Maddox, Henry	1	1	5		13
Molyneaux, Reverend Robert	6				64
Miles, Edward	2	2	4		12
Miles, Nicholas	2				1
Morris, James, Senior	1				
Moreland, Henry A	1		3		
Murphy, Hezekiah	1	1	3		
Maddox, Notley, Senior	2	2	3		7
Montgomery, Eleanor		1	2		
MacGlue, Elizabeth	1	1	4		
Macpherson, Lieutenant, Mark & Company	26				
Miles, Joseph	3	2	6		6
Mudd, Jeremiah	1		1		1
Muschett, Mungo	1	1	2		17
MacCoy, Mary		2	7		
MacDaniel, Theophilus	1		1		
Mitchell, Captain John	2	1	3		21
MacBane, John	1		5		
MacDaniel, Archibald	1		1		
McDaniel, Allen	1	2	7		3
MacDaniel, Daniel	2	2	6		3
Moreland, Zachariah	2	1	8		
Middleton, Horatio	2	1			20
McEvoy, John	1	1	3		
Marshall, Thomas, Senior	2		1		14
Marshall, John, of Thomas	1		1		5
Macpherson, Basil	1				3
Marshall, Thomas Hanson	1	1	3		49
Munroe, Thomas			1		1
Munroe, John	2	3	4		
Macpherson, Walter, Senior	2	2	6		23
Moore, James			1		13
Moreland, Samuel	1	2	4		
Moreland, Mary	1		2		
Miles, James	1	2	6		
Middleton, James, Senior	2	1	4		49
Middleton, James, Junior	1	1	1		14
MacDaniel, Nathaniel	1		3		
Montgomery, Joshua	2	1	7		
Montgomery, James	2	2	2		
Moreland, Jacob	1	3	4		
Miles, Eleanor	1		2		2
Miles, Edward, of Henry	1				
Miles, Barton	2	3	5		1
Maddox, Edward (Nanjemoy)	2	3	1		3
Maddox, Henry (Nanjemoy)	1	1	3		2
MacDaniel, Rebecca		1	4		
Middleton, Theodore	1	2	1		7
Middleton, Smith	1				5
Mudd, Mary	1		5		10
Moore, Matthew, Senior	1		2		6
Montgomery, Mary	1		3		
Montgomery, John	1		4		1
Montgomery, Henrietta			3		
Montgomery, Rebecca		2	3		
Miles, Nicholas	1	1	1		
Miles, Henry	1	2	2		5
Mudd, Roswell	1	1	2		3
Moreland, Isaac	1	3	5		
Moreland, Theopilus	1	2	3		
Moreland, Patrick	2		1		2
Martin, Mary	2	1	4		
Moreland, Richard, Junior	3	2	9		
Montgomery, Thomas	2	1	3		
Moreland, Philip	1	2	3		
Moreland, Joseph	1		2		2
Moreland, James	1	2	4		
Mahorney, Millborne	1		2		
Moore, Matthew, Junior	1	3	5		
Moore, Elijah	1	3	4		1
Montgomery, Barnaby	1	2	3		
Mahorney, Basil	1	1	2		
MacDonnaugh, James M	1		1		8
McCoy, Johnston	1	3	2		8
Mudd, James, Junior	1	2	3		3
Macpherson, William H	1		7		11
Macpherson, Kitty G	1	4	2		9
MacAtee, Susanna	1		2		
MacAtee, Mary	3		3		2
Marshall, Philip	1	1	3		12
Mchorn, Velindar					
McAtee, John, Senior	2		2		4
McAtee, Thomas, of John	1				
McLean, William	1	3	2		1
Mason, William, Pomonkey (Qua. James Lorney Overseer)	1				5
Marbury, Francis H	2		1		10
Marbury, Henry	1	1	1		6
Moreland, William	1		3		6
Mudd, Richard	2	1	3		
Mudd, Bennett	3	1	4		11
Mudd, Henry J. (of Thomas)	2		3		12
Mudd, Mary	1		5		11
Mudd, Henry T	1	3	3		
McDaniel, Jonathan	2	1	4		
Mudd, Ann			1		5

TERCENTENARY YEAR 1958

NAME OF HEAD OF FAMILY.	Free white males of 16 years and upward, including heads of families.	Free white males under 16 years.	Free white females, including heads of families.	All other free persons.	Slaves.	NAME OF HEAD OF FAMILY.	Free white males of 16 years and upward, including heads of families.	Free white males under 16 years.	Free white females, including heads of families.	All other free persons.	Slaves.
Mudd, Henry, Senior	2		5		9	Maddox, Basil	1		3		
McGruder, Mary (her Quart. no Overseer)					7	Moredock, Samuel	1	3	3		
						Maddox, John (Chickamuxen)	2	3	3		15
Moran, John, Senior	1				9	McAtee, Sarah			3		2
Maddox, James, Senior	1	1			9	Macpherson, John, of Daniel	1	1	4		
Moran, Meveril	2	1	2		7	Marr, Martin	3	1	4		
Moran, Gabriel	3	2	2		13	Millstead, William	2		3		12
Moran, Andrew	4		3		11	Maddox, John, of John	1				2
Macpherson, Elizabeth		1	3		10	Marstin, Jane	1	1	3		
Morris, Ann		4	4			Mason, Lott	1		4		3
Marshall, Benjamin	2		6		9	Mordocke, James, Senior	1		5		
Mollahorn, John W.	1		1		2	Maddocke, James, of James	1	3	3		
Murphy, Daniel, of James	2	5	4			Marshall, William, Junior	1	2	4		5
Mattingley, Ralph	1	1	2			Macpherson, Samuel, Hanson	3	1	3		12
Mudd, Bennett, Newport	1					Middleton, Samuel	1	2	3		32
Mason, John	1	1	1			Mason, Martin (Carpenter)	1				
Macpherson, Captain Alexander	1	3	5		18	Meek, John B.	3		2		27
Midley, John	1	1	3		12	Mitchell, William	3	1	1		3
Morris, Joshua	1	3	3			Maddox, Len	2	2	3		
Montgomery, William	3	1	2		1	Mayhew, Catherine	1	2	4		5
Montgomery, Joseph	3	2	6			Moredocke, Godfrey	2	4	2		3
Murphy, Walter	1	1	2		1	McGregor, Walter	1		1		1
Massey, Mary			1			Millstead, John B.	1		1		
Montgomery, Charles	1	2	1		1	Moredock, William	2	1	4		1
Moore, Jane			3			Moredock, Wiliam, Junior	1		1		
Murphy, Nathaniel	1		1			Maddox, Richard	1		1		
Molton, Joseph	1	4	2		9	Maddox, Rhody	2	2	5		1
Molton, George	1	4	2		8	Martin, Allen	1	2	2		5
Moran, Jonathan	1	2	1		4	McPherson, Daniel, of Daniel	1	3	4		
Moran, Charles	1		3		4	McLeannam, John	1	1	3		1
Moran, John	2	1	6		17	Millstead, Noah	1	2	2		
Monroe, John	1		4		7	Mason, Richard	7				24
Molton, Elizabeth			2		1	Mankin, Charles	1	3	5		14
Murphy, Samuel	1	3	3		3	Norder, William	2	3	3		
Matthews, Thomas	1	3	3		6	Nally, Shadrac	1	1	3		1
Murphy, Daniel, Senior	4		3		9	Nace, Negro, the property of Thomas Young, prince George County, and his family			4		3
Mattingley, Zachariah	1	2	5								
Mankin, William, Senior	3		1								
Maddox, Noah	1	1	3		2	Newman, Edward	1		4		
Mason, William (his quarter, John Delozier, overseer)			6		20	Notier, Michael	1	1	3		
May, William	2		6			Nellson, Thomas	2	5	5		10
Maddox, Henry (Nanjemoy)	1	2	3		1	Knott, Justinian	2	4	4		4
McConchie, William	4	3	7		50	Nettle, James F.	1		1		1
Marshall, Robert	1	2	3		16	Nally, Dennis	2	4	4		9
Mastin, Huse	1	1	3		26	Newman, William	1	2	4		1
Mahorney, Clement	1	2	3		1	Nally, Leonard	2	2	4		1
Maddox, Eleanor		1	4		11	Nally, Gustavus	1	1	2		6
Minitree, Paul	2	2	3		8	Nally, Susanna	2	2	4		
Marshall, Thomas	1		4		13	Nottingham, Eleanor	1	3	2		3
Maddox, John (Pickawaxen)	2	1	4		24	Noble, Zachariah	1		4		
May, Richard	1	1	3		1	Noble, William	1	2	2		
Marshall, John, Senior	2	1	2		23	Nally, Barnaby	1		3		
Marshall, William, Senior	2		4		14	Nally, William	1	1	7		1
Mead, Tobitha	2		3		2	Nally, Thomas	1	1	3		1
Macmillion, William	1	3	3			Nally, Thomas, Junior	2	2	2		3
Martindale, Elizabeth	2		4			Newman, William (Mulatto)				4	
Miller, George	1		1			Newbury, John	1				
Muschett, Captain John	1	4	1		17	Nellson, Joseph	2	2	7		2
Millstead, Elizabeth	1	1				Nellson, Frederick	1	1	1		3
Millstead, Samuel	2	2	5			Nicholson, Henry	1	1	1		3
Millstead, Thomas	1	1	4			Nally, John	1	2	5		
Maddox, Samuel	2	2	4		2	Nettle, Thomas	1		3		1
						Norwood, Garner	1	1	2		

CHARLES COUNTY, MARYLAND

NAME OF HEAD OF FAMILY.	Free white males of 16 years and upward, including heads of families.	Free white males under 16 years.	Free white females, including heads of families.	All other free persons.	Slaves.	NAME OF HEAD OF FAMILY.	Free white males of 16 years and upward, including heads of families.	Free white males under 16 years.	Free white females, including heads of families.	All other free persons.	Slaves.
Neale, James................	2	3	4	..	30	Padgett, John..............	1	2	3	..	..
Neale, Bennett.............	1	2	1	..	20	Padgett, Henry.............	1	1	3	..	1
Neale, Edward.............	1	..	..	..	..	Padgett, Elizabeth..........	1	2	2	..	1
Neale, John (Cob Neck)....	3	1	4	..	18	Padgett, Jonathan..........	1	3	5	..	..
Neale, Joseph (Cob Neck)...	2	3	7	..	13	Padgett, Aaron.............	1	1	5	..	..
Nellson, John...............	1	..	2	..	1	Pye, Joseph................	1	..	1	..	10
Neale, Sarah................	1	2	2	..	..	Pye, Charles................	4	3	3	..	23
Nellson, Thomas, of Thomas.	1	2	2	..	..	Perry, Sibba................	1	..	3	..	..
Nally, Richard.............	1	2	4	..	2	Peacock, William...........	1	1	4	..	4
Noiry, Daniel...............	1	3	3	..	10	Proctor, Thomas and Samuel Collins (Mulattos).........	..	..	..	12	..
Nellson, Hannah (Mulatto)..	..	..	..	1	..						
Owenbread, William........	1	..	2	..	..	Pierce, Charles.............	1	..	4	..	1
Ostree, Thomas.............	2	2	3	..	1	Pierce, John................	1	2	2	..	2
Ogle, Benjamin.............	2	1	..	1	..	Parker, Jonathan...........	2	1	3	..	3
Ostree, Philip..............	2	..	1	..	..	Power, Jesse...............	1	1	1	..	..
Owen, Joseph...............	1	3	2	..	3	Paddy, John................	1	2	1	..	..
Owen, Elizabeth............	..	1	6	..	9	Perry, Edward..............	1	4	5	..	..
Ogden, Jonathan............	2	3	6	..	..	Perry, James A.............	1	..	..	..	..
Osborne, Thomas	1	3	5	..	2	Perry, Hugh (Benedict).....	1	4	4	..	3
Osborne, Rhody.............	1	..	2	..	1	Proctor, Charles (Mulatto)..	..	..	..	7	..
Osborne, Jeremiah..........	1	2	1	..	..	Penny, Ann (Mulatto)......	..	..	..	1	..
Osborne, Walter............	1	3	1	..	2	Posey, Elizabeth (Newport).	1	..	2	..	12
Owen, Richard.............	2	3	3	..	1	Proctor, Joseph (Mulatto)...	..	..	..	6	..
Ogden, Benjamin............	1	3	3	..	8	Proctor, Francis (Mulatto)..	..	..	..	1	..
Osborne, Henry.............	1	3	2	..	..	Proctor, Michael (Mulatto).	..	..	..	1	..
Oden, John.................	2	..	..	..	..	Proctor, Eleanor (Mulatto).	..	..	..	2	..
Oden, Isaac.................	2	5	3	..	..	Proctor, Thomas (Mulatto).	..	..	..	5	..
Oliver, William..............	1	1	2	..	2	Proctor, Henry (Mulatto) ..	..	..	..	6	..
Oliver, James...............	1	..	1	..	1	Poston, Benjamin...........	1	1	5	..	1
Othrington, Caleb (Mulatto).	..	..	..	8	..	Proctor, Milley (Mulatto) ..	..	..	..	1	..
Oden, Elias.................	1	..	1	..	5	Proctor, Tenney (Mulatto) .	..	..	..	1	..
Posey, Henry of Humphrey..	1	1	2	..	10	Proctor, Isaac (Mulatto) ...	..	..	..	1	..
Oakley, John................	1	4	3	..	2	Proctor, Jennett (Mulatto) .	..	..	..	1	..
Oakley, Joseph..............	1	..	1	..	1	Proctor, Elizabeth (Mulatto).	..	..	..	1	..
Osbourne, Thomas, Junior...	1	..	5	..	..	Proctor, Chloe (Mulatto) ..	..	..	..	1	..
Pickerell, Samuel...........	1	1	2	..	..	Proctor, Jacob (Mulatto) ..	..	..	..	1	..
Pickerell, Joseph............	2	..	3	..	1	Paddison, John.............	1	1	2	..	..
Padgett, James..............	1	4	4	..	..	Poston, Priscilla............	1	..	2	..	10
Power, Joseph..............	1	..	2	..	4	Poston, Mary...............	1	..	3	..	4
Peers, Nicholas.............	2	..	3	..	6	Poston, Bartholomew.......	1	..	1	..	1
Price, Thomas..............	2	2	1	..	4	Poston, Solomon............	1	3	3	..	..
Poston, William.............	1	3	4	..	4	Poston, John...............	1	1	2	..	4
Permillion, James...........	2	..	2	..	..	Proctor, William (Mulatto)..	..	..	..	5	..
Posey, Thomas..............	1	..	2	..	5	Plummer, Judith............	1	4	2	..	..
Posey, Henrietta............	1	..	4	..	3	Proctor, Susanna (Mulatto).	..	..	..	1	..
Power, Mary Ann...........	..	1	5	..	..	Penny, Sarah (Mulatto)....	..	..	..	1	..
Philips, Isabell..............	..	1	4	..	..	Price, Zachariah............	1	1	3	..	13
Proctor, Leonard (Mulatto).	..	..	..	1	..	Penn, Major Jerred.........	1	1	3	..	41
Penn, William (Newport) ...	1	2	3	..	1	Penn, Mark................	2	5	2	..	..
Pye, Walter................	2	2	1	..	14	Penn, Stephen..............	1	..	4	..	..
Philpot, Hanson H..........	1	..	4	..	5	Philpot, Elizabeth...........	..	..	2	..	13
Pyles, Reverend Henry (Newport)...................	1	..	..	..	28	Posey, Belain...............	1	6	3	..	23
Parnham, John, Esquire	2	2	3	..	26	Penn, John.................	1	1	7	..	2
Proctor, James (Mulatto) ...	..	..	..	1	..	Posey, Rhody...............	1	1	3	..	..
Penn, Mark H..............	2	1	3	..	..	Posey, Benjamin, of Uzziah.	1	1	1	..	..
Power, John................	1	2	5	..	..	Posey, Benjamin V.........	1	3	3	..	7
Porteus, Martha............	..	..	1	..	9	Price, Henrietta............	1	1	2	..	5
Pickerell, John..............	1	5	2	..	..	Posey, Thomas, of Thomas..	1	1	1	..	..
Padgett, Joseph.............	1	..	1	..	1	Posey, James...............	1	..	..	..	..
Padgett, Benjamin, of William	1	4	4	..	..	Posey, Elizabeth............	..	1	3	..	..
Padgett, Eleanor............	..	..	1	..	..	Perry, Francis..............	1	..	..	..	..
Padgett, Benjamin, of Ben ..	1	..	..	..	..	Posey, Jacob................	1	..	1	..	..
Padget, Benjamin...........	1	5	2	..	..	Posey, Francis..............	1	..	..	..	..
						Picking, John....:.........	1	2	1	..	..

NAME OF HEAD OF FAMILY.	Free white males of 16 years and upward, including heads of families.	Free white males under 16 years.	Free white females, including heads of families.	All other free persons.	Slaves.	NAME OF HEAD OF FAMILY.	Free white males of 16 years and upward, including heads of families.	Free white males under 16 years.	Free white females, including heads of families.	All other free persons.	Slaves.
Posey, Mary Ann	1	1	5			Robey, Penelope			3		
Posey, Burdett	1	5	3		2	Rawlings, Sarah	1	1	2		
Perry, John	1		2		2	Reeves, Hezekiah	1		1		26
Posey, John	2					Robertson, James	1	2	2		5
Perry, Robert	1	1	2		2	Robertson, Benjamin	1	1	4		4
Posey, Rogor	1	2	1		1	Reeves, Courtney	1		2		31
Posey, George	1	3	2			Robey, William, of Richard	3	4	4		1
Posey, Thomas	2		2			Richards, Richard	1		1		
Posey, William	1	2	3			Richardson, Mark	1	3	3		
Perry, Mary			2			Richards, William	1	1	1		
Posey, Humphrey	3	2	6		4	Richardson, William	1		1		3
Picking, Sarah	1	1	2			Roberts, Henry	1		4		
Perry, Thomas	1		2		9	Reeder, John	1	3	5		
Posey, Uzziah	1	2	2		8	Ray, Thomas (Mulatto)				6	
Perry, Hugh (Nanjemoy)	1	2	3			Richards, Samuel	1		2		2
Philberd, John	1	1	3		1	Robey, John, of Josias	1	1	4		1
Posey, Ann	1		3			Roe, William	1	4	3		2
Quade, Thomas	1	2	4			Rowland, John	3		3		
Queen, Walter	1	4	4		12	Robertson, Elijah	1	1	4		
Queen, William	1		6		18	Risen, Elizabeth			3		
Ruston, James (Mulatto)				3		Robey, Joshua	1		4		1
Russell, James	3		2		5	Richards, Thomas	2	1	6		6
Russell, Thomas	1		1		4	Rawlings, Martha			3		
Robinson, William (Son of Ben)	3	2	3		6	Rutter, Joseph	1		1		
Ray, Charles (Mulatto)				4		Reeves, Leonard	1	3	6		3
Reeder, Richard R	1	1	5		21	Reeves, Samuel	1	4	6		3
Riney, James	1	1	3		5	Robertson, William G	2	3	5		
Richardson, Josias W	1		4			Richardson, Luke	1	1	2		
Robey, Zachariah	1	3	4			Robertson, William (Pickawaxen)	1	2	5		1
Robey, Benjamin of Richard	1	1	6			Rebbitt, Francis	1	1	3		
Robey, John, of Richard			3		8	Ratcliffe, John	1	4	3		2
Robey, Samuel, of Richard	2	5	4			Reeves, James	1	3	2		
Ridgate, Elizabeth			3		12	Rock, James	1				
Robey, Hezekiah	1		2		1	Reeves, Thomas	1	1	4		9
Robinson, William	1	1	4			Russell, John	1	1	6		6
Robey, Alexander	2	4	3		5	Risen, Peter	1				
Robey, Barrack	1	1	1			Risen, Ann		3	3		
Robey, Basil (Poor House)	6	8	20		9	Renn, John	1	2	3		
Rains, Robert (Mulatto)				5		Ratcliffe, James	1	1	4		2
Rock, Charity		2	4		2	Robertson, William (Nanjemoy)	2	2	5		1
Reed, Thomas	2	1	4			Ratcliffe, Quinton	1				3
Robey, Jesse	1		2			Ratcliffe, Shadrac	1	2	1		3
Rogers, Robert	1	2	8		11	Ratcliffe, Joseph	3	5	6		
Ray, Daniel (Mulatto)				2		Risen, Chandler	1	4	5		
Reeves, Bennett, Newport	1	2	1		2	Ratcliffe, Samuel	1				
Robertson, Mitchell	2	1	2		4	Ratcliffe, James (Carpenter)					
Reeves, William	1		1		5	Ryan, Ignatius	2		5		32
Reeder, Benjamin	3		3		11	Robertson, John	1	3	2		24
Ray, James (Mulatto)				5		Rye, John	1	2	4		
Robey, Jeremiah	1		1			Risen, Philip	1	1	5		6
Robey, Samuel, of John	1	2	4			Rye, Rawley	2	3	3		
Robey, Lessly	1	1	1		6	Rye, William	1		4		
Robey, John A	3	1	4			Risen, Lancelot	2	1	2		
Robey, Joseph	1	1	3		1	Rice, William	3	1	1		
Robey, Jacob			1		1	Rye, John	1	1	4		
Robey, Leonard, Senior	2		2			Ratcliffe, Burdett	1	1	1		6
Robey, Richard, Senior	1	2	4		5	Ratcliffe, Ignatius	2	6	2		4
Robey, Barton, of Richard	1					Ratcliffe, Francis	1		1		
Robey, Thomas	2	4	3		2	Ratcliffe, Rhody	2	3	3		1
Robey, William, Senior	1	4	2		2	Rye, John	1	3	3		2
Robey, Aquila			6		5	Rye, Warren	2		2		5
Robey, John N	2	2	2		8	Ratcliffe, Winnefort					
Reeves, Upgate	2		2		1						

CHARLES COUNTY, MARYLAND

NAME OF HEAD OF FAMILY.	Free white males of 16 years and upward, including heads of families.	Free white males under 16 years.	Free white females, including heads of families.	All other free persons.	Slaves.	NAME OF HEAD OF FAMILY.	Free white males of 16 years and upward, including heads of families.	Free white males under 16 years.	Free white females, including heads of families.	All other free persons.	Slaves.
Shelton, John S.	1	1	3	..	12	Semmes, Mark	4	3	5	..	10
Sewall, Charles	2	...	2	..	27	Sute, Walter	1	1	3	..	2
Simpson, Ignatius	2	1	3	..	8	Scallion, John	1	4	5	..	..
Stone, Thomas, Senior	1	2	3	..	15	Scott, James (Newport)	1	3	3	..	5
Sandiford, Thomas	3	4	4	..	4	Scott, Christian	1	...	2	..	8
Smith, Sarah	...	...	1	1	1	Simpson, Catherina	...	3	3	..	3
Smith, Elizabeth	1	...	3	..	2	Simpson, Thomas (Newport)	1	...	1	..	2
Stockett, Thomas	1	1	2	..	3	Swann, Edward (Senior)	3	2	3	..	..
Semmes, Marmaduke	1	...	4	..	19	Semmes, Thomas (Port Tobacco)	2	3	9	..	23
Stuart, Ignatius	1	1	2	..	1						
Stonestreet, Edward	1	1	2	..	2	Smith, Henry	1	1	1	..	..
Smoot, Edward, Senior	1	1	4	..	19	Smallwood, James	1	2	4	..	9
Sanders, Thomas	1	1	5	..	..	Simpson, Joseph	1	3	1	..	..
Smith, Walter	5	3	5	..	8	Smith, James	1	...	4	..	3
Smoot, Josias	1	3	1	..	22	Smith, Electius	1	...	1	..	3
Sanders, Edward	2	...	1	..	5	Smith, Elizabeth	...	2	4	..	5
Stone, William, Senior	2	2	5	..	8	Smith, Basil	1	2	4	..	6
Sanders, John	2	3	7	..	9	Sansbury, Isaac	5	2	6	..	9
Shurden, John	1	3	...	..	...	Stuart, William	1	4	3	..	1
Simpson, Thomas	1	1	1	..	9	Simpson, Thomas	1	1	3	..	..
Stewart, Henry	1	2	6	..	5	Smallwood, Susanna	1	...	2	..	6
Semmes, Ignatius	3	1	6	..	13	Smallwood, Walter	1	...	...	..	4
Smith, Josias	1	...	5	..	1	Smallwood, Henry	1	...	2	..	1
Simpson, Charles	1	3	3	..	5	Smith, Thomas (Blacksmith)	3	2	5	..	..
Semmes, Bennett B.	1	...	1	..	6	Smallwood, Ann	...	...	1	..	12
Swann, Charity (Mulatto)	...	...	...	1	..	Smallwood, John, of James	1	...	2	..	..
Swann, Elizabeth (Mulatto)	...	...	...	5	..	Spalding, Basil	2	...	4	..	19
Swann, Linder (Mulatto)	...	...	...	1	..	Spalding, Edward	1	...	3	..	6
Swann, Elizabeth, Junior (Mulatto)	...	...	...	1	..	Spalding, Basil, Junior	1	1	2	..	4
Semmes, Jame, of Thomas	1	...	2	..	1	Sinnett, (Major) Robert	2	...	3	..	28
Stone, Hanson	2	1	2	..	10	Swann, Samuel, Junior	2	1	3	..	2
Stone, David	2	...	...	..	9	Smith, Vernon	1	4	3	..	5
Swift, Gordon (Virginia), no Overseer	...	...	2	..	7	Sanders, Bennett	1	1	6	..	1
Stone, Mary	1	...	2	..	23	Steward, Philip	1	...	...	..	33
Smallwood, Captain Thomas	2	1	2	..	7	Smallwood, Ann (Widow of John)	...	...	1	4	3
Smallwood, Ledstone, Junior	1	1	2	..	7	Slater, Samuel	1	...	1	..	..
Smallwood, William M.	2	2	2	..	1	Slater, John	1	1	6	..	1
Stuard, Ann	...	...	3	..	1	Smallwood, Basil	1	1	2	..	1
Shackorley, William	1	1	4	..	4	Stone, John, Senior	1	1	2	..	9
Smithson, William	2	4	3	..	..	Sullivan, John	1	...	...	..	..
Semmes, William, Senior	1	2	4	..	1	Smith, Clement	1	3	4	..	7
Smoot, William B. (of Thomas)	3	4	2	..	16	Stonestreet, Henry	2	3	3	..	17
Scott, James	1	5	3	..	..	Slater, William	1	3	1	..	5
Skiffington, Roger	1	...	...	..	..	Smith, Simon	1	3	6	..	3
Smallwood, Ledstone, Senior	1	1	4	..	..	Smallwood, Thomas, of Thomas	1	1	6	..	..
Smallwood, Pryor, of Ledstone	2	1	7	..	1	Smallwood, Hezekiah	1	1	4	..	1
Simpson, Henrietta	...	...	4	..	...	Smallwood, Pryor, of Thomas	1	...	...	..	..
Smallwood, Bean (of Pryor)	1	...	...	..	...	Smallwood, Bean, of Thomas	1	2	4	..	..
Swann, William (Mulatto)	...	...	...	3	..	Savoy, William (Mulatto)	...	...	...	5	..
Scrogin, Dorothy	...	5	4	..	...	Savoy, Archibald (Mulatto)	...	...	...	9	..
Shikerley, Thomas	1	...	2	..	6	Shaw, John (Pomonkey)	1	2	2	..	..
Shervin, Mary	3	...	1	..	19	Shaw, William (Pomonkey)	1	1	5	..	..
Stone, John H., Esquire	1	1	6	..	24	Stoddert, Thomas	1	...	1	..	5
Stone, Walter	3	...	...	..	2	Stoddert, Elizabeth	...	...	...	..	13
Semmes, Robert D.	3	2	...	..	10	Stamp, John	1	1	3	..	1
Semmes, Mary	...	...	4	..	7	Smith, Henry (Bryantown)	2	...	1	..	7
Scott, John Day	1	4	3	..	1	Smith, Jane	...	...	1	..	2
Shepherd, Francis	3	...	3	..	7	Smith, John L.	1	2	2	..	..
Sly, Robert (Newport)	2	1	5	..	11	Shepherd, Philip	1	1	4	..	..
Smoot, Isaac	1	...	...	..	9	Sothoron, Levin	3	1	3	..	13
						Slye, John	1	...	...	..	..

TERCENTENARY YEAR 1958

NAME OF HEAD OF FAMILY.	Free white males of 16 years and upward, including heads of families.	Free white males under 16 years.	Free white females, including heads of families.	All other free persons.	Slaves.	NAME OF HEAD OF FAMILY.	Free white males of 16 years and upward, including heads of families.	Free white males under 16 years.	Free white females, including heads of families.	All other free persons.	Slaves.
Sothoron, John	1				20	Scott, Samuel	1		2		1
Smith, Charles S.	1				10	Shanna, James	1		4		
Smith, Henry (of Charles)	2		1		14	Smoot, William (of William)	2	2	4		4
Smith, Richard	1	3	1			Sutherland, Ignatius	1	2	4		
Shanks, John	1	1			3	Skinner, Jeremiah	2		1		5
Sothoron, Henry G. (his Quarter at Benedict: Leonard Branson, Overseer)					23	Stromatt, Captain John	2	1	5		8
						Speake, Hezekiah	1		3		1
Smoot, John N	2		6		9	Stoddert, Major William	1		1		23
Smoot, Hendley	2	2	7		14	Simms, Thomas (Nanjemoy)	1	5	1		7
Scott, Creey (Mulatto)				1		Skinner, Walter	1	1	1		
Simms, John	4	2	4		1	Simms, Joseph (of James)	1	4	3		12
Sinclair, Mary	2		2		3	Sothoron, Walter	1	2	2		7
Simpson, Rachael			1			Skinner, Elisha	1	1	1		1
Savoy, Martha (Mulatto)				2		Smoot, Eleanor			2	1	
Sute, John	1	2	5			Smoot, Richard	1		3		
Simpson, John L.	1		3		1	Steward, William (Nanjemoy)	2	4	6		1
Simmonds, Samuel	1	1				Smallwood, (General) William	1	2	5	7	56
Steward, Henry (Benedict)	1		3			Speake, Captain Joseph	1	1	4		8
Sanders, Ann (Widow of Joshua)			2		28	Speake, John T.	1				9
						Speake, Henrietta			1	1	9
Scott, Joshua (Mullatto)				3		Speake, Captain Francis	1	1	3		15
Spalding, Ignatius	2				15	Skinner, Thomas (of William)	2	2	3		
Smoot, Arthur	1	2	4		5	Skinner, Thomas (of Thomas)	1	2	6		
Smoot, Barton	1	2	1			Skinner, John, Senior	1	2	4		
Seager, Benjamin	1		1			Speake, Henry	3	1	2		13
Semmes, Edward	1		2		5	Skinner, Edward	2	1	2		3
Smoot, Mary			2		2	Skinner, Jesse	1	1	1		
Shicklesworth, John	1	1	4			Skinner, James	1		4		6
Smoot, Samuel	1		2		4	Skinner, Manning	1		3		1
Savoy, Francis (Mulatto)				1		Skinner, Ann, Senior			1	5	5
Sothoron, Ann			1		9	Simmons, Aaron	1	2	5		
Scallion, Peter	1	1	4			Smith, John (Nanjemoy)	1	2	3		1
Swann, James	2	3	2			Skinner, John (Junior)	1	2	2		4
Swann, Chloe	1		3		1	Shields, Thomas	1	3	7		1
Swann, Thomas	1		7			Skinner, Joseph, at William Jones	1				
Swann, Samuel H.	1	1	1		1	Stone, Samuel, Senior	2	1	2		8
Swann, Charles	2	1	5			Sisson, Caleb	1		2		
Somerville, Philip	1	1	2			Smith, Eleanor (Mulatto)				4	
Swann, Thomas (Senior)	1	3	4			Skinner, Hezekiah	1	2	6		
Steward, George	1	1	2		4	Strange, Charlotta	1		1		24
Steward, Walter	1	6	4			Simms, James	2	5	5		18
Smallwood, Mary	3	2	6			Smoot, William Barton (of Charles)	1	2	4		26
Swann, Mary, Junior (Mulatto)					11	Thompson, George (Shoemaker)	2	3	2		1
Speake, John, Senior	1		2			Turner, John B., Esquire	1	2			1
Sanders, Jordan	1	2	5			Turner, Zephaniah	2	2	3		15
Shaw, Sarah			1	1		Tuson, Robert (Mulatto)				5	
Stone, Matthew	1				5	Timms, Charles	3	3	3		3
Swann, Jennett (Mulatto)				4		Timms, John	4	1	6		2
Smoot, Alexander	2	3	1		9	Tier, William	2	1	3		9
Smith, James	2	2	4			Tier, Charles	2	2	4		8
Smith, John	2	1	3		1	Tier, Francis	2	1	2		5
Smoot, William, of Edward	2	3	5		10	Tier, Joseph	1		2		9
Smoot, John, Senior	2	4	4		11	Thompson, Matthew	2	1	6		
Smith, Elizabeth	1		1		6	Thompson, Joseph Green	1	1	2		21
Scrogin, Barton	1	1	2			Tier, Sarah, (Mulatto)				1	
Simms, Mary (Pickawaxen)	1	1	5		6	Tubman, Eleanor	1		1		10
Smith, John (Cob Neck)	1	1	3		2	Tubman, Samuel	1	1	1		8
Shaw, William	3	1	6		7	Thompson, John B.	1	2	2		25
Simpson, Jane (Pickawaxen)			1	4		Thompson, Joseph	2				
Swann, William (at the mill)	3		1		14	Taylor, William (Mulatto)				5	
Scott, John	1	1	3		2						

CHARLES COUNTY, MARYLAND

NAME OF HEAD OF FAMILY.	Free white males of 16 years and upward, including heads of families.	Free white males under 16 years.	Free white females, including heads of families.	All other free persons.	Slaves.	NAME OF HEAD OF FAMILY.	Free white males of 16 years and upward, including heads of families.	Free white males under 16 years.	Free white females, including heads of families.	All other free persons.	Slaves.
Thompson, Thomas (Mulatto)				1		Thompson, Thomas (Chickamuxen)	2	4	3		1
Thompson, Alexander (Mulatto)				1		Thomas, William (Senior) (Chickamuxen)	1		4		
Thompson, Mary (Mulatto)				4		Thomas, Clem	1	4	2		1
Tier, Ann	2		3		6	Templeman, John	1	1	1		
Taylor, James	1	2	3			Turner, Joseph (Port Tobacco)	1	4	5		11
Thompson, James	1	2	3		6	Thomas, Colonel John (Nanjemoy)	2		2		24
Thompson, George	2	3	2		1	Taylor, William (Nanjemoy)	1	1	4		
Thompson, Ann			3		4	Thompson, Ann (Nanjemoy)	1		2		
Thompson, Ann (Junior)			2			Talmash, Judith	3	1	3		1
Turner, Samuel	4		5		3	Taylor, Sarah		1	3		
Thompson, Thomas	2	3	7			Thompson, Alexander M.	1		1		
Tench, Joshua	1	1	4		3	Thompson, William	1				
Thompson, Smallwood	2	1	1		2	Williams, Jeremiah	1	1	1		
Thomas, John Mattoman	1	1	4			Wedding, Philip	2	1	3		
Tench, Thomas	1	1	3			Ware, Edward Scott	2	2	4		
Tyler, William	1	2	3		13	Wallace, Judith	1	3	3		4
Thompson, Charles	1		1		6	Wages, Mary			1		
Thompson, John (of George)	1	1	4		5	Wright, Thomas	1				
Thompson, James, of James	1	1	1		3	Wheeler, Richard	1		3		1
Turner, Jonathan	3	2	5		2	Wheeler, Charles	1				7
Taylor, John	1	1	1			Webster, Thomas (Mulatto)				3	
Tubman, Richard	4	2	3		13	Wheeler, Clement	2	1	4		7
Thompson, James	1		1			Welch, William	1		1		
Thompson, Leonard	2	4			1	Wheeler, Ann	2		1		7
Timpson, Benjamin	3		4		1	Ware, Francis M	1	3	3		5
Thompson, John (Bryan Town)	1		2		1	Wills, John Baptist	2		3		4
Turner, William	1	3	3		12	Warthen, Priscilla			3	1	
Thomas, Kenelm	1		4		7	Ware, Francis (of Jacob)	1	2	3		
Taylor, Mary	2		3			Ware, Jacob	2		2		
Thomas, Thomas	2	2	5			Weems, Reverend John	1	1	2		5
Tubman, Henry (Quarter)					12	Warthen, William	2	3	5		1
Thomas, Mary	1		1		6	Whitter, William	1				5
Thomas, Nathaniel	1	1	2		7	Whitter, Buckley	3		5		
Thomas, James, Junior	1	1	2		7	Wheeler, Ignatius	1	2	3		13
Thomas, James, Senior	1				8	Warthen, Ignatius	1	5	1		
Thomas, Catherina	2	2	5		4	Wills, Ignatius I	1		2		5
Thompson, Henry (Mulatto)				6		Ware, Coloniel Francis	1		4		18
Thompson, William (Mulatto)				1		Wheeler, William	1				18
Thompson, Joseph (Mulatto)				1		Wood, James (Newport)	2		5		4
Tench, Leonard	1		3		2	Wood, Philip	2	1	4		8
Turner, William (Junior)	1	2	2		2	Watts, Doctor William, (Quarter)	1				5
Turner, John	1	1	1			Warthen, Baker J	1	1	4		
Turner, Williamson	1		1			Wildder, Margaret		1	4		7
Turner, Randall	3	2	9		1	Wiseman, Zacharian (Mulatto)				1	
Thompson, Ann (Mulatto)				1		Warthen, Bennett	2	1	5		2
Thorn, Abaslom	2	3	3		3	Warrington, James	1				
Thorn, Elizabeth	1	1	3			Windsor, Mary			1		1
Tippett, Ely	1	1	2			Winter, John	2		1		22
Tubman, George	1	1	1		22	Winter, Captain Walter	1	4	6		14
Thompson, Mary (Chickamuxen)			3			Winter, Elizabeth			1		12
Timms, Joseph	1	1	2			Warder, William	1				
Turvey, Joshua	1					Thomas, Philip	1	3	5		10
Taylor, Henry	1		3			Williams, John	1	2	3		1
Thomas, Philip	1	3	5		10	Wedding, Thomas	1		3		2
Tomkins, John	1		4		1	Wedding, Thomas, Junior	1	3	2		1
Thompson, Joseph	2	6	3		19	Wight, Isle of	1	1	3		5
Thomas, William (Nanjemoy)	1					Wright, John	1	1	3		
Thompson, Leonard (Nanjemoy)	2		4		1	White, William	1	3	3		2
Taylor, William (Chickamuxen)	1		5		13	Wedding, John, Senior	1	3	8		
						White, John	1		4		

NAME OF HEAD OF FAMILY.	Free white males of 16 years and upward, including heads of families.	Free white males under 16 years.	Free white females, including heads of families.	All other free persons.	Slaves.	NAME OF HEAD OF FAMILY.	Free white males of 16 years and upward, including heads of families.	Free white males under 16 years.	Free white females, including heads of families.	All other free persons.	Slaves.
Wilkinson, Alexander	2				8	Wheeler, Benedict	1	3	3		12
Wilkerson, Walter	1	1	6		1	Ward, Ignatius	1	3	3		2
Willett, George	2	3	3			Ward, John (of Augustus)	1		2		9
Wedding, William	2	1	7			Ward, Susanna	2		3		5
Wheeler, Ignatius (Junior)	1		4			Williams, Jeremiah	1	1	1		
Welch, Edward	1	3	3			Wildair, John B.	1	2	3		4
Wilkerson, Bennett	1	3	2		1	Windsor, Zachariah	1	1	6		
Willett, James	1	3	2			Wildair, James	2		1		9
Wood, James (Son of Sorrow)	5		1		25	Wood, Jane (Mulatto)				5	
Williams, John (Mulatto)				1		Winman, Edward	1				
Welch, George	1	1	2		1	Warder, James	2	2	4		
Wood, John (of Richard)	1	1	4			Warden, Acey	2		3		6
Ward, Thomas	1		7		5	Wheeler, Samuel	1	2	3		5
Wood, James (Pomonkey)	2		1		1	West, Henry	1		5		
Wright, Joseph	1	2	1		2	Woodward, Henley	2		1		7
Wright, John	1				2	Whaland, Jeremihah	1	2	2		
White, John	2					Woolford, Vinney			3		
Wood, Margaret	1		2		13	Woodward, Samuel	2	1	2		2
Wood, Peter	1	2	2		16	Wright, Mary	1	1	4		
Wilkinson, Captain William	2	3	5		29	Winter, Walter (Nanjemoy)	3		1		12
Whetely, William	1	3	3		16	Williams, Elizabeth			1		3
Whetely, Francis	1	3	2		7	Wapole, George	3	1	2		
Wallace, Cornelius	1		4		4	Wapole, John	1	2	5		
Wallace, Richard	1		2		6	Wright, John L.	2		2		3
Wood, Benjamin	3	1	5		8	Wright, Gorry	1				
Waters, Randolph	1		2		2	Wapole, George, Junior	2		2		
Williams, John, Junior	1	2	4		1	Woodward, William	1	2	2		
Warthren, Marma D.	1					Wapole, James	1	1	5		
Wathen, Barton, Junior	1	2	2		2	Wapole, William	1		4		
Warthen, Clement	1	1	7			Wheatley, Samuel, Negro and family					3
Warthen, Bennett, Junior	4	3	6		3	Woodward, John	1		1		
Whetely, Mary			2			Wright, John (Nanjemoy)	1	2	2		
Wathen, Martin	3		3		2	Williams, John (Overseer for William B. Smoot)	1	1	3		
Williams, Salary			1			Vincent, Philip	2		3		
Whetely, Francis	3	1	4		7	Vincent, Rhody	1	1	5		
Wathen, Barton	1	3	4		2	Venables, Mary	1	2	6		1
Waters, Gustavus	1	2	1		3	Venables, Ezekiel	2	1	1		1
Waters, James, of Joseph	1	2	4		7	Voulls, James	2	1	3		
Waters, Joseph	1	2	4		2	Vane, William	1		6		
Waters, James (fuller)	4	1	5		1	Vincent, William	1		2		8
Waters, Edward	1	2	2		3	Young, Robert (his Quarter) James Chatham Overseer			1		9
Waters, Zephaniah	2	1	3		14	Yates, Josias	2		1		1
Weatherington, Richard	1	2	5		1	Young, Elizabeth		1	1		8
Waters, Thomas	1	5	3		1	Yates, Elizabeth			6		65
Waters, Mary			3		2	Young, Joseph	1	1	3		13
Waters, William	1	2	4		24	Yates, Charles	1	2	5		12
Wallace, James	1				1	Young, James	3	2	2		
Waters, John C.	2	2	7		1	Upton, William (Mulatto)				3	
Weatherington, James	1		1		1	Vardin, John	2	3	4		8
Wheelan, John	1		1		13	Vane, John	1		4		1
Wood, Margaret, Junior		3	2		13	Spalding, Edward (Negro)					2
Watson, James	2	3	5		5	Jenifer, Daniel, Esquire	1				22
Wiseman, James (Mulatto)				1							
Wood, Leonard (Newport)	1		6								
Wood, (Doctor) Gerrard	1	3	1								
Ward, Mary		1	4		5						

INDEX

Acton, John, 104
Adams, Daniel Jenifer, 52, 55, 56
Adams, Francis, 39
Adams, Henry, 9, 15, 17, 19, 32
Adams, Capt. William F., 74
Addison, John, 39
Agricultural Fair of 1848, 111-112
Algonquin Indians, 3
Allanson, Thomas, 31
Allen, John, 17
All Faith Parish, 73
Allen's Fresh, 101, 105, 112-113, 124
Allward, James, 39
Anderson, Joseph, 52
"Aqueenseek", 68
"Araby", 63
Atwikses, Humphrey, location of first County Court, 15
Atzeroth, George A., Lincoln conspirator, 130

Baker, General L.C., on Civil War conditions in County, 124
Baker, Thomas, 15
Baltimore and Potomac Railroad, 138
Barnes, Richard, 52, 109, 113
Barnes, William C., 113
Barton, Capt. William, 32
Bayne, see Beane
Beall, John, Jr., 48
Beall, Rezin, 56
Beane, Edith, wife of Rev. Matthew Hill, 37
Beane, John, 32
Beane, Ralph, 35
Beane, Walter, 35
Belcher, Henry, 39
Benedict, or Benedict-Leonard Town, creation of, 33; War of 1812, 102-105; mention on maps, 101, 105, 112
Bladensburg, Battle of, 104
"Blenheim", home of the Lees, 98-99
Boarman, Henry, 55
Boarman, Major William, 31, 35
"Boarman's Manor", 31
"Boarman's Rest", 35
Boats, 24; see also Ferries, and Steamboats

Booth, John Wilkes, flight, 130-133; search for, 131-132
Bowden, Hugh, 39
Bowling, William F., 127
Bracco, Bennett, 56
Bray, Rev. Thomas, 40, 41
Breet, George, 39
Bricks, for houses, 23, 24
Bridges, over Zekiah Swamp, 61; see also Potomac River Bridge
Brent, George, 113
Brent, Mother Mary Margaret, 71
Brent, Robert, 71
Brooke, Baker, 12
Brown, Gustavus, the elder Dr. Brown, 52, biog., 82-83
Brown, Dr. Gustavus Richard, biog., 83-87
Brue, John, 52
Bryantown, 35, 105, 106, 111, 112, 113, 131, 133
Bullox, Joseph, 39
Burford, Thomas, 32
Burgess, Thomas, 104
Burnham, Nathan, 121

Callock, Jon, 39
Calvert, Cecil, 1, 9
Calvert, Charles, 9
Calvert, Philip, 12, 13
Calverton Manor, erection, 9
 sale of, 50
Camp Stanton, Benedict, Civil War, 129
Campbell, Rev. Isaac, 45, 46, 52, 73
Campbell, James, 52
Carrico, Dr. Louis Carlyle, 143
Carrico, Theresa, 108
Catholic Church, 17th cent., 33-35; 18th cent., 67-72; mass in private homes, 68; 19th cent., 106; see also names of individual churches
Causin, Causine, Cawsin or Causeen
 Nicholas, 8
 Ignatius, 19, 20, 32
 Gerrard B., 52, 61, 67, 76
"Causine's Manor," 8
Cawood, Benjamin, Jr., 52
Cawood, Stephen, 30
Caye, Jon, 39

198   CHARLES COUNTY, MARYLAND

Census, of 1712, 43;
of 1790, 66-67; 8
Chandler, Job, 15, 31
Chandler, William, 32
Chandler's Hope, patent to Job Chandler, 31; as temporary Carmelite convent, 71; home of the Neale family, 69.
Chandler's Town, or Chandlee's Town, 32
Chapel Point, 6; establishment of chapel, 34; Union troops at, 122; occupation troops at, 133.
Chapman, John Grant, biog., 113
Chapman, Pearson, 53, 63
Chapman, Robert F., 139
Chapman's Landing, 63
Chapman Town, 112, 132
Charles County, boundaries, 10; boundary change of 1748, 48; convention of 1861, 121; creation of, 9-10; physical description, 1-2; settlers, 23.
Charles Town, see Port Tobacco
Charlotte Hall School, 45-46, 73
Chicamuxen, 5
Chief Justice of County Court, 13
Christ Church, 40; moved to La Plata, 143
"Christian Temple Manor," 31
Chunn, Capt. Samuel, 47
Chunn, Zachariah, 52
Civil War, 119-135; troops in county, 122-123; conditions in 1861, 123;
Civil War, aftermath of: restrictions on residents, 134; Oath of Allegiance, 135; defeatist attitude, 136; effect on politics, 136-137.
Clagett, Richard, 52
Clarke, Gilbt, 39
Clothing, of settlers, 24; of Indians, 4
Cole, Giles, 30
Commissioners, selection of, 13; Oath, 10; first named, 9; duties, 9; present at first court, 15, 16
Communications, 17th cent., 24; 18th cent., 49; 19th cent., 115, 116, 140; see also mail, transportation, etc.

Complaints against British, in 1776, 58; in 1812, 102
Compton, Barnes, 137, 142;
Compton, Stephen, 52
Compton, William, 52
Compton, William F., 52
Confederate Agents, Miss Olivia Floyd, 128; Thomas A. Jones, 125
Confederate States Army, First Maryland Artillery, 126
Contee, Benjamin, biog., 95; executor of McDonough Fund, 109.
Contee, P.A.L., 127
Copely, Lionel, 37
Copely, Rev. Thomas, S.J., 6, 8, 33
Cornall, Joseph, 32
Cornish, Jno., 39
Cornwallis, Thomas, 9, 144
County Court, meeting places, 16,17; duties, 14, 15
County Seat, first site, 16, 17; established at Port Tobacco, 46; removed to La Plata, 141-142, 143
Courby, John, 39
Courtney, Father, 106
Court House, survey of, 22; first building, 17-18; building at Port Tobacco, 46; new building of 1821, 105; moved to La Plata, 142; La Plata building, 1896, 143.
Court Records, 13
Court Riot of 1786, 65-66
Courts, John, 20
Cox, Col. Samuel, 122, 131
Cox, F. M., 138, 142, 143
Craig, John, 55
Craik, James, 46, 52, 53, biog., 95-96
Crain, Gerald W., 113
Crain, Peter W., 113
Crescent, 142, 143
Cresswell, Nicholas, 83-85
Crime and punishment, 16, 156

Darnall, Henry, 31
"Darnall's Manor," 31
Davis, Capt. Allen, 47
Davis, George W., 104
Davis, Henry, 52
Debating Society of Port Tobacco, 75
Declaration of Independence, signing, 59; celebration, 60
Dement, William Fendlay, 126

Democratic Party, 137
Dent, Alexander, 104
Dent, George, 52, 53, 54, 55
Dent, George, Jr., 52
Dent, Rev. Hatch, 73; biog., 95
Dent, Hezekiah, 52
Dent, John, 51, 52, 53, 54, 66
Dent, Peter, 48, 52
Dent, Dr. Stoughton W., 125
Dent, Warrent, 52
Deyzer, S., 39
Dickenson, Frances, (Mother Clare Joseph of the Sacred Heart), 71
Digges, Eugene, 120
Digges, Dr. John T., 126
Digges, W. Mitchell, 143
Doages Indians, 3
Dodd, Richard, 39
Dorsett, James A., 126
Doughty, Rev. Francis, 36
Dunnington, Roger, 104
Durham Parish, 40; effects of Revolution, 73

Dye, Reuben, 52
Dyke, Matthew, 39
Dyson, Bennet, 52

Eatbey, Arthur, 39
Education, 17th cent., 44; 18th cent., 44-46; 19th cent., 110-111
Eilbeck, Ann, 63
Eilbeck, Widow, 63
Episcopal Church, 17th cent., 37-43; 18th cent., 72; effect of Revolution, 73-74; 19th cent., 108
Episcopal Parishes, 40; see also by name

Farrall, T. R., 139
Fendall, Benjamin, 52
Fendall, Henry, 52
Fendall, Josias, establishment of the county, 9; rebellion, 11-13
Fendall, Phillip Richard, 52, 53, 54, 55
Fendall's Rebellion, 11-13
Ferguson, James, 113
Ferguson, Richard, 109
Ferries, 17th cent., 25; 18th cent., 49-50
Fithian, Philip Vickers, visits Squire Lee, 98
Fleet, Capt. Henry, 3

Floyd, Miss Olivia, 111; biog., 128
Floyd, Robert Semmes, 128
Food, 18th cent., 76
Forbes, James, 52
Forestry, native growth, 2; as an industry, 161
Fowke, Gerard, 52
Franciscan priests, 34
Franklin, Francis B., 52, 74
Franklin, Henry, 39
Franklin, William, 104
Friendship Landing, 5
"Friendship Manor," 31
Frost, Will, 39
Funeral Customs, 17th cent., 29

Gaidge, Dr. Matthew, 29
Garner, Capt., 74
Garner, Benjamin W., 121
Gerard, Thomas, 8
Gerston, Edward, 39
Gibbs, John, 39
Gill, Robert, Jr., 55
Goasby, John, 39
Gouge, John, 32
Gray, George W., 143
Gray, William Jeremiah, 74
Gumey, John, 39
Gwinn, John, 52

Haggat, Humphrey, 17th cent. medical treatment, 26-28
Haislip, James, 143
Halkerston, John, 56
Hamilton, Alexander, Scotch merchant, 65
Hamilton, Alexander, Sec. of Treasury, 91
Hamilton, Burdet, 52
Hamilton, John, 112
Hanson, Hoskins, 52
Hanson, John, President of U. S. In Congress assembled, 64; biog., 92
Hanson, John, Jr., 60
Hanson, John, youngest, 52
Hanson, Randolph, 20
Hanson, Samuel, 53, 54
Hanson, Samuel, Jr., 56, 66
Hanson, Samuel of Samuel, 56
Hanson, Sarah, 61
Hanson, Walter, 51, 52, 53, 56, 65, 74

Hanson, Walter, Jr., 52, 60
Hanson, William, 47, 52
Harbin, Thomas H., 125
Hardy, Hen., 39
Harris, George, 16
Harris, John, 56
Harris, Thomas, 52
Harris Lot, 113
Harrison, Ensign (Perhaps Richard), 48
Harrison, Joseph Hanson, 51, 52, 53, 54, 57
Harrison, Capt. Richard, 47
Harrison, Robert Hanson, biog., 90-91
Harrison, Samuel, 50, 52
Harrison, Samuel, youngest, 52
Harrison, Walter Hanson, rector of Durham, 92
Harrison, William, 55, 56, 57, member of Congress, 92
Harrison, Col. William D., 105
Hatch, John, 9, 13
Hawkins, Henry S., 32, 39, 52
Hawkins, Josias, 46, 51, 52, 53, 54, 56, 57
Hawtan, William, 39
Henley, Mr. Robert, 32
Henson, Josias, 119
Henson, Matthew, 145
Herold, David E., 130
Hill Top, 101, 105, 112, 123
Hill, Edith Beane, 37
Hill, Rev. Matthew, 36, 37
Hill, Valentine, 39
Hinson, Randolph, 39
Hobart, Moses, 52
Homes of settlers, 24
Honeyman, Robert, journal, 55
Hooe, Robert T., 51, 52, 53, 54, 56, 57
Horse racing, 18th cent., 50; 19th cent., 112
Hoskins, Bennet, 31
Hoskins, Col. John, 50
Hughes, John J., 113
Hundreds, 9
Hunley, Robert, 9
Hunter, Rev. George, S.J., 67
Hunter, Rev. William, S.J., 35
Hussey, Thomas, 16, 20, 21, 22
Hutchinson, Will., 39

Indenture System, 152-155
Independence, resolution for, 57; signing the Declaration, 59; celebrating, 59
Independent Democrats, 137
Indians, 3-7
Industry, water and its products, 147; Naval Powder Factory, 144-145
Ingle, Capt. Richard, 6, 33

Jail, first, 18; at Port Tobacco, 46; new jail of 1811, 101
Jenifer, Daniel, 51, 52, 53, 54, 76
Jenifer, Daniel of St. Thomas, comm. for use of Potomac River, 64; signer of the Constitution, 65; Intendent of Revenue, 65; biog., 93-94
Jenifer, Daniel II, 111, 114
Jenifer, Walter H., 52, 53
Jenkins, George P., 113
Jenkins, John, 15
Jenkins, Joseph, 30
Jesuits, 6
Johnson, Joseph C., 143
Jones, Rev. Hugh, 45
Jones, Samuel, 52
Jones, Thomas A., Confederate communications, 124; escape of Booth, 131-133
Jones, Williams, 74
Joy, Joseph, 52

Kean, Thomas, 47
Keech, George, 52
Key, James, 52, 53
Keybert, John, 52
King and Queen Parish, 40
Kingsbury, James, 39
Knolewater, John, 39
Knott, John N., 52

La Plata, growth, 139; name, 139; county seat, 142
Lancaster, John, 55
Land, Richard, 39
Landings for boats, 17th cent. 24; 140. 141
Langley, Samuel P., 146
Lee, Capt. Arthur, 47
Lee, James, 29, 30
Lee, Philip, 97

Lee, Philip Thomas, 100
Lee, Squire Richard, 98-99
Lee, Richard Henry, 98
Lee, Richard H. (1814), 100
Lenton, Joseph, 15
Lenton, Mrs. Joseph, 29, 30
Lewis, Lt. William, 9
Libraries, layman's, 44; Charles County Public Library, 147
Lincoln's Assassination, 130
Lindsey, Lindsay or Linsey, James, 9, 15, 30
Lindsey, Lindsay or Linsey, Edmund, 15, 16
Livestock, 154, 155, 156-157
Lomax, Thomas, 15, 30
Lomax, Osborne, 39
Love, Samuel, 52, 53, 54
Lower Zachaia Parish, 106
Loyalty to Union, editorial, 123; persons, 128
Luckett, Ignatius, 52
Luckett, Legran I., 111
Lumbroso, Dr. Jacob alias John, 29
Lynes, Philip, 20, 21, 22, 39

McConochie, Rev. William, 44, 52, 73
McDaniel, Horatio M., 104
McDonough, Maurice James, biog. 108-110
McDonough District, 108-109
McDonough Institute, 110
McKarter, Alexander, 39
McPherson, Alexander, Jr., 52, 54
McPherson, John, 52
McPherson, Thomas, 52
Maddox, James, 52
Maddox, Notley, 52
Mail service, 17th cent., 25; 18th cent., 49; 19th cent., 116, 117
Mankin, Charles, 52
Mankin, Stephen, 39
Manning, Joseph, 39
Manor Grants, 8, 9, 31; see also name of manor
Manors, Proprietary, 8, 9; sale, 50
Map of Charles Co., R. W. Williamson (1861), 123
Marshall, Hall, 5
Marshall, John, 52, 56
Marshall, Thomas Hanson, 52, 53

Marten, John, 39
Maryland Independent, 142
Maryland Line, 60
Mason, George, 63
Mason, William, 63
Mastin, Francis, 52
"Mattawoman Neck", manor grant, 9; site of Naval Powder Factory, 144
Mattawoman Parish, 106
Matthews, Anne (Sister Bernardina Theresa Xavier), 71
Matthews, Ann Theresa (Sister Mary Aloysia of the Blessed Trinity), 71
Matthews, George W., 113
Matthews, Rev. Ignatius, 69
Matthews, Susanna (Sister Mary Eleanora of St. Francis Xavier), 71
Matthews, Thomas, 8; as commissioner, 17, 19; holds and returns St. Thomas Manor, 33-34
Matthews, William, S. J., 107
Medicine, 17th cent., 26-28
Meeke, John B., 52
Merrick, William, 113
Meteorite, 105-106
Methodist Church, 18th cent., 74; 19th cent., 118
Middleton, Edward, 39
Middleton, William J., 121
Militia, 17th cent., 30; 18th cent., 47; French and Indian War, 48; War of 1812, 102, 104
Mings, Edward, 32
Mitchell, Capt. John, 74
Mitchell, John H., 143
Mitchell, Walter, 113, 122
Mitchell, Walter J., 143
Moore, Rev. Mr., 40
Moore, Henry, 17
Moore's Lodge, court house at, 19; 20
Moran, John, 55
Mount Carmel, establishment, 71, 72; in the 19th cent., 107
Mudd, Dr. George Dyer, 137, 142
Mudd, Dr. Samuel, 130, 131, 133
Mudd, Sydney E., 142, 143
Mudd, Sydney E., Jr., 143
Mudd, William A., 121
Munn, John, 32

Muschett, John, 52
Mynock, Michaell, 39

Nanjemoy, 5, 101, 105
Nanjemoy Parish, 40
Naval Powder Factory, 144-145
Neale, family of Chandler's Hope, 69-70
Neale, Anthony, 68
Neale, Rev. Charles, S.J., 70, 71
Neale, Edward, 48
Neale, Rev. Francis, S.J., 70
Neale, Henry A., 112
Neale, Capt. James, 8, 32, 55, 154
Neale, Rev. Leonard, S.J., 107, 70
Negroes, first in county, 43; no. in 1790, 67; unrest due to slavery, 119; taken by Union troops, 124; Negro regiment trained at Benedict, 129; in post Civil War politics, 136; effect on agriculture, 153; 158
Newman, George, 39
Newman, Riva, 39
Newport, 101, 105, 112, 124
Newspapers, *State Register*, 111; *Port Tobacco Times*, 111; *Crescent*, 142, 143; *Times-Crescent*, 143, *Maryland Independent*, 142
Newton, Richard, 39
Non-Importation Association, 51
North Pole, discovery, 145

Oath of Allegiance to State, 62
Oath of Allegiance, Civil War, 135
Old Warehouse Landing, 6
O'Neill, Hugh, 36
Organ, Church, St. Thomas 67; Port Tobacco Parish, 73
Oversee, Simon, 31
Owen, Richard, 104

Pamac river, 6
Pangiah Manor, 9, 50
Parker, Thomas, 39
Parnham, John, 52, 54
Parishes, see Parish name; also Episcopal parish
Parks, Edward, 9, 16
Patobanos Indians, 3
Payn, John, 39
Payne, Robert, 32
Peary, Robert E., 145

Penn, Jezrell, 52
Pennsylvania Railroad, 138
Peers, Nicholas, 76
Peers, Valentine, 76
Philpott, Edward, 39
Philpott, Benjamin, 52
Picawaxen creek, 5
Pickawaxon Parish, 40
Pile, Joseph, 31
Piscataway Creek, 6
Piscataway Parish, 40
Pleasant Hill, 105
Plebe, George, 39
Pomfret Church, 68; present church built, 106-107
Pomonkey, 5
Pope's creek, 43, 112, 124-125
Pope, Francis, 29, 43
"Popleton", 37
Port Tobacco, as a port, 31; made county seat, 46; commerce, 46; social life (18th cent.), 46, 47; theater, 47; description (1775), 55; change of name, 105; description (1807), 101; life (mid 19th cent., 115, 112-113
Port Tobacco area, 5, 6
Port Tobacco Parish, 40, 72-73
Port Tobacco Times, 111
Ports, 17th cent., 31
Posey, Adrian, 129, 142, 143, 144
Posey, Belain, 52, 54, 62
Posey, Benjamin, 39
Posey, Richard B., 112
Potomac River, 6; commission for use by Maryland and Virginia, 63-64
Potomac River Bridge, 147
Potopaco, 3, 6
Powder Mill, Revolutionary War, 60-62
Powell, Robert, 39
"Poynton Manor", 8
Presbyterian Church, 17th cent., 35-37, 18th cent., 74
Proprietary Manors, *see* Manors, Proprietary
Protestant Petition of 1689, 38, 39
Pye, Mr. Edward, 32

Racing, 50, 112
Railroads, 138-140
Ratcliff, John, 39

Reddish, John, 32
Reeder, Richard R., 52
Reeder, Robert S., 113-114
Republican Party, 136-137; 120
Religion, see name of denomination
Revolutionary War, military districts, 56; pay of soldiers, 56; rations, 57; service of Maryland Line, 60
"Rice Manor", 8, 31
"Rich Hill", 131
Riddle, Charles, 127
Ridgate, Thomas Howe, 76
Roads, 17th cent., 24; 18th cent., 49; 19th cent., 117
Roberts, J. Hubert, 143
Rochefort, Law, 39
Rookewood, Edward, 39
"Rose Hill", 128
Roser, Benjamin, 16
Rye, Walter, 55

St. Ignatius Church, 7
St. John's Parish, 40
St. Mary's Church, Bryantown, 106, 35
St. Mary's Church, Newport, 34
St. Peter's Parish, 106
St. Thomas Manor, 8, 33-34, description (1775), 55; description (1784), 69; 111
Sanders, Edward, 32
Sanders, Joshua, 55
"Sarum", 31
Scott, Rev. Robert, 44
Semmes, Adm Raphael, C.S.N., 127
Servants, indentured, 153; trading in, 154; punishment of, 155
Settlers, clothing, 24; homes, 24; types of people, 23
Sennett, Robert, 52
Seventh Regiment Infantry, U. S. Colored Troops, Maryland Volunteers, 129
Shawe, Ralph, 39
Shepard, Charles, 39
Silk, cultivation of, 158
Sims, Thomas, 55
Sine, William Barton, 39
Skelton, John, 55
Slavery, 119, 158, 43
Smallwood, James, 32, 39

Smallwood, William, revolutionary activities, 51-56; on Court Riot, 66; no. of slaves, 67; Durham vestry, 74; biog., 87-89
Smallwood Foundation, 89
Smith, Charles S., 52
Smith, Capt. John, 2, 3, 6
Smith, William, 32
Smithsonian Institution, 5
Smoot, Edward, 56
Smoot, George C., 52
Smoot, Dr. James J., 143
Smoot, John Nathan, 56
Smoot, Richard M., 130
Social life, 25, 75-76, 158
Southerland, L. M., 127
Southern Maryland Electric Cooperative, 146
Southern Maryland National Bank, 144
Southern Maryland Railroad, 140
Spalding, Basil, 127
Spalding, Catherine, 107
Spaniards, 2, 150
Speake, Richard, 52
Speake, Captain T., 74
Stamp Act, 50
Spikeman, William, 39
Steamboats, 116, 140
Stoddert, Benjamin, 50
Stoddert, Benjamin, sec. of Navy, 94-95
Stoddert, John (Capt.), 47
Stoddert, John T., 113
Stoddert, Kenelm T., 52, 56
Stoddert, William Truman, 74, 89-90
Stone, Frederick, 113
Stone, Dr. John, 29, 32
Stone, John Hoskins, 52, 53, 56, 81-82
Stone, Michael Jenifer, 76, 82
Stone, Samuel, Jr., 52
Stone, Thomas, revolutionary activities, 51, 52, 53; signing the Declaration of Independence, 57, 59; commission for use of Potomac, 64; biog., 77-81
Stone, Gov. William, 8, 35, 36, 39
Stone, William B., 112, 113
Stonestreet, Nicholas, 113
Susquehannocks, 4, 6

Taxation, British, 50, 51
Taylor, William, 39
Theater, 47
Theobals, Clement, 16
Theobold, Capt. William, 47
Thomas, Capt. John, 47
Thomas, John Allen (lawyer), 65
Thompson, Col. Francis, 120
Thompson, George, 15, 29
Thompson, Robert, 39
Thompson, Col. William, 112
Thomson, James, 39
Thornton, Thomas, 52
Times-Crescent, 143
Toag Indians, 3
Tobacco, 17th and 18th cent. cultivation, 149-152; 19th and 20th cent., 159-160; slaves and tobacco (18th cent.), 67; part in Fendall's Rebellion, 12
Tools, agricultural (17th cent.), 153, 154; Indian, 6
Tournaments, 112
Towns, creation of, 32
Transportation, 17th cent., 24, 25, 31; 18th cent., 49; 19th cent., 115, 138-141; air, 146, boat, 140-141, 116; boat landings, 140-141; railroads, 138-140; roads, 117; Potomac River Bridge, 147
Trappe, 112
Trinity Parish, 73
Troop, Robert, 15
Truman, Nathaniel, Gent., 31
"Truman's Place, Manor of", 31
Tubman, Rev. George, 40, 41, 55
Turner, Edward, 39
Turner, J. Samuel, 142
Turner, James, 39
Turner, Samuel, 52
Turner, Zephaniah, 52, 53, 76, 113
Tyne, James, 32

Vanderdonck, Mary Doughtie, 29, 36
Voting Districts of 1868, 136
Wade, Richard, 39

Wakefield, Thomas, 39
Waldorf, 140
Walker, James, 9, 16
War of 1812, 101-105
Ward, Capt. Francis, 47
Ware, Francis, 46, 51, 52, 53, 54, 56
Waring, John W., 143
Warren, Capt. Barton, 47
Warren, Edward, 52
Warren, Father Henry, 34
Warren, Humphrey, 32, 39
Watson, Maj. Roderick, 125
Weems, Rev. John, 73
Wells, Elijah, Jr., 111
Wentour, Robert, 24
We-sorts, 7, 8; origin of name, 8
"Westwood Manor", 31
Wharton, Jesse, 31
"Wharton Manor", 31
Wheeler, James, 32
Wheeler, John, 20, 32
White Plains, 140
White, Father Andrew, 4, 6, 7, 33
Wichaley, Thos., 39
Wicomico River, 5, 8, 9
Wilkinson, Gen. James, 96-97
William and Mary Parish, 40
Wills, Dr. Francis R., 112
Wills, Mr. P. R., 143
Wilmer, Rev. Lemuel, 108, 128
Wilmer, Dr. W. R., 136, 142
Wilson, John, 39
Wincott, John, 39
Winter, Walter, 52
Winter, William, Jr., 52
Wirt, William, 73
Wolfe, William, 143
"Wollaston Manor", 8
Wolves, 151

Yates, Jonathan, 52
Yates, Theophilus, 52
Young, Col. Bennett H., 129
Young, Robert, 52, 54

Zachia Manor, Zekiah, or Zachaia, 9, 50

www.ingramcontent.com/pod-product-compliance
Lightning Source LLC
Chambersburg PA
CBHW071433150426
43191CB00008B/1112